Dustin Lance Black is a filmm [...] wn for writing the Academy Award-winning screenplay of the Harvey Milk biopic *Milk* and for his part in overturning California's discriminatory Proposition 8. He divides his time between London and Texas.

Mama's Boy

'An utterly compelling account of growing up poor and gay with a thrice married, physically disabled, deeply religious Mormon mother, and the imprint this irrepressible woman made on the character of Dustin Lance Black. Their extraordinary bond left me exhilarated – it actually gave me hope for the future'

JON KRAKAUER, author of *Into Thin Air*

'Fascinating' *Gay Times*

'This beautifully written memoir is a wonderfully optimistic story of tolerance and positive change for today's divided times' *Bookseller*

'Bittersweet and surprising' *Women and Home*

'A beautiful, original book' PANDORA SYKES, *The High Low*

'Black's tender and heartfelt love letter to his remarkable mother is an act of courage and reclamation. It's a well-deserved tribute'
New York Journal of Books

'A fast read with witty observations, and all the emotions to go along ... [A] testament to the powerful impact a good parent has on children [...] e unlikeliest of child [...] *co Chronicle*

34 4124 0018 9670

'A fascinating and poignant combination of memoir and family history . . . Both personal and universal . . . Finding common ground is indeed the powerful throughline in *Mama's Boy*'

Salt Lake City Weekly

'The story of how a mother and son came to reconcile their differences and realize the importance of family' *NPR*

'Dustin Lance Black's memoir comes at exactly the right time; his complicated, surprising, and ultimately touching journey with his mom is a great example in our ideologically divided times'

ANDY COHEN, author of *Superficial* and *The Andy Cohen Diaries*

'Black provides a wholly engrossing account of how a mother and son evolved beyond their potentially divisive religious and political beliefs to uncover a source of strength and unity through their enduring bond. A terrifically moving memoir of the myriad complexities of family dynamics' *Kirkus Reviews* (starred review)

'A beautifully written, vastly entertaining, and moving memoir . . . Black seems incapable of writing a dull word as he evokes his stirring life and times, ultimately inspiring comity by word and example'

Booklist (starred review)

Mama's Boy

A MEMOIR

Dustin Lance Black

JOHN MURRAY

First published in Great Britain in 2019 by John Murray (Publishers)
An Hachette UK company

This paperback edition published in 2020

1

A CIP catalogue record for this title is available from the British Library

Paperback ISBN 978-1-473-66545-3
eBook ISBN 978-1-473-66546-0

Printed and bound in Great Britain by Clays Ltd, Elcograf S.p.A.

John Murray policy is to use papers that are natural, renewable and
recyclable products and made from wood grown in sustainable forests.
The logging and manufacturing processes are expected to conform
to the environmental regulations of the country of origin.

John Murray (Publishers)
Carmelite House
50 Victoria Embankment
London EC4Y 0DZ

www.johnmurraypress.co.uk

FOR TOM, ROBBIE RAY,
AND MY WILD AND WONDERFUL AMERICAN FAMILY

Contents

Mama's Boy

Prologue

A hot, gauzy morning in the late summer of 1987. That was the first time I ever laid eyes on the streets of Los Angeles. I was thirteen years old but looked ten at best—an agonizingly shy Texas boy with eyes like water, hair like the sun, and a tanker truck's worth of secrets. I was jammed in the backseat of my mom's massive yellow Malibu Classic between my little brother, Todd, and our stinking cat, Airborne. My mom said we were "on the move." Others would have called it "on the run."

Days earlier, my family had packed up what little we had of value and vanished without notice from our lives in the Lone Star State—leaving behind my middle school in San Antonio and our Mormon church in the Randolph Ward, heading west. My mom was behind the wheel, her hairspray-stiffened curls resting on worried shoulders as she worked the hand controls to speed up and slow down her beast of a car: a colossal artifact from a former life that now had to be wrested into submission by a woman who walked on crutches, her legs in braces, her spine fused and held together with metal bars hidden just beneath the scars that ran the length of her body.

My big brother, Marcus, sat up front beside her. His hair was just as long as hers but kissing a black leather punk-rock jacket covered in pins and buttons that shouted obscenities my mom had miraculously (if not willfully) grown blind to. He had a map spread out on his lap. We were lost. We were scared. But in good Southern, Mormon fashion, we kept our terrors to ourselves.

Here's the thing: we'd been taught our entire lives that places like Los Angeles were filled with folks who'd traded their souls and salvation for fame, booze, drugs, cash, cars, hetero sex, group sex, and dirty, filthy faggot sex. Los Angeles was the embodiment of an unfamiliar, exotic America that we'd been warned to avoid: liberal, often coastal, a place for sinners and moral relativists. For our ragtag family on the run, passage through this city was a test of spiritual strength. So we plugged our noses in back, Marcus did his best to navigate up front, and my tiny runaway mom rotated the hand control that turned the gear that pressed down on the gas pedal that she hoped might propel us to safety.

Two hours later, Marcus and my mom finally spotted the entrance to the 5 Freeway heading north. The terrain grew steeper as we headed into the hills and over the Grapevine, a stretch of highway out of L.A., where the snarl of traffic gave way to golden grasses, a reservoir lake, ranches, and a meadow filled with wildflowers. These were more familiar sights. This felt more like home. My mom looked up into her rearview mirror, found my eyes, and with all of her mighty love and warmth, sent me a strong, silent message: *You're safe now, my Lancer.*

I took a breath or two, pulled out a pen and a spiral notebook, and wrote a letter to a girl back in San Antonio. She and I had recently participated in a one-act drama competition. She'd played Eve. I'd played Adam. Her mom was our drama teacher. I described Los Angeles as the "second gayest city in the world." It wasn't a compliment. I was already fairly certain that San Francisco was in first position thanks to AIDS hitting the national news when Old Hollywood heartthrob Rock Hudson fell out of his closet and into his grave. Since then, even the news shows in Texas had started offering up images of emaciated gay men, most in San Francisco, but others in New York and Los Angeles, dying terrible deaths thanks to their "lifestyle choices." So yes, it seemed that San Francisco was the closest to hellfire, but I was fairly certain Los Angeles wasn't far behind. I suppose I felt it necessary to let someone in Texas know I'd survived our journey through this foreign land.

But as we reached the top of a mountain, something in my God-fearing heart stirred, and I looked back toward the city. It was calling to me. If I'm being honest, it had started calling well before we set out on this adventure. If Los Angeles was dangerous, I was curious. How true were the stories I'd heard? Did the people there really do so many strange things to their bodies, their minds, and one another? Did they really make all of those movies and TV shows I'd fallen in love with on the rare occasions we were allowed to watch them? And the most dangerous question of all: Did the nation's current teen heartthrob, Ricky Schroder, with his golden hair and ocean-blue eyes, actually live somewhere down in all that chaos?

That question, and all of its invasive roots and sticky webs, lingered longest in my mind as I watched the city glimmer and shine in the morning sun until it slowly disappeared behind a veil of blue-white smog.

Thirty years have passed since that drive, and for more than two and a half decades of that time I've called this City of Angels my home, with all of its sunshine, celebrities, workers, artists, headaches, egos, booze, dreams, lies, cigarette butts, body parts, hot tubs, invitations, hangovers, trophies, and yes, reliably progressive values. And like most Angelenos, I've spent much of that time in my car getting from place to place, tucked inside my bubble. Isolated. And in a hurry.

So whenever I heard a siren, I did what most Angelenos do: look forward, left, right, check my rearview mirror, and keep on driving. As an Angeleno, the last thing you want to do is tap the brake. The clock is ticking. We have places to be, coffees to order, deals to make, and great things to accomplish by lunchtime.

But something happened a few years back to strip me of that habit. I was driving home down Hollywood Boulevard when my mom called. I hit the icon on my dash to answer. She sounded gloomy and called herself a "dinosaur" twice. I'd rarely heard her in such a state. I was worried. So I added a three-day layover via Dulles Airport in Virginia to my next love-fueled flight to London to see the Brit I was fast falling head over heels for. It was a little surprise visit to lift my mom's spirits, and a big birthday present to myself.

My mom now lived in Manassas Park, in a house built right on top of the bloodied Civil War battlefields of Bull Run, where more than twenty-four thousand soldiers gave their lives in the debate over whether all men are created equally—a scar on our nation, reminding us of how divided we once were, and in many ways still are.

My mom cried with joy and relief when I walked into her bedroom. I spent all three days with her there. We blew out candles. We ate cake. We ordered in from a local restaurant and enjoyed our dinners on her bedroom floor. Then I opened the presents she'd ordered off her laptop from her perennial perch atop her bed.

She wasn't feeling well, but that was nothing new. For a variety of reasons, big and small, she'd long been forced to use her not inconsiderable strength to fight off this illness or that. We'd done this ailment dance many times. We simply took advantage of her sleepless nights to share stories, watch *NCIS*, check out the Home Shopping Network's jewelry specials and buy a few pairs of earrings she couldn't afford on a military retirement check, sneak far too many Oreo cookies, and witness a sunrise. Her spirits were lifted by the company. So were mine.

Just before I left, my stepdad arrived home from work to take her to the doctor for a checkup, and get her some antibiotics for what she felt sure was a bladder infection. Love hungry and London bound, I ordered a cab to the airport.

It was a markedly quiet ride. I don't remember music ever even being turned on. But then my cell phone rang. The caller ID said "Mom." Nothing unusual. This was her regular call to say she missed me already, and I would say the same, because it was true. Instead, when I said hello, my stepdad's trembling voice rang in my ears: "Your mother collapsed. In the garage. Her heart stopped. The medics got here. They did CPR and revived her, but she isn't conscious. It's bad, Lance. It's really bad."

I couldn't process it. This was the same brave mom who had successfully slayed the City of Angels years earlier with three little boys and no use of her legs. It was impossible to imagine her having to be revived by anyone. My mom was the one who kept everyone else safe and strong. Her tough, stubborn heart didn't need a stranger's help to keep going.

Choking out the words, I told the cabdriver what I'd just heard, and bless his heart, he plowed right over the grassy center median and turned back the way we'd come. Soon we heard the siren. Then we saw an ambulance take a left turn off of my mom's road, racing away from us toward the local Manassas hospital. That's when I noticed that, like they did in Los Angeles, the drivers in this small, polite, Southern town mostly didn't bother to pull over for ambulances either. Maybe a brief pause to let it pass, then a chase to make up their lost time in its wake. As we raced to catch up, I grew more and more distressed by this surprising similarity. My mom, my best friend, my rock was inside of that ambulance fighting for her life, and even here in her treasured South, no one seemed to give a damn. Our terror was their inconvenience.

Just like my mom, when things get bad, I get quiet. The worse they get, the more silent I become. The cabdriver looked back. I hadn't taken more than half a breath since I told him to turn around. I must have looked like a ghost. And with far too much peace in his voice for my comfort, he said, "What is meant to be now, will be."

I started to shake. Until then, I hadn't considered that she might die. Everything I'd ever built was thanks to that stubborn heart of hers, and there it was, racing away from me in the back of an ambulance. Suddenly, I didn't know if I'd ever again feel the warmth of her hand, know the might of her will, or stand atop the foundation she'd built for our family with the strength of her steel-clad spine.

My mom had grown up in the South. Louisiana and Georgia. She had been deeply religious. Baptist, then Mormon. She had worked for the U.S. military. She had voted for Ronald Reagan and Bush Senior. I now had spent decades living in that wicked city she'd refused to let us set foot in when I was thirteen. I had gone into the arts. Heck, I'd outright fought for progressive causes like marriage equality. To outsiders, in this day and age, my mom and I should have been enemies. Our house should have been divided—North versus South, red versus blue, conservative versus progressive, coasts versus mountain or plains, or however you choose to name such tribes. Instead, my mom and I fueled each other. Her oil lit my lamp, and eventually mine lit hers. The tools I learned to wield growing up in her conservative, Christian, Southern, military home were the same ones I'd used to wage battles that had taken me from a broken-down welfare apartment where gunfire sang me to sleep to the biggest stages in the world, and to the front row of the United States Supreme Court to fight for LGBTQ equality.

Although my mom and I had often disagreed politically and personally, she'd led our family by example, instilling in us a can-do attitude that often defied reason—an optimism many would call foolish, ignorant, and naïve, but an optimism that occasionally shocked our neighbors and our world with its brazen veracity. She was my reason.

It's not something I've shared until now, and I know it may sound silly to some, but I had often hoped our relationship was like a pebble thrown into a pond, breaking the surface and sending ripples to the water's edge. If my mom and I could set foot on the bridges between us, then perhaps our neighbors and those closest to us could too. Perhaps our diverging Americas wouldn't be doomed to destroy each other the way our news shows and politicians would have us believe. And perhaps more could find a higher plane than politics.

So I let the cabdriver know that I'd pay for any ticket he got, but that if he didn't push his pedal to the floor, he was asking for a big old can of whoop-ass from yours truly. He didn't need much convincing. My red eyes had already made the stakes abundantly clear. My mom had to live. Because deep in my gut, I feared a storm was coming. Beyond the headlines of the day, I could just make out the sparks of division catching fire in the disparate places we called home, and I knew that my mom and I had much more to discover and build if we were going to help our neighbors and family weather the terrible schisms this storm would bring.

So I held my zen-like cabdriver's gaze until he looked back out toward the ambulance that was now racing away from us, and he hit the gas.

PART I

CHAPTER 1

Still Water

I

This may come as a surprise to some, but I've always excelled at math and science. It was 1988 when my high school physics teacher told me that nothing in the universe ever gets moving without being moved by an outside force. This was hardly a news flash. I'd already heard a lifetime of stories, most set in the small, Southern town of Lake Providence, Louisiana, that taught me that little ever moved or changed for our kin, at least not without dying. Death had long been the only reliable mover where our family tree was planted. But as I was to math and science, I was drawn to these stories. And thanks to one in particular, I knew of an exception to our family rule. It was buried in the true tale of an outside force that had arrived with very little warning, and got things moving in terrible, surprising, and bewildering ways.

It was February 28, 1948, and no screaming could be heard from inside the small paper-brick home. There were only the sweaty sighs of an adolescent farmboy and a four-year-old girl as they worked alongside a thirty-something farmer who smelled of whiskey to gather bloody rags and place them in a bucket. The house's floors were unfinished—plywood, mostly. You could see clear through many of the walls to their wood-and-wire innards. And to protect it from floods that never came, the tiny house sat perched atop cinder blocks on the dusty cotton farm this family of sharecroppers called home.

Seemingly far older than her thirty-three years, Edith Corene Whitehead, the matriarch of the clan, was known to most as Cokie. She was a small, sturdy woman with curly dark hair who sewed herself dresses from scraps for special occasions, and wore cat-eye glasses with "jewels" in the corners to see right. She'd found the frames at a secondhand shop. She'd just given birth to her seventh child, six of whom were still alive, three still under her roof. Sweaty and weak, propped up on her elbows in bed, she used what strength she had left to pull herself upright, slip on her bejeweled glasses, and help mop up the rest of the bedroom. Her home was unfinished, but she insisted it be clean.

As she worked, her strength slowly returned, and thank goodness, because there were beans to boil and cornbread to bake, and perhaps one of the many chickens roaming the backyard would get its neck twisted before sundown. Meat was an extravagance in Cokie's home, but this was a day to celebrate. So: an afternoon of feather plucking, frying, and then beans and cornbread with tomato and onions, shared among five hungry mouths. As always, Cokie would claim the chicken's back as her own, saying she liked it the best, though of course it was the worst. She wanted her children to have the juicy legs and wings and the prized breast pieces. Their needs, their survival, had to come first.

Later that day, as evening threatened, Cokie's husband, Victor, handed the baby to her four-year-old sister, Martha, and asked her to rock the newborn back to sleep in the old family rocking chair. Sweet Martha instantly fell in love with her little sister. But when it came time for dinner, Victor had vanished. He was already off drinking somewhere. Fine by Cokie. One less mouth to feed.

When the dishes were done, Cokie finally took a moment for herself. She walked into the back bedroom, dipped her hands down into the old iron crib, and picked up her brand-new baby girl—little Rose Anna Whitehead.

Cokie hadn't always been the warmest or easiest mother to her brood; life was too demanding for any slack or too much affection. But she caught herself gazing at this baby a bit differently than she had the rest. Sure, Rose Anna was a quiet, beautiful child, the kind born with her eyes wide open to the world, but that wasn't it. In fact, it wasn't anything special about the child at all. It was a wisdom and acceptance that had begun to dawn on Cokie with age: there would be no rising above circumstances here in Lake Providence, a town buried deep in poverty. She would see no American dream come true. She was the wife of an alcoholic sharecropper living on a tenant farm her boys tried their best to keep up in his absence but only seemed to lose more ground on each month.

That night, looking into Rose Anna's wide blue eyes, the baby's ten perfect, wiggling toes and fingers all reaching out to her mother, Cokie accepted the truth that so many good Southern mothers of her means had to: love was about the only thing she might ever earn in her life. Then and there, in ways she feared she hadn't with her other children, she dedicated herself to putting love first with this child. She was going to give all she had to her perfect little "Rose."

I never got to meet Cokie, but she was my grandmother, born in Greenway, Arkansas, on October 4, 1914. Raised by distant, indifferent relatives, she was for all intents and purposes an orphan, with little love or family and no home to call her own. So when a dirt-broke, dusty-blond, blue-eyed, sixteen-year-old boy from a logging family confessed his love for her, she didn't hesitate. At the ripe old age of fourteen, Cokie Landrem married Victor Willie Whitehead and soon had a daughter, Hattie Faye, then a son, Billie-Ray. But Billie-Ray died of mysterious causes that neighbors and relatives called a "rare heart condition." Most now admit it was likely a simple case of appendicitis that these young parents didn't have the know-how to handle.

Cokie had gone only as far as the fifth grade, and Victor had made it only to the third. With few skills and even less knowledge, Cokie and Victor tried their hand at sharecropping on a wealthy man's tenant farm in Lake Providence. In the South at the time, many landowners still paid the tenant farmers who worked their land with only food and clothing up front and the promise of shared profits at the end of each season. But when that time came, those sharecroppers were often told they'd earned nothing more than the food and clothing they'd already been given. Others were told they hadn't worked hard enough and now owed their landowners a debt.

Cokie and Victor were a rarity among sharecroppers in their community in that they, like their landowners, were white; most in their occupation were black, descendants of slaves who were supposed to have been liberated by a civil war but had instead met this new injustice. And, like their black neighbors, each year Cokie and Victor's debts grew larger no matter how hard they toiled. The way Victor coped was not a rarity either: he turned to drink.

But by the time Rose Anna turned two years old, she was still far too young to know the family farm was anything but heaven. It had little yellow chicks wobbling out of an incubator, baby pigs that grew bigger each month before they inevitably "found new homes," and ample dirt and rain for all the mud pies a little girl could dream of baking. Beyond their house were fields of clover with white pom-pom blossoms on them. Sweet Martha lovingly showed Rose Anna how to use her fingernails to make slits in the stems, weaving one into the next to build long strings of pom-pom-blossom jewelry.

But the truth was, their father's alcoholism had taken its toll. He was rarely home, and when he was, he was no longer a helpful presence. The eldest boys did their best to keep the farm going without him, but it was a failing enterprise.

Luckily, the family owned a milk cow, so there was butter to be made. But they never ate it; Cokie would churn it, press it into a mold, and sell it. There were pecan trees, so the kids would pick the pecans up off the ground, put them in a burlap sack, and sell those too. Cokie even took a job at the dime store as a cashier, working six days a week for twenty-five dollars. She paid ten of that to a neighbor named Gertrude, who looked after Cokie's kids and her own while Cokie was at work. Gertrude was a small black woman with a few missing teeth, pigtails, and who liked to chew tobacco. She became a second mother to Cokie's little ones, and Cokie gave her free rein to do so. She didn't see Gertrude or her mothering as inferior in any way. There was simply no space for racism in her home. She and Gertrude were sisters of survival above all else.

Although not thoughtful or considered, Cokie's perspective on race was extraordinary in 1950s Lake Providence. Sitting atop Louisiana's northeast corner, the town has a terrible history of slavery, racism, and poverty that continues to this day: in 2013, CNN reported that it was the poorest city in the United States, with the added honor of having the greatest wealth disparity. In the last half century, the population has hovered around four thousand souls, and although African Americans had been the majority since General Grant

marched in with his Union soldiers, Grant gave all of the supposedly liberated land to white folks. Until 1962, black people weren't
even allowed to vote. During the time Cokie was raising her children,
there was still an almost total separation of the races. But it was tough
to see this divide in her home or in Gertrude's. Gertrude even listed
Cokie as "next of kin" when she died. So the youngest children in
Cokie's home grew up perilously naïve about the deeply racist world
around them.

Martha would eventually get a job at the town's Dairy Queen. She
walked there every day after school, and on weekends. The cook was
a black woman, and Martha liked her very much. They talked all shift
long about anything and everything, so Martha came to believe they
were best friends.

Then one day, Martha and her best friend walked into town after
work. They hadn't gone far before a white shop owner launched
out of his store and lit into Martha: "What the hell kinda show ya
puttin' on?!"

"We were just walking, sir," Martha said in her slow, notably well-
enunciated way.

He looked at them both, his eyes red with rage, then he turned
to Martha's friend and began bellowing and cursing, demanding
that the frightened young black woman get out of his sight. Martha's
friend had no choice but to run for her life.

Martha's walk hadn't been some kind of protest or demonstration for civil rights. She hadn't known that she and her friend were
doing anything radical by walking together. But it *was* radical in that
time and place, and now she was getting a frightening crash course
in bigotry.

In her soft, still immaculately enunciated words, I could still hear
the anger and fear in sweet Martha's voice as she told me this story
over half a century later. "That is where you come from, Lance."

Even as life grew increasingly difficult, Cokie stayed true to her quiet
promise to try to love her new Rose a bit better than she had her
older children. Come payday, Rose Anna occasionally received a
piece of citrus fruit. Her mom would tell her it was "a real expensive

treat shipped all the way from a place called California. Out on an ocean called the Pacific. Where the movie stars live."

Of course, Rose Anna's special treatment didn't go unnoticed by her siblings. One night, just before her third birthday, Rose Anna was busy throwing a fit because she had to share the sofa with her big brother Don. She complained that every time he moved, jumped, or bumped around, it was hurting her legs and arms. It was absurd. Don adamantly defended his right to wiggle about, but their mom took Rose Anna's side again. Don was banished from the family couch. Yet even after he was long gone, Rose Anna continued to cry and fuss that she was unbearably uncomfortable. It made no good sense.

A great many things soon stopped making sense to Cokie. Rose Anna never stepped into the bedroom she shared with Martha that night. And when Martha woke up the next morning looking for her beloved baby sister, she found only Gertrude in the kitchen. With the tone of a woman who'd long since stopped losing tears over tough turns, Gertrude stated: "Your mama and Annie gone 'way to the hospital last night, honey. Don't know when they gon' be back."

It turned out that soon after Don and Martha had fallen asleep, little Rose Anna's aches and pains had become excruciating, and when Cokie asked her to straighten her legs, she couldn't. They were frozen. Worse, she was struggling to breathe.

That night, without a single soul knowing it, an outside force had arrived in Lake Providence, and now that force had a death hold on Cokie's precious Rose.

In the middle of the night, Cokie rushed her Rose to the hospital in town, and doctors hurriedly put in motion prescribed emergency procedures—procedures not to save the child, but to isolate her. Cokie was forced from the room and made to strip off her clothes, and those clothes instantly vanished, likely to be burned. It seemed that her Rose was showing all the symptoms of the potentially deadly, disfiguring, and immobilizing virus called polio.

In 1950, that word struck terror in the hearts of parents across the nation. Starting in 1916, a polio epidemic had swept through at least one region of the country each summer. Cesspools of still and polluted water were polio's favorite breeding grounds. Wealthy cities quickly made advances in sanitation and sewage to help prevent outbreaks. But few considered improving the infrastructure of a shrinking city of mostly "Negroes" a priority. Rose Anna's hometown was riddled with just such pools of dark, still water. Now her lifeless legs were an omen that a Louisiana outbreak was brewing.

Most folks who were exposed to the polio virus never got sick. The 5 percent who did usually experienced only flu-like symptoms. But for the unlucky 1 percent Rose Anna now belonged to, the virus would ravage their motor neurons, leaving their limbs, lungs, and throats paralyzed—some so severely that they died. This 1950 outbreak would kill nearly three thousand people in the United States, and over the next decade, polio would paralyze or kill over half a million people worldwide, every single year. There was no cure. And there were no truly effective treatments.

The Lake Providence doctors' primary responsibility now was to keep Rose Anna quarantined while she was still contagious. Whether Rose Anna lived or died wasn't up to them; it was up to her own luck and will. She'd already lost the game of luck to even contract the disease, much less start losing mobility, so if she was going to live, her will was what she had left.

Kept from her daughter's side, Cokie felt her heart breaking. Rose was her chance at a rebirth, a chance to turn love and care into a life's purpose. But like it had so often, life had less charitable plans for Cokie. Preferring her church's deep-fried feasts to regular Sunday attendance, Cokie wasn't the most devoted Baptist, but now she put pride aside, got down on her knees in the waiting area, and apologized to God for a surprisingly long list of sins. Then she prayed for what she was really after: her child's life.

That night, with her mother praying to a savior who thus far had shown her little generosity, and with no one at her side to calm her terror and pain, little Rose Anna Whitehead gasped for air and lost consciousness. But she did not lose her will. No, sir. It turns out her will burned far too hot for dying.

I I

The bellows groaned as it sucked air out of the goliath iron cylinder. At a glance, the contraption looked ripped from a science fiction film. Taking a closer look through the small windows in its sides, nurses could see a little body lying on the "cookie tray" inside, its chest expanding in the vacuum the suctioning bellows created, drawing into the body what its muscles no longer could: life-sustaining oxygen. The groaning stopped, then it began again, this time forcing air into the cylinder, the pressure pushing air out of the tiny body. Over and over.

Weeks after surviving her isolation in Lake Providence, Rose Anna had been moved to a hospital in Vicksburg, Mississippi, where an iron lung was now doing her breathing for her. Of course, if you ever asked little Rose Anna if she'd lived in an iron lung for the weeks it took for her body to stop the virus's immobilizing march, for one-quarter of one lung to regain enough strength that she could breathe on her own again, she would vigorously deny it. "Why would I need anyone's help to breathe, thank you *very* much." For the rest of her life, this "Thank you *very* much" would be her genteel replacement for "Kindly go fuck yourself." She'd be provided with ample opportunities to use it.

Rose Anna's performance of her iron lung lie was so convincing that save for one photo of her asleep in the contraption, her doll-like head sticking out of one end of the massive metal beast, her secret would have been safe. But perhaps it wasn't a deliberate lie. To an oxygen-deprived three-year-old separated from her mother and siblings, perhaps it all just seemed like a nightmare, too horrible to be real: something to wake up from, not remember.

She would have opened her eyes on occasion to check her toes and fingers, to see what still wiggled and what had stopped responding. While her hands, arms, and lungs slowly regained some strength, her legs and torso seemed to grow worse. She must have feared what would happen if the paralysis reached her chin and overtook her head. She surely would have seen what was done to the children who began losing that fight. A knife would slice a hole in their windpipe, a tube would be shoved into it, and a nurse would pump a bag to keep the child's brain alive as long as possible before the child's body gave up, the frightened child unable to call out for her mother.

For those lucky enough to survive polio's degenerative, contagious period, it was a leap from the frying pan into the fire. Survivors would be transferred to long-term-care facilities to endure years of painful, further-disfiguring surgeries and rehabilitation. And thanks to the nature of how and where this virus often spread, most parents proved too poor for regular visits. Survivors became orphans of circumstance, left to brave terrible surgeries to fuse bones, cut away dead muscles, and transplant ligaments in often futile attempts to salvage limbs—all of this in a time before modern anesthesia or effective painkillers.

If it hadn't been for Franklin Delano Roosevelt, there would have been little hope of waking Rose Anna and her wardmates from their living nightmares. A survivor of polio himself, the thirty-second U.S. president stood with braces on his legs when he took the oath of office, stealthily holding on to the lectern for support.

A decade before becoming president, Roosevelt had opened the nation's first full-fledged rehabilitation institution for polio patients, in Warm Springs, Georgia. He had long felt that the country needed a home for modern advancements in polio treatment. He found his answer in Elizabeth Kenny, an Australian nurse who was pioneering a polio therapy that sought to eliminate the need for aggressive surgeries or immobilizing limbs with casts, splints, metal bars, and leather straps. Her belief was that hot baths and warm wet packs could relieve pain and spasms, and that by stretching and exercising what muscles remained, some patients might regain some movement. These methods didn't yield great gains either, but at least they didn't lean on the pain and further disfigurement of scalpels.

The steaming water bubbling up out of the ground in Warm Springs made it an ideal home for Roosevelt's toughened tribe of young polio survivors. Everyone around Rose Anna knew that this was the only place she might find an advanced, humane shot at recovery. But the Whiteheads were dirt-poor, the cost an impossibility for Cokie. Once again, FDR would indirectly help.

Roosevelt had founded the March of Dimes in 1938 as an alliance between doctors, scientists, and volunteer fund-raisers to support polio research and education and help patients who couldn't afford Warm Springs. After a wildly successful national push, the March of Dimes' efforts became localized. Chapters popped up in thousands of counties across the nation, each asking Americans to send in one dime during the Christmas season to help.

It must have felt like an answer to Cokie's late-night hospital prayer when the local March of Dimes, operating out of her own Lake Providence Baptist church, came knocking to say they'd raised enough money to pay for Rose Anna's full-time care in Georgia. It was Cokie's first turn of luck in a good long time, but it came at a cost. Warm Springs was an eight-hour drive from Lake Providence, and she might only afford to make that kind of journey twice a year at best: maybe for a birthday, maybe for Christmas. That would be it. And how long would Rose Anna be there? No one had a good answer to that question.

But here's the extraordinary thing about Cokie Whitehead: she could find hope in the smallest cracks and crevices. Before there was ever a shot at recovery at Warm Springs, three-and-a-half-year-old Rose Anna was allowed a rare trip home from the hospital in Vicksburg. Within minutes of being home, she had found her old wooden potty chair, and without any instruction pulled herself up onto it, then, using its back like a walker, started scooting it forward with her arms, dragging her limp legs behind. Repeating those steps, she began moving freely about the house under her own power, showing an incredible amount of ingenuity and determination. It was a major event in the family, and thanks to Cokie, it was the topic of discussion on porches for a mile around that night. "And her daddy said she'd never walk again! Look how wrong he was! She's walking!" Cokie said to anyone who'd listen, and even louder to those who wouldn't. Her daughter was going to beat the odds. "My Rose will walk again, and all on her own. You mark my words."

Letting her unbridled optimism lead, Cokie dropped her precious Rose off in Georgia certain that her stay would be brief. But hope for a quick recovery slowly faded over the weeks that became years. The only consistent contact mother and daughter would have was their long distance Sunday phone calls. Cokie had to limit those to three minutes each if she was going to put food on the table for the rest of her family. So she and her Rose grew expert at packing every bit of gossip, tears, and encouragement into those three precious minutes. But if Cokie's hope was fading, she never once let a soul hear about it, because she refused to let her daughter's hope fade.

As much as Rose Anna looked forward to those calls, she was despondent for days afterward. Privately, so was Cokie. Because when you have little material wealth, and even less hope of ever finding any, family becomes absolutely primary. It's partly what built the great Southern traditions that "family comes first" and "blood is thicker than water." Of course, folks from all over will say their families come first too, but until you've lived in the kind of town my grandma called home, where any kind of personal ambition, career, or education comes a very distant second to being there for your children, parents, siblings, uncles, aunts, cousins, and even second and third cousins, you haven't yet experienced the passion and power of absolute familial primacy.

Not to say Southern folks don't hurt our own; we most certainly do. That's why the repercussions of such lapses in familial allegiance cut so incredibly deep. And there's a dark side to this "family comes first" coin: if mine comes first, then what about other families? Might they be seen as a threat? Indeed. Such fidelity gave rise to the most famous family feuds in American history: the Hatfields versus the McCoys of Kentucky and West Virginia, or the Lees versus the Peacocks of Texas. And this dark side of "family first," born out of love and protection, can be seen in modern attacks on new outsider families that some fear are just too foreign or different—new families labeled as threats, even when they aren't at all.

But Cokie wasn't thinking about politics or family feuds. She was focused on a family divided by disease, and her search for solutions. A terrible outside force had started things moving in dire ways in

Lake Providence, and now Rose Anna was stuck in a heartrending situation. A true daughter of the South, what she wanted back more than her motility was that most precious thing there is where I come from: her family. That great need, and her mother's imperishable optimism and confidence, are what would fuel little Rose Anna's impossible dream to one day come unstuck from stillness.

CHAPTER 2

Safety's Sound

I

Still strapped down to her hospital bed at night for her own safety, six-year-old Rose Anna woke before sunrise to listen for the faraway sound of angels singing. With all of the other sick children still fast asleep, she often thought she could hear them.

The voices were actually those of missionary ladies singing morning hymns in a chapel well beyond Rose Anna's Warm Springs ward, but unable to get up and go find them, Rose Anna preferred to imagine they were guardian angels. Their voices helped her feel safe and gave her hope that joy, love, and beauty might still exist someplace. If not inside her ward, then perhaps just beyond it.

When Rose Anna had first arrived at Warm Springs, all of the nurses, doctors, teachers, and aides had quickly fallen for their new golden-haired girl. Rose Anna couldn't move most of her body at all back then, but she understood the power of a well-batted eyelash. And she was bright. She was expert at math by six years old, and by seven, though she still couldn't move her torso much, she understood most of the science behind her care. Thanks to her circumstances, she was the first in her family in generations with access to a proper elementary school education, and it became clear that a Whitehead's mind was capable of far more than scratching dirt and drinking. When tempted with knowledge and good teachers, it was as thirsty as a fish in a fryer and sharp as a tack.

But Rose Anna offered the staff challenges as well. By the age of eight, she'd regained control of her arms and hands, a blessing that suggested increased autonomy in her future but also marked the beginning of her reign as ward heartbreaker. She could now fix her golden hair, what she called her "crown and glory," as well as her makeup, her clothes, and whatever else she could reach with her outstretched arms. So she made herself and her surroundings "perfectly pretty, and with plenty of flowers around the edges." It looked as if a Rose Parade float had crashed down wherever she dropped anchor. If a new staff member dared object to the garden growing on her bedside table, Rose Anna would shoot back, "Flowers ought to live anywhere and everywhere they like, sir, and I like them right where they are, thank you *very* much." And that was the end of the conversation.

The boys on her ward, with their own frozen limbs, would linger, stare, stammer, and flirt with the princess in bed number nine. Soon, so did the able-bodied young "push-boys" who manned the wheelchairs or fetched crutches when the patients fell during walking lessons. Whenever Rose Anna fell, there were always boys racing to help her. So when a cute one came around, well . . . Rose Anna might let herself fall, and fall often.

But despite her floral surroundings, somewhere around this time, Rose Anna decided that she no longer wanted to be called Rose. The sound of it reminded her too much of the mom and home she missed so terribly. Besides, here in Warm Springs, she thought perhaps she could make something special of herself. Here everyone was perfectly imperfect—their battle scars, casts, crutches, or wheelchairs worn like merit badges. Here, afflictions, stitches, and braces didn't earn the label of "freak" or garner stares and disgust; they were symbols of one's will to survive. In this extraordinary place, young polio survivors got a glimpse of what a "normal" childhood might have been: crushes, squabbles, laughter, tears, and heartbreak. So these lonesome survivors formed a tight, absolutely unique family of outsiders, and at the center of it all, like some Hollywood ingénue, eight-year-old Rose Anna shortened her name to simply Anna. Because here she felt sure that Anna could be a star.

With so many patients arriving and disappearing, Anna began keeping an autograph book to stop her friends from vanishing altogether. I'd long heard stories of the brave children, nurses, and doctors who filled Warm Springs and Anna's treasured book. I finally found that book at the bottom of an old dresser, buried under pressed flowers. It hadn't been opened in nearly half a century.

I've built most of my career out of the stories of those who came before, so to me, any such object is sacred. It might hold wisdom, shortcuts, and battle-tested solutions to today's challenges. When I carefully opened this one, I found each page filled with children's ghosts. A few had simply signed their names, but most had left long inscriptions—evidence of the depth of Anna's relationships, the power she held, and the young woman she was becoming.

A boy named John filled a page with: "*Roses* are red, violets are blue, sugar is sweet, and so are you."

On a page marked "Reserved for Abray (your push-boy)," Abray had eventually written: "Good luck to a very sweet and very cute girl. Abray Bell."

In Spanish, another boy wrote out an entire poem that ended with: "Your 'roses' on my path have brought me joy. A forest of a thousand flowers. I love you." Another broken heart.

A roommate wrote: "Rose Anna now, Rose Anna forever. Whitehead now, but not forever! Susan."

An aide on the ward wrote: "Always remember the good and bad times we had in Warm Springs." She signed it "Grandmama Moody." She was as close to a grandma as most of these children would ever know.

Anna's recovery wasn't quick or easy. No matter how hard she worked, her legs and spine refused to grow strong again. And nearly ten years after she first fell ill, new roommates were still coming and going, still writing their names in her book, while there she remained.

"My little 'Rosebud,' I've known you since I came here. Three summers ago! Now you have grown up into a young lady . . . I like you very much. Meryl."

"To a sweet girl. I have enjoyed being in the room with you during surgery. Get well soon. Your roommate, Lynn. 1960."

"Roses are red, violets are blue, I have polio, and so do you. Connie, 1961."

And from another long-term survivor: "Rose Anna, I hope that our friendship will continue to grow as it has since we first met in Vicksburg in 1951. It will be ten years that we have known each other this November. Love, Nat."

In the book's final pages, there are fewer and fewer mentions of when Anna might ever go home, or ever regain the use of her legs.

And in the very back of her autograph book lives a heartbreak: dozens upon dozens of hand-drawn calendars marking every day, week, month, and year Anna was hospitalized, with infinite little *x*'s as she counted down the never-ending days until she might get better and finally be home again.

I I

I n one of the few photos of seven-year-old Anna from her Warm Springs days, she's leaned up against a brick wall outside a hotel room next to her mother, who's holding a doll. It was Christmas morning. Despite the bleak backdrop, they look happy enough. Cokie and Victor had gotten a divorce by then, the farm was now bankrupt, and Cokie's bad financial situation had become impossible. Cokie had spent nearly every penny she had to get that cheap hotel room in Warm Springs. She'd spent her last cents on dolls for Anna and Martha, who'd made the long journey with her to see her baby sister. One cheap hotel room, only one of her five siblings, and two inexpensive dolls. It was the best Christmas Anna would know for quite a long time; as seldom as she received visitors, a visit home herself was far more rare because her tiny body demanded constant medical care.

On the Christmases when Cokie couldn't swing a Georgia hotel, she did her best to make the most of what little she had for the rest of her kids. She spared no expense come time for dessert, building them the most extravagant treat she knew: a real fruit salad. To her children, the big, burgundy glass bowl her annual fruit salad was served in—the bowl that came out of its secret hiding place only once a year—was their family's great treasure.

Cokie would carefully pick out the best fruit on her way home from work the day before Christmas, and then just as carefully peel and chop it up on Christmas morning, making sure not an ounce was wasted. She'd add a can of fruit cocktail and a quarter cup of granulated sugar, cover the bowl with plastic wrap, and pop it in the refrigerator to chill.

But the Christmas of 1961 promised to be the most special yet. Despite all of Anna's doctors' passionate appeals, Anna had refused to use a wheelchair. "I don't want to be down there. I want to be up with everyone else. And my arms are stronger than any working legs, thank you *very* much." And so by her thirteenth birthday, with her strong arms and the help of metal braces on her legs, torso, and neck, Anna had become fairly proficient on crutches, using them in much the same way she had her old potty chair. Her arms became her legs, her braced legs swinging like a pendulum beneath her torso. Most days she could make it clear across the ward without falling, and she didn't mind all the bruises and stitches on her chin from her many epic crashes. They were her battle scars from a war she was determined to win.

Come 1961, thanks to Anna's hard-won proficiency with crutches, and the mountain of assurances Cokie gave Anna's doctors, Anna was cleared to go home for Christmas. She wasn't going home for good—not yet—but this was a step in that direction. The announcement of her yuletide return was received with elation and brought all her grown siblings back home to Lake Providence.

By that year, searching for some stability of her own, Cokie had gotten remarried, this time to a man she valued more than she loved. He owned a little house and took home a modest paycheck. In turn, she'd given him two new daughters, Mary and Nannette, but the family still needed a second income, so Cokie had kept her dime store job. Once Anna arrived home for Christmas that year, Cokie walked the mile home from work in record time.

Each afternoon, Cokie would burst through the front door, push her dining room table to the center of the room, put quilts on top of it, and get Anna up there to go through the series of exercises the doctors had prescribed. Some required two people, so Martha held her sister down by the hips while Cokie moved and stretched Anna's limbs.

In the bathroom hallway, there was a harness with a series of pulleys that Cokie's new husband had bolted above a door. The harness would go around the back of Anna's neck and under her chin, and then weights were added. Anna had to hang there for a long time in hopes of straightening her spine, which had begun to bend and twist from her atrophied muscles—a severe form of polio-induced scoliosis. Cokie was determined to get this right so the doctors would let her Rose come home more often. But no one realized how painful these exercises and hangings were, because Anna never complained. She bore them because she was tough, because she didn't want to scare her mom, and because she welcomed their pain—she'd suffer anything not to appear more twisted or "freakish" to the world outside of Warm Springs.

Anna hadn't come home empty-handed. She'd returned with a special Christmas surprise for her mom. And on her second day home, during one of her stretching sessions, she pointed to the toes on her right foot.

"Look, Mama."

"What am I looking at, honey?"

"My toes."

Cokie looked at them, but she didn't know what she was supposed to be seeing.

"Look closer."

Her mom leaned in, and Anna wiggled a few of her little toes. After a decade of dedicated, painful work, Anna had regained the use of a few of her toes. She wiggled them like mad, grinning from ear to ear, as proud as she could possibly be.

The room fell silent, and Cokie began to cry. Anna received her mother's tears and kisses as joy and praise, but when the tears kept coming, Anna saw them for what they were.

After a decade of sacrifice and hope, Anna's wiggling toes finally forced Cokie to accept what she had always feared most: her precious Rose would never get better. No amount of work at Warm Springs could force that miracle. And just as her liquor-stinking ex-husband had predicted, Rose Anna Whitehead would never walk without crutches again.

Anna's smile fell with her mom's tears. "I'm sorry, Mama."

When she heard that, Cokie's tears suddenly ceased, and she snapped back, "Don't you *ever* apologize for who you are ever again.

Not to me, and not to anybody. You're my Rose, and I am so proud of you right now I just can't keep my tears inside me."

To cement her lie as truth, Cokie invited neighbors from a mile around to witness Rose Anna's "miraculous progress." Anna wiggled her toes one by one for neighbors, postmen, and preachers. And if any failed to celebrate the accomplishment to Cokie's satisfaction, or dared to belittle it behind Anna's back, that poor soul got a sweaty dose of hell from Cokie. Because when you grow up poor in the South, you have two options: you either sink into your misery and die, or you celebrate every little thing you can and live. With the latter option, there's little time for self-pity; you have to "get up and get on with it." That's what Cokie had to teach her Rose to do now.

This was most certainly what Anna's second-oldest sister, Josie, had done, and they'd all seen how it had paid off. Josie was a family inspiration. She had grown up in the dirt, rarely complained about it, and worked her tail off to become a registered nurse. She'd married her childhood sweetheart, James Ray Mosely, and they had three wild and wonderful kids together: Sandy, Debbie, and James Lynn. And with all of their success, Josie and James had actually bought a car of their own—the very car they'd let Cokie use on her eight-hour road trips to see her baby girl in Warm Springs twice a year.

Anna fell in love with Josie's husband the moment she laid eyes on him. James was likely only five foot five, but to Anna, he was tall, dark, and handsome. Anna had never met a man who could talk to anyone and everyone, and who everyone actually seemed to like talking to. He had genuine Southern charm. So on the very few occasions Anna got out of the hospital, she insisted on a trip to Texarkana to see James and Josie.

When Anna stepped foot in James's home, things worked a whole lot differently than anywhere else in the world. James wouldn't let Anna get away with a thing his own daughters couldn't, and if his girls could do something without his help, then darn it, so could Anna. To outsiders it may have seemed cruel or insensitive, but it was the main reason Anna loved him so dearly.

Each summer, Josie, James, and their kids drove their homemade pop-up trailer to Bard Springs in the Ouachita Mountains of Arkansas for a week of camping. Once the campsite was set, it was an hour's

hike to the clear springs the kids loved to swim in. So how does a
good old Southern gentleman like James carry a paralyzed girl up a
mountain for one hour?

"Oh, heck no. If my girls can walk it, she can walk it too," James
would say.

Next thing you knew, little Anna was walking like a pendulum all
the way up that rocky path to the crystal-clear springs. And when
Josie's little ones dawdled or complained, Rose Anna sped up. Not
only was she going to show them she could do it, she was going to
beat them all to the top.

And she nearly did.

Reaching the springs for the first time ever, Anna watched with
a tinge of jealousy as Josie and James's kids jumped into the cold,
clear water. Josie put a life jacket on Anna and they watched from the
shore. They sat there together in silence. Then Anna felt it: James's
strong arms lifting her up off the ground. And before she knew what
was happening, he'd slung her into the air and out into the middle of
that ice-cold water.

Splash! She was screaming bloody murder as her head went under.
James didn't panic. He just watched and waited. And when Anna's
head finally surfaced, she screamed again. But it wasn't in terror. She
was screaming like any little girl who'd just hit water that damned
cold. It was a scream of liberation and unbridled joy. There she was,
floating down that spring-fed river just like the rest.

Josie pointed it out first: "James, her lips are turnin' real blue."

James quickly waded in, pulled her out, and looked at her real
close. "You're right, Josie. Her lips are turnin' real blue."

Anna's heart broke. She didn't want this to end. James saw it in her
eyes and added, "They're real blue, Annie . . . just like everyone else's
lips." And he chucked her right back into the water! She squealed
with delight. He must have thrown her in forty times that day.

So when Cokie broke the big news that Josie, James, and every one
of Anna's other siblings were coming home for Christmas in 1961,
Anna was beside herself. Cokie pulled out all the stops. There were
countless new handmade decorations, and Santa even put an apple
and an orange in Martha's, Anna's, Mary's, and Nan's stockings that
Christmas morning.

When the time finally arrived for Christmas dinner's main event, Cokie stepped to the fridge and emerged cradling her revered burgundy bowl. The fruit salad was piled high this year. She could smell the sweetness of it before she'd even taken off the plastic wrap.

But one step from the fridge, Cokie's hands shook. Then, the heavy bowl, slick with the dew that had collected on its cold glass, slipped from her fingers. Time seemed to slow as the treasured bowl headed toward the hard, unfinished kitchen floor. When it finally hit, it hit hard and loud. *Smash!* It must have been a terrible sound. Impossibly loud. I can almost hear it echoing more than half a century after it shattered into a million tiny pieces.

The room, filled with so many, went silent.

Cokie's burgundy bowl, which had slept in its safe spot high above the chaos and heartbreak of their daily lives, waiting patiently to share its uncommon excellence, had been the symbol of the family's hope—hope that despite circumstance, something better surely lay ahead. It quietly spoke of crazy dreams and unbridled possibility, the source of whatever foolish optimism this family dared hold on to when whispering about brighter tomorrows in shared beds late at night. And there it lay, destroyed, its exotic treasure mixed in with shards of blood-red glass.

Not a word was uttered. Cokie sat down while Josie and James gathered the remains. Anna grew incredibly still, the crash continuing to ring in her ears. Where were her guardian angels now? How could they have let such hope be crushed? She watched as the blood-red shards vanished into a bucket, perhaps fearing what would soon prove to be true—that the cherished bowl's passing was an omen, that hope was indeed receding, and that new tragedy would soon fill the void.

CHAPTER 3

Our Suffering

I

For nearly a decade, the March of Dimes had helped Anna avoid polio's most brutal surgeries, and although her recovery was proving Cokie's optimism too bold, with the vigilance of Warm Springs' caretakers, she could now "walk" upright with crutches and braces. The March of Dimes had even made her into a Louisiana poster girl to help raise more funds for others. Anna's grateful smile radiated off newspapers around the South—her angelic face framed by a leather strap under her chin, and supported by steel bars locked into an orthopedic corset that kept the weight of her torso from bearing down on her increasingly fragile spine.

All of this made the news from Anna's local March of Dimes chapter seem impossibly cruel. A volunteer at the Baptist church that ran Anna's chapter had been skimming off the top. By the time the crime was discovered, the chapter had gone broke. Anna's spine refused to stop twisting from the polio-related scoliosis, and suddenly there was no more money to send her back to Warm Springs to receive the care it demanded.

Cokie's heart broke all over again. She did all she could to find new support, but with few resources, connections, or know-how, she came up dry. Truth is, if you don't have an education, and if no one has ever taught you how the system works or introduced you to people of influence, how can you be expected to navigate the system when it starts to fail? You most likely can't. You likely fail with it. And so the powerless stay that way. The poor get poorer. The sick get sicker. And when the men at the local Lake Providence hospital said that Anna's only option was to go to the nearest Shriners Hospital for their free treatment, Cokie believed them.

Anna would never see her adoring Warm Springs push-boys, tend her bedside flower garden, or hear her angels' voices ever again. Her new hospital was way down in New Orleans, and its scalpels, drills, and surgical horrors would make Georgia's hardships seem like an all-too-pleasant dream.

I I

As on most nights in her new, unfamiliar New Orleans hospital, Anna was in bed and her eyes closed, but she couldn't
sleep. Unlike at Warm Springs, the children living alongside
her here weren't exclusively polio patients; they had suffered every
kind of affliction or accident. Many were missing limbs. Her new
roommate had no legs, and only one arm. She used that arm to push
her body around on what amounted to a homemade skateboard.
They made quick friends, but few children here dared get close. Too
often, doctors and nurses would walk in unannounced and roll one
of Anna's new friends away—off to a surgery he or she didn't know
was coming, had never agreed to, and had no power to stop. Some
simply never returned. At Shriners, the scalpel ruled.

Anna's new ward nurse had seemed kind enough at first, with a
soft Southern drawl that felt familiar, and a gentle touch as she spoke
about the "hard truths" Anna needed to accept. Because of her condition, Anna wouldn't be able to attend school with the "regular"
kids, so college was out of reach. And her body would never be able
to perform full-time work. But Anna shouldn't worry too much: the
government had programs to support people like her.

Anna absorbed these losses, and turned to other hopes: love and
family. She had often dreamed of having children of her own. But like
a thief, that same nurse snatched those dreams away too: "My sweet
dear, you won't be able to have little ones. Your body couldn't carry
them. It'd kill you and the baby."

This cracked Anna's heart wide open. But what she found inside
wasn't sadness. It was something new: rage. The weakness in Anna's
muscles had created opportunities that had made her mind and heart
grow strong, and now she was being told that those strengths would
be of little use—that love, marriage, and children were all hopes too
big. Her only future, she was told, was on the government dole. She
couldn't bear this news, so she wouldn't accept it, and that little spark
of rage began to burn and glow.

From all the years Anna lived in hospitals and rehabilitation wards, she saved only two things: her autograph book from Warm Springs and an eleven-page essay from New Orleans titled "Our Suffering." I only recently found it, next to her birth certificate and a childhood attempt at a family tree, locked in an old leather briefcase shoved in the back of a closet. No author is credited, but it seems to have been written by a patient. Perhaps Anna contributed herself. Regardless, it clearly meant a great deal to her—its corners were bent, its pages well worn from repeated readings. Another rare and sacred clue from the past. So I sat down and tried to read it with the same care she might have fifty-five years earlier in a loud but lonesome hospital far from home. Among its words lives a deeply personal, intimate look into the lives of these frightened children. Several passages leap from it, passages that became touchstones in Anna's struggle to survive, such as:

> Nature does not intend that a *rosebud* remain as it is. In order for it to be truly beautiful, it must open and expand. We are like the rosebud, for God wishes for us to open and expand, to grow and not to remain as we were or as we now are. And we must not cling to our present condition as if it were final. We suffer because we do not see far enough ahead. But in order to see far ahead, we must accept the voice, the presence, and the love of God.

In the absence of any tangible signs of hope, Anna was being told to put her hopes in the hands of a higher power in order to keep moving forward. This wasn't unique to Anna's situation; it's a common practice in the world I come from, a world where many have little but their beliefs, where the fullness of God more than makes up for an empty bank account. It's partly why Sundays were and still are so central to our kind of American life, why we still find such community and comfort in our churches. It's a big part of why I loved going to church as a child. And in New Orleans, Anna turned the blind optimism she'd inherited from her mother into something new: faith. Few in her family had been particularly devout. Hospital-bound most of her life, she hadn't learned to pray in her family's local

Baptist church. Anna was a child with no denomination. Yet she began praying to God each morning and night, beseeching Him to let a brighter tomorrow come.

The trouble was, a child living in Anna's new ward needed a hell of a lot of God and faith to chase away all of the fears this place provided. The New Orleans doctors rarely shared their designs with the children. Anna would be wheeled away without notice, only to wake up with fresh new incisions running the length of her limbs, decorated with gruesome staples and stitches like some kind of Frankenstein's monster where doctors had cut back more muscle and bone, or attempted to graft tendons and ligaments into her legs. And the only cure for her pain was morphine, which filled her dreams with ants—swarming and devouring what little she had left of her body.

The horrors of Anna's time in that New Orleans hospital are worthy of their own book, a book about the right to health care and the rights of children, but this is not that book. And most of the stories from New Orleans were so painful, Anna refused to share them for fear of making them real again. But we do know this: she always put on a brave face for her mother. Perhaps too brave. On a rare visit to the New Orleans hospital, Cokie stepped away for a moment, and Anna confided in her big sister Martha, who had joined her mom on this visit. The doctors were considering a major new scoliosis surgery, and Anna didn't think their mom understood just how painful or dangerous it would be. She told Martha that the patients who'd survived it said it was like having a "tractor run down your back." This was as scared as Martha had ever seen her little sister.

The next morning, when Cokie and Martha were well into their journey back home, the doctors came for Anna again. Anna's heart quickened with panic. Sweaty and trembling, she was wheeled into an operating room that by today's standards looked medieval: crude blades, suction tubes, clamps, and a terrifying apparatus made of stainless steel bars and bolts intended to live inside her if she made it out alive.

She held no love or affection for these doctors and nurses. So she refused to allow them the gratification of comforting her for their crimes that morning. If she was going to die today, she would do it on her own terms. She knew that if she could control nothing else, she could control her tears. They were hers. So she refused to cry for them that day.

Soon the too-familiar cold, wet, stinking rag hit her face. There was no proper anesthesia at the time, no gas, just a cloth dipped in chloroform and pressed down over her mouth and nose. She was told to breathe in the noxious vapors. Little Anna held her breath, taking one more moment of her own, one more moment of life, then she put her fate and future in "the voice, the presence, and the love of God," and breathed in the horrible vapors. Her life and body were in His hands now—hands that to date had shown her little protection.

Word arrived in Lake Providence a day later. Once Anna's back had been cut open from neck to tailbone, her spine proved far more twisted than the doctors had anticipated. Implanting the "straightening and strengthening" device became nearly impossible. They had managed it, but the complications meant she'd lost a lot of blood. She was still unconscious, and her blood pressure was dropping. The doctor rang one of Cokie's neighbors who owned a phone to let her know that Anna's passing was now more a matter of when than if.

Billie-Ray, Cokie's second child, had died when Cokie was barely a teen. With the wisdom that accompanies age came the knowledge that there was far more she should have done to save her son. Privately, she blamed herself for his death, and now she felt she owned the blame for her Rose's condition too: for letting her get the disease in the first place, for all of the pain and isolation she'd endured, now magnified tenfold in New Orleans. And with this new turn, all of her daughter's bravery would be rewarded with a lonely, horrific death because her mama was too ignorant and poor to do better for her.

Cokie hadn't told anyone that she'd started getting dizzy at work, that she'd have to sit down to keep from fainting, or that a doctor had told her a part of her heart wasn't working right anymore. It likely hadn't been for a long time, but now aggravated by stress and age, it was giving out. Cokie had purchased a heart-shaped locket, which she wore around her neck, filled with the "emergency pills" her doctor prescribed. When she felt her chest tighten and her breath go, she had to take a pill and quick. When word arrived from New Orleans,

Cokie's heart broke. It literally broke. And she could hardly steady her hand to open the heart-shaped locket to save it.

Martha was equally devastated by the news. Half a century later, she had to pause to keep from breaking down as she talked with me about this moment in our family's history. In the South, we tell each other stories to help make us stronger, and we build our stories up to match the dire nature of our situations—difficult times demand the most inspiring stories. Rose Anna had become the family's story. She was their light, their pint-size survivor, their reason for strength. "If little Rose Anna can survive shit like X, Y and Z, with a smile on her goddamn face, then we damn sure can survive this or that." All of her sisters, brothers, aunts, and uncles had uttered some version of that sentiment at one point or another to their own children, or privately to themselves in hours of need.

And beyond our family, Anna's story had given more than a few of her neighbors strength and hope too. Now this story was about to be taken away. Anna slipped into a coma late that night. It seemed that life had finally delivered an injury too deep, even for her mighty will.

III

Most of the folks working in the New Orleans children's hospital were black, and many spoke Creole. Willie was one of those aides, and the ever-present bird perched on his shoulder had picked up more than a few of Willie's choice expletives. During her months of living on Willie's ward, Anna had in turn picked up a few of the bird's most beloved dirty words.

Willie had long since learned not to talk much with the kids in the hospital. It was best not to get attached. But perhaps sparked by the first-rate education Warm Springs had provided, Anna was proving to be a curious child, and she was fascinated by Willie and his colorful bird, so from the moment she met them, she'd batted her eyelashes and worked her charm to make sure they came to visit her whenever Willie was on a shift. Before he knew what was happening, he had fallen hopelessly under Anna's spell.

Fueled by Anna's infectious curiosity, Willie soon figured out how to sneak Anna out of the hospital and down to the famed Café Du Monde—a big, bustling café nestled between Jackson Square's bright gardens and the mighty Mississippi River. Together, they'd listen to street performers play jazz, drink milky coffee, and stuff themselves with New Orleans's deep-fried, sugar-powdered beignets. Like her old brother-in-law James, Willie never treated Anna with kid gloves, so she quickly learned to love him even more than his bird. And for the short while they had together, he was like the father she'd never really known.

When Mardi Gras arrived, Anna begged Willie to take her out to see all the floats and bawdy costumes, to hear the hullabaloo of wildly exuberant music. A little white lie to the doctors, and Willie put Anna in a wheelchair so they could navigate the rowdy, drunken crowd. For this special occasion only, and under his trusted control, Anna accepted the indignity of two wheels.

They arrived midway through the parade. Anna stared up, mesmerized by the colorful feathers, masks, and beads. Women in the crowd were exposing their breasts in hopes someone would toss down a strand from a float or balcony as reward. A few men flashed their wares too. It was loud, unbridled, vivacious. Anna was in the midst of something she felt sure no one else in her family had ever experienced, but unlike all her other firsts, this one wasn't painful, it was magical. Then, from a towering float, a woman began flinging out gold and silver Mardi Gras coins into the crowd.

"Are they real gold?" Anna asked Willie.

"They look real to you, sugar?"

"How the heck should I know?"

"Well, I don't think they real gold, baby. No."

"They look real enough to me, Willie." And she wanted one.

From high atop a float, a woman popping out of a sequined gown spotted little Anna down below and waved. Anna enthusiastically waved back, and that busty woman threw a fistful of beads and "real" gold and silver coins down toward Anna's wheelchair. Anna quickly rolled out from under Willie's control, positioning her chair over as many of those beads and coins as possible, and then glared at anyone who dared try to grab such treasure from a girl in a wheelchair. "Get 'em, Willie!" she cried out. Willie gathered up every last one. The trick to this game figured out, Anna waved like mad at every passing float, and by the end of the parade, they had collected a massive cache of treasure for themselves.

This was the only story Anna ever readily shared from her time in New Orleans—never the traumas, just Willie, his swearing bird, their beignets, and the acquisition of her "real" gold coins. The rest I had to dig and beg for. I suppose that's the spirit of a survivor, of an eternal optimist—despite all the "nos" and "nevers" thrown at her, she was always looking to the bright side, or for some hopeful sound to grab ahold of.

Two days into her coma, she thought she heard one.

The sound was far away, but she locked onto it and wouldn't let it go. It was a parrot, swearing in Creole. And following the sound of Willie's cussing parrot, Anna slowly made her way out of that coma her doctors had said she would never escape. A few days later, tough old Willie, who claimed to have seen it all, shed tears when he saw his Anna smiling up at him again.

One of the most well-worn pages in Anna's long-saved essay "Our Suffering" contains this passage:

> We can rebel against our condition and make ourselves
> and those around us miserable. Or we can accept it with
> resignation and patience, and derive great benefit from our
> suffering for ourselves and others. This patience is *not a passive
> acceptance* of our suffering and a meaningless surrender to our
> wills. But it is an *active and energetic exercise of the will*. . . . We
> must continue in our efforts, not despairingly, but *hopefully
> aware* that one day our struggle will end and we will be
> victorious.

I can only imagine how those words buoyed Anna's spirits in the months to come as doctors built a cage for her body: steel bars down both legs from hips to feet, then bolted into shoes. The metal inside and out would take the place of hamstring, calf, abdominal, and back muscles—a body remade of steel, aluminum, leather, and copper. Rubbing braces would build thick calluses on her legs and feet. Bolts would stain her flesh as they corroded. The curving of her spine would slow but never improve, lifting one leg far higher than the other. And in that time, Rose Anna Whitehead would rename herself once more. She was no longer an Anna. That was a girl's name. By her own decree, she was now a woman. A survivor. And she would be called Anne.

Her spine now made of steel, Anne refused to cry or complain any longer; she refused the morphine that gave her such horrible nightmares. Because somewhere in her coma, she had found her mother's sturdy, some say foolish optimism buried deep inside of her. And once awake, she put that optimism next to the rage she'd found in her broken heart, and made a decision to use her hopefulness and energetic will to prove every one of this hospital's staff of realists wrong in every possible way.

I understand the mighty power and dangers of Anne's rage and foolish optimism all too well. They live deep inside of me too. Because just to my left, keeping me company as I type these words, are four of Rose Anna's shimmering gold Mardi Gras coins. Because, of course, despite many more trials ahead, and every assurance that she'd never fall in love or have and raise children of her own, tough little Rose Anna Whitehead grew up to be my mom. And that inheritance, from mother to daughter to me, would prove a force with the strength to move things in directions few in our world would have ever dared imagine possible.

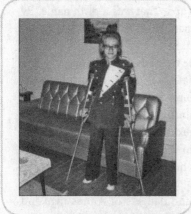

CHAPTER 4

A Body in Motion

I

The same high school physics teacher who taught me that nothing starts moving without an outside force getting it going also taught me that a body in motion won't stop moving without something forcing it to slow down.

At the age of fifteen, nearly thirteen years after her nightmare began, Anne finally found herself on the long-awaited ride back home to Lake Providence, free of all of the hospitals' terrors for good. On that journey, she made a list of things she'd been told she'd never do. It included walking with her own two feet, having a "normal" boy fall in love with her, going to prom, going to college, driving a car, traveling abroad, holding a full-time job, getting married, and having children. While Anne had come to accept that suffering would always be a part of her life, she refused to accept these limitations. So each morning, she dedicated herself to receiving her suffering with an open heart, then got to work proving everyone wrong.

Anne was finally home, but she'd be damned if she was going to sit still.

Lake Providence had changed since Anne left. In the years she was away, Anne's black neighbors had won the right to vote, and her high school had been integrated, but racism there was far from dead. Many white folks left town when integration arrived. The remaining white kids headed to a new private school that could charge tuition their parents hoped the black families couldn't afford. Anne's family most certainly couldn't afford it, so that fall, Anne walked like a pendulum into her mostly African American public school.

For Anne, it wasn't strange to be a minority. She already knew what it meant to be different, and she once told me that it felt like her black classmates didn't gawk at her the way the white kids in town did. Her new classmates understood what it was like to be judged on appearance over character, and perhaps they didn't want to pass that pain along.

What Anne could no longer ignore was her white neighbors' bigoted remarks and racist slang. When she asked them about it, some would say, "That's just the way it's always been." Others outright argued the superiority of the white race—ideas they'd learned from their parents and grandparents. Anne knew better. She'd already seen more of the world and met more kinds of people than most here ever would. Polio had given her that unexpected gift. And because polio didn't discriminate, Anne had grown up surrounded by diversity. Hell, her life had been saved by a black man and his foulmouthed bird—why wouldn't she share a classroom with a child who shared his shade of skin? But as her big sister Martha knew too well, in Lake Providence, this kind of attitude made Anne dangerously unique in a whole new way.

Anne had only about half of her high school days left, but she made up for lost time. She made the honor roll, went to football games, and joined the band—and not just any band, the marching band, for which she figured out how to balance on her crutches so she could play her clarinet standing up. And when prom arrived, she didn't lament her single status but had her mom get out needle and thread. Anne wasn't going to let that New Orleans nurse be right about her missing prom. Cokie tailored a spectacular dress—tight up top to straighten Anne's back, and in regal princess fashion, with a billowing cloud of baby blue chiffon below.

The night of the prom, Anne posed for a portrait on the family sofa. Cokie helped her sit up nice and straight, then spread out all the blue chiffon, perfectly covering Anne's braced legs. Cokie stepped back and pressed her camera's shutter, and the zirconium flash cube burned up in an explosion of light. Her Rose looked like an honest-to-God movie star that night, and that's not hyperbole. I have the photo on my desk, and I've worked with many a movie star. My mom looked absolutely stunning.

Over the next two years, Anne did everything she could to eclipse the label of "cripple," but on occasion it proved too tall an order. Martha can remember a high school football game Anne was supposed to meet her at. Martha arrived late and chatted up the ticket boy to try to find out if Anne had already gone in. She had to think, "What makes Anne distinctive?" She described her sister: "She has beautiful blond hair, blue eyes, with glasses, cat-eye glasses . . ."

At this school, that should have sufficed, but a friend walked up and told the boy:

"You can't miss her. She has polio."

Martha was furious: "Of all the things you could say about my sister, of all the things she's done, why the hell would you say that?!"

It's true that Anne's hard work was partly an attempt to build a smoke screen, but that smoke screen began paying dividends most dared not dream of in her hometown. At seventeen years old, Anne hadn't seen her father in years, so she wrote him a letter that included this shocker: "I graduate in May, you know. I can hardly wait. I plan to start college at Northeast in the fall. I went and took a scholarship test there and I got a letter from them last week and they asked me to come for an interview."

Cokie and Victor couldn't have imagined finishing elementary school, and now their most challenged child was packing up a baby-blue piece of secondhand luggage with her few earthly possessions, on the cusp of doing what few in their town or family had ever done: leaving for college. Cokie was in awe. The nightmare that had stolen her daughter's limbs, and nearly taken her life, was now revealing its flip side: Anne, though immobilized—or perhaps thanks to that—was becoming a genuine mover in a town where little ever moved.

The following spring, an item appeared in the local Lake Providence newspaper: "CLAIMED BY HONOR SOCIETY. Roseanna Whitehead (Northeast State College) was among the 26 freshman women initiated recently into Alpha Lambda Delta, national honor society. . . . Miss Whitehead, a graduate of Monticello High School, aspires to be a doctor of medicine." Nowhere in the article is there a mention of disability. Hot damn. She'd finally eclipsed that characteristic with her academic excellence.

But good grades aren't enough to build a full life, and Anne hadn't become an expert flirt just for sport. She loved boys. And tall, dark, and handsome was her thing.

The war was raging in Vietnam, and like so many others, Anne began writing letters to the young soldiers over there. If one wrote back and asked politely, she'd send a photo of herself from the shoulders up. She was beautiful in those photos, so she had little trouble getting letters and photos back. Most of the young men would ask to meet up in person when their tours of duty were complete, and that's when Anne's replies would slow. Or occasionally a young man would stop writing her, likely wounded or killed in combat. To those who had lost limbs but still wrote, Anne might reveal her own condition in hopes of comforting her new brother in that struggle.

Anne filled a gold, wallet-size photo book with the pictures of the men she wrote to and fell for in college. Years later, it surfaced, and we flipped through it together. I called it her "golden book of boys," and I pointed out a stunningly handsome young man near the back. Tall, with thick dark hair and a square jaw, he looked like an absolute teen idol. When I asked her if they'd ever met in person, I could feel her heart sink. "Yes . . . that was Don."

Anne hadn't met Don through a letter-writing campaign where she could easily hide her most visible difference; she'd met him in college, in person. He knew what her legs and body looked like, and he didn't seem to mind. From the day they met, she began waking up an hour earlier each morning to stand in front of her dorm room's mirror, leaning on a crutch to put on her makeup, roll her hair with giant curlers, and get herself just right. And guess what? It worked. Don began asking Anne out on proper dates. And after one such date, Don leaned in and kissed her full on the mouth. It was wetter than she'd imagined, but it still seemed too good to be true. The most handsome boy in school was pursuing her. This wasn't supposed to happen. It seemed everyone but her mom had warned her it never would.

It quickly became clear to anyone who met Anne and Don that they were getting serious fast. Don had even whispered the words "marriage" and "kids" once or twice, and now he wanted to come home with her to Lake Providence to meet her family over the summer. He was a proper son of the South and wanted to show Anne suitable respect before going any further. Anne had dreamed of getting married one day, and occasionally even imagined the more medically dangerous idea of having children. Now a man was suggesting they might try both.

Anne finished her spring semester in late May and headed to Texarkana to visit Josie and James. Their daughter, my cousin Debbie, was a teenager then. She remembers Anne "writing all these letters to Don, and Don writing all these letters back." Debbie would lie on her bed listening to Anne read them out loud, fascinated if not tantalized. Anne even had a picture of Don that she put up at the head of her bed. And when Don finally arrived in person, he was everything Anne had promised, if not more. Even James, Anne's fiercest protector, thought he was "grade A."

Don loved Anne and wasn't afraid to show it or talk about it with anyone. But no matter how high love soars, it can dig holes twice as deep.

When Anne finally met Don's folks, Don's mother was kind to Anne's face, but once Anne left the room, she expressed a deep concern: "How will she ever give you children?" Don pushed back, but just like Anne's doctors, Don's mom was certain that Anne's body couldn't handle a pregnancy. By the end of the summer, she had done her homework to prove her case, and had convinced her son that Anne could never give him a family or her the grandkids she deserved. So, his own heart breaking, Don ended things with Anne.

Anne's grades suddenly plummeted from As and Bs to Ds and an F. She was devastated. She even reached out to a young priest named Embry whom she'd met in New Orleans. He had been a handsome teenage priest-in-training who little Anna had tried to tempt with love letters to leave the seminary for her. He had successfully resisted her charms. Now she needed to know how he had accepted that he would never love a woman, never get married, and never have a family. A week later, he wrote Anne back:

> The best one can do is to love more, beyond what might be
> expected in return. One must see his own value and self-worth
> to become of value to others. This value and worth we have
> is from God. He loves us, and that's something. And we have

things to do in this world, even if it's not big, because we have
responsibilities as Christians. But it's tough to be a Christian; it
takes blood, sweat, tears, and the sacrifice of life.

Anne had never been a very religious young woman, but her prayers to God in New Orleans had worked out well enough. And so, after receiving Embry's letter about God's love and purpose easing heartbreak, she began visiting churches near campus.

She would forever begrudge the local Baptist church for having stolen the money that forced her from Warm Springs. Now she yearned for a new church, a more holy and uplifting Christianity, but despite her numerous Sunday outings to this chapel and that, none seemed to fit. It was all too hellfire and brimstone, and she'd had more than enough of that in this life already.

As it turned out, all of her searching would prove to be in vain. The faith she was after didn't require any footwork. It came knocking.

At the very back of my mom's "golden book of boys," there was a picture of one of the most handsome young men I'd ever seen—shiny dark hair, a distinctive jaw, and crystal-blue bedroom eyes. I tried my best not to make my keen interest too clear, and thank goodness, because when I casually asked, "Who's he?" my mother took a long, thoughtful breath and said, "That's your father, Lance."

11

Two cute, clean-cut men in pressed white shirts, black slacks, and name badges that deemed them "elders" despite their hardly being out of their teens knocked on Anne's dorm room door one day. They were the picture of perfection. Kind and polite, they didn't preach about hellfire but spoke of a new and everlasting restored gospel of Jesus Christ that claimed all men were inherently good, and that things like love and family didn't end when we died. "We will all be reunited in heaven. Because family is forever." To Anne's Southern heart, this meant her family would now come first for all of eternity. It was very appealing for a young woman who knew too well the pain of not having her family near.

Anne had a thousand questions. They had every answer. The point of life was to pass a test: to see if you could stay true to the word of God despite temptation. It was also for Heavenly Father's souls in heaven to come down to Earth and get bodies. One look at Anne's legs and torso and they knew what to share next: "And in heaven, the bodies we get here on Earth will be healthy and perfect again, forever." Much like mine, my mother's "too-good-to-be-true" filter often fails. She was happy to believe that in these Mormons' Celestial Kingdom (the highest floor of their multilevel heaven), she would have a perfect body and be surrounded by her family forever.

Anne immediately began attending services at the Church of Jesus Christ of Latter Day Saints. Coming from an alcoholic home, she loved its rules against drinking and smoking. Her life thus far had been so messy; the tidy structure of this new brand of Christianity with its adherents' well-ironed Sunday clothes, sharp haircuts, and love of all things "celestial" and white, must have felt like sweet relief. Earthly life had shown her only chaos. This church was so very orderly.

It didn't hurt one bit that her missionaries soon introduced her to another young man on his mission in Louisiana. He had grown up in Provo, Utah, the heart of Mormondom. And he was just about the best-looking young man Anne had ever laid eyes on: tall, dark, and handsome. If he wanted to talk to her about Jesus, the Holy Spirit, or Heavenly Father, she didn't mind one bit. He could have recited the phone book and she would have said "Amen." His name was Raul N. Garrison. When she got up the nerve to ask what the N. stood for, he paused, a sly grin creasing his bedroom eyes, and answered, "Nothing." And he meant it. His parents hadn't given him a middle name, so he'd added the initial himself. It's worth noting that this is how contemporary Mormon prophets present themselves: Thomas S. Monson, Gordon B. Hinckley, Spencer W. Kimball. He was trying to elevate his stature by taking on a middle initial like all the best "men of God" do. It was LDS bold. He was confident, and a rebel to boot. What a dream.

Mormon missionaries aren't supposed to engage in romance of any sort while on their two-year missions, but Raul was different. Everything he did and said felt like flirting. Now he'd met his match. Anne was a master flirt. She'd leaned on that skill for nearly two decades. So Raul and Anne started going to meals together outside of church and meeting up in ways that seemed an awful lot like dates. He told her no one could know. That wasn't music to her ears, but she agreed, and they did their best to keep what increasingly looked like a budding romance from the good folks at church. But when Anne's family found out she'd met someone new, they were all eager to meet him.

If James Ray Mosely didn't like somebody, everybody knew it, and quick. And in contrast to how he'd felt about Don, James couldn't stand Raul. He didn't trust "that rat" as far as he could throw him. But James could tell that Anne was falling hard for Raul, so in this instance alone, he chose to hold his tongue. He would live to regret that silence.

It was true that Anne seemed genuinely happy. Here was a handsome young man from a good family who seemed to love her despite her condition, and when she told him she wanted a family more than anything in the world, and that she would try her best to have children for them one day, he said, "Okay"—but that if it wasn't Heavenly Father's design, he would be all right with that too.

When Raul finally did propose, he made it clear that there was a clock ticking on the offer. His mission in Louisiana was coming to an end. He'd soon have to return home to Utah, where he would be subject to the draft—unless, of course, he married a disabled woman. That kind of a marriage would earn him a deferment. Though far more practical than romantic, his deadline did make good sense, so Anne did her best to push back any concerns it may have raised.

Cokie wrote letters begging Anne to finish school: "You're only months away from graduating, my love. You don't know when you might need something to fall back on." Anne's entire family thought she was throwing away the greatest opportunity any of them had ever had. But now Anne had an offer of marriage, perhaps even children, and an eternal family in a church that promised her a perfect body in the afterlife. It was everything she'd ever been told she would never have, all laid out in front of her. So, even faced with passionate objections from her family, how could she say no?

On January 6, 1969, while most people her age were expanding their consciousness, resisting a war, neck-deep in a sexual revolution, and still feeling the glow of a summer of love, Anne took off her braces, let go of her crutches, and waded into a baptismal font in the Monroe branch of the LDS Church. An elder named Terry cradled her small body, said a few prescribed words, and submerged her fully. I can imagine the hope that must have filled her heart when she was under the water. With this act, she belonged to a new family of Latter Day Saints. With this act, she'd be allowed to marry a good Mormon man in one of those monumental, glimmering LDS temples. And with this act, she would have a perfect body in heaven.

Anne never returned to classes. And when she filled out the marriage application, she put all of her names together as one: "Roseanna." After all, this moment would be the culmination of everything Rose, Anna, and Anne had survived. And on May 30 in a small ceremony in Lake Providence, the young woman who'd been told she'd never experience love, marriage, or children was legally wed to Raul N. Garrison for time and eternity.

It was the happiest day of her life, though even her dear sister Martha did not attend.

There was a job waiting for Raul in California, the land where her mom had once told her precious Christmas fruit came from. Anne knew full well that nothing much in Lake Providence ever moved or changed without dying, and that only by facing that terrible outside force called polio with hope and optimism had she broken the mold and set herself into motion. Now she was determined to keep moving. So she packed up what little she owned into her baby-blue suitcase, kissed her tearful mother goodbye, and began her first journey of adulthood.

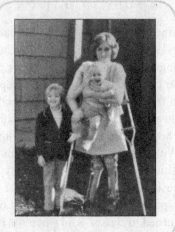

CHAPTER 5

Bedrock

I

It was 1970. Each Sunday morning, Anne and Raul's new neighbors in Sacramento, California, beheld a peculiar sight: a rail-thin woman with long blond hair, dressed for church, stepping out of the smallest house on the block with braces and crutches and a massive beach ball–shaped protrusion around her midsection. Less than a year after saying "I do," Anne had dispensed with all the medical experts' sage advice and started trying to get pregnant. Doctors had warned her countless times that her body couldn't handle a pregnancy and that she would likely lose the child if not her own life. And polio had long since robbed her of any "pushing" muscles, so there was no possibility of a natural delivery, and doctors were far from certain that her body could bear a cesarean section.

But having a family was my mom's number one dream. It was what polio had denied her during her own childhood; it was what those cute Mormon missionaries had guaranteed she'd have for "time and eternity" if she converted.

By late winter, Anne had to stretch her crutches far out in front of her to maintain balance as she swung her big belly like a pendulum beneath her. Everyone worried. Her mom and sisters did their best to prepare her for the inevitable miscarriage. Come spring, her deeply concerned doctor made the call that to let this pregnancy continue threatened both mother and child. Thinking only of her unborn baby, Anne relented, and on April 2, she let the doctor slice her open and pull out little Marcus Raul Garrison, a good many weeks early.

Marcus could have fit in your hand. His lungs refused to work. He was purple-yellow and just clinging to life when Anne first looked through the incubator's curved glass. He was in agony, fighting for air, untouchable. Now she worried that the naysayers had been right: this dream wasn't only selfish, it was damn cruel, and she was the architect of Marcus's pain.

Maybe it was the nurses' vigilant care, my mother's prayers, or even the blessings administered by the two Mormon boys who came by the hospital every few days, but Marcus's lungs slowly got stronger, and so did he.

Weeks later, when Anne finally held her "brave little man" on their way out of the hospital, the doctors went on and on about how lucky she was, and warned her never to try this again. The last thing she said to those doctors was stern: "There was no luck to it, thank you *very* much."

Four years later, her belly was even bigger, and on June 10, 1974, she was prepped for surgery all over again. This time, she had a run-of-the-mill chest cold. But there's nothing run-of-the-mill about a chest cold for a polio survivor. She had only a quarter of one lung working well, so any pesky flu phlegm was potentially fatal. Her coughing fits were endless, alarming to strangers, and a real concern for her new doctors.

That morning, Anne tried hard to get all the phlegm up, to hydrate, to sneak any medications that might thin the mucus, listening for doctors coming up the hall so she could stifle her terrible cough. She didn't want to give those men any reason to delay the procedure and risk her second child's health.

Shortly before 1:00 p.m., Anne was wheeled into the operating room. The room was modern, the medications far more gentle than what she'd experienced as a little girl, but midway through the procedure, whatever willed her to breathe through such clogged lungs fell asleep with her. Her blood pressure dropped precipitously. Her heart threatened to give out. A breathing bag went over her face. The nurse started pumping while doctors rushed to deliver the child before it met a similarly grim fate.

Soon a blood-streaked, vernix-covered baby emerged from the slice in her flesh. He was deathly quiet and still. The doctor quickly examined him: despite his silence, he was very much alive.

A breath. Another. An angry coughing fit, and Anne began breathing on her own again, gasping for air. More irritated than frightened, she showed little interest in the fact that she'd nearly died on the operating table. She wanted to know, "Is the baby okay?"

The nurse handed Anne her second son, wrapped up tight. The next few moments proved fodder for a story she'd spin for me for years to come:

"You didn't cry. Your big blue eyes were wide open. Like flying saucers. And they just stared up into mine like you had so much to teach me. And I just knew, I knew you were going to teach me so many things."

Raul interrupted the transcendent moment. "Look. He has crinkled-up little ears." He had just ensured that the first words his second son's "unusual" ears heard from his father were critical.

As it turns out, many years later the nurse at my elementary school would figure out that my ears were like that for a reason. I had likely refused to let go of them because I have abnormally sensitive hearing. I can hear things too high-pitched or too quiet for most. That might sound like a superpower to some, but it's mostly been a torture. Faraway noises and conversations most find inaudible can drive me crazy. High-pitched sounds actually hurt my bones. And my unusual ears often overhear critical whispers and gossip not intended for them.

But as I lay in my mom's arms in my first minutes of life, she paid my crushed ears no mind. To her they were perfectly different.

Raul wanted to name me Dustin after the actor Dustin Hoffman. As a good Mormon wife, Anne knew she had to put her preferred name in second position. So Dustin Lance Garrison filled in the birth certificate blanks. But not one to ever truly give in, she only ever used "Dustin" in public. In private, I was always her Lancer. It's a moniker wrestling match that's alive and well today, leaving me to choose who will remain in the "Dustin" camp of strangers and who will become a member of that select group I allow access to the real "Lance."

Having barely survived birth number two, any realistic, reasonable person would have raised her two boys and counted her blessings. But not Anne. On March 4, 1978, she gave birth to her third son, Todd Bryant Garrison. This time the surgery went flawlessly, the baby was perfectly healthy, and perhaps because of the ease of things, with no one screaming for her to stop this madness, she told the doctor to tie her tubes. They gladly did as they were told.

Anne couldn't drive, she didn't have a job or a college degree, but she did have a husband and a family. Item by item, she was proving her childhood naysayers wrong.

. . .

It turned out that my silent first moments were predictive. I said little to anyone outside of our home for the first decade of life. I was so painfully shy that family reunions were spent hiding behind couches, lured out only by my aunt Josie's promise of a bowl of ice cream in her quiet kitchen. I refused to wear bright colors or shirts with words or illustrations for fear of someone commenting. Big groups of loud human beings were my worst nightmare.

My safe haven was a quiet room with my mom's craft box. Tape and glue were my pals, and I could spend days on end with them building peep-show boxes of faraway worlds or sock puppet friends with glued-on googly eyes. My mom was the beneficiary of countless "masterpieces" built of construction paper and felt. And although I refused to speak, I loved to listen, especially to my mom's voice. I would curl up next to her in bed, secretly sucking on my left index and middle fingers while twirling my white-blond hair as she read aloud to me. Book after book, story after story, my mom and I traveled to the most extraordinary places, met the most fascinating people, and encountered and conquered the most terrifying foes. Neither of us was a particularly good fit for this world. So we became masters at transporting ourselves to other worlds, and in those worlds, we were adventurers and heroes. Her hopeful stories were our escape, our salvation. And so I fell in love with the magic of storytelling.

These moments sit atop the most treasured memories of my life. Because, although I was only six years old, they would prove to be my final hours of safety and innocence—the last moments before everything broke apart.

I I

I have only a few vague memories of Raul. He was a traveling salesman, and too busy with his job (and whatever he got up to with other women on work trips) to spend much time with my brothers and me. For my mom, having children was the fulfillment of an impossible dream; I'm afraid Raul saw us as the fulfillment of his Mormon duty to propagate. Raul wasn't bright. He struggled to stay employed. And in that pursuit, he moved us from Sacramento to Stockton, and then from El Paso to San Antonio, where he finally landed a job selling toys.

Late in the summer of 1980, word came that an aunt on my father's side, who I had never met or even heard of, was coming to visit us in San Antonio with plans to take us to the zoo. Her name was Louise. My mom wanted the house flawless for her visit, so we all shifted into full preparation mode. Chores in our home weren't a learning exercise. We were our mother's arms, legs, and muscles. But Marcus was ten years old now and already adept at a too-cool-for-school act he'd eventually perfect. So that week, our mom announced that I was now grown-up enough to take over Marcus's vacuuming duties. I was beside myself with pride. Marcus knew it was a trick, and he rolled his eyes as I dedicated myself to leaving perfect rows in the family room carpet in an effort to prove that her faith in me was well placed.

In addition to my standard chores, I was also tasked with looking after one-year-old Todd. I loved Todd from the get-go. He was my chief project. So between cleaning duties, I attempted diaper changes, following all of the instructions my mom had carefully spelled out and demonstrated. And even with Marcus sneaking off to a friend's house, we were well ahead of schedule for Aunt Louise's arrival.

But while I was helping to scrub out the cracks in the kitchen floor, my mom told me that Aunt Louise wasn't an aunt at all; she was actually Raul's first cousin. Such intentional misnaming seemed rather ridiculous to me, but I was happy to call her a mashed potato if her visit meant we got to go to the zoo. My opinion didn't change much when, upon her arrival, "Aunt" Louise proved to be an especially unremarkable human being: plain dress, plain hair, not much to say of any real interest, and features fixed in a constipated expression.

So I quickly put her out of mind as I distracted myself with the easily irritated bald eagle, the curious little monkeys, and all the thick-skinned elephants at the zoo. Most of all, though, I was mesmerized by the machines that looked like jukeboxes, with glass tops and quarter-eating slots, that for the right price would press a waxy, plastic toy gorilla, panther, or elephant right in front of your eyes.

We were broke and we were Mormon, so we were thrifty. I already knew that I would never own one of those wax figures. I satisfied myself with watching the machine press other kids' toys, smelling the hot waxy plastic cool from afar as the children casually snatched the finished products from the machine's guts. And that's when Louise did her one remarkable thing: she pulled out a big stack of quarters, fed the coin slot, and told me the next wax gorilla would be mine. I was stunned.

Out of habit, I looked to my mom for permission, but on this occasion I was met with a tight smile. Crap. It had never mattered that I rarely used words; my mom and I didn't need them. We could read each other's minds. But as special as that sounds (and it was special), it also meant there was no hiding anything from each other. I knew then and there that she had nothing against the red gorilla; there was something about Louise she didn't care for.

I stifled my joy as I felt the bright red gorilla cool in my hands, and as quickly as I could, I found a fatal flaw in it: Why would they choose red wax for this gorilla machine? Everyone knows gorillas are black and silver. This error would have to be corrected.

That afternoon, I carefully laid out newspaper on the back patio, chose my paint colors from Marcus's vast collection of model paint, and set out to bring my gorilla more realistically to life. My mom was not normally one to interrupt such creative endeavors, but on this afternoon she opened the sliding glass door, stuck her head out, and said something that for better and for worse would stick with me for far too long:

"Wouldn't you enjoy doing the fun stuff more once you've finished your chores?"

I thought about it. The answer was no. I had the creative itch to do this right now. But that wasn't the answer she wanted. She wanted me to stop doting over Louise's gift. And maybe she was right. Perhaps I actually would enjoy painting more with all of my work done, completely carefree. So I put my painting aside and got to work picking up the house, helping change my little brother's diaper again, and setting the table for Louise's enchilada dinner.

Afterward, my mom tucked us all into bed early, but there were none of the usual bedtime stories or endless "I love yous." She seemed distracted. I didn't fall asleep but sat up thinking for hours. I heard voices. I heard the front door open and close.

When I woke up the next morning, Marcus wasn't in his bed. That wasn't normal. The sun was already shining through the wood shutters, turning our room a deep amber. Why had no one woken me up?

When I walked into the family room, there was a surprise waiting: my actual aunt Josie. My heart leaped. Sometime in the middle of the night she had made the seven-hour drive from Texarkana to San Antonio. She gave me a giant squeeze of a hug . . . but then she walked outside without any explanation. That moment remains crystal clear in my memory, because it marks the end of a bright chapter—the last beat before I realized how fragile love can be.

As I stepped a bit deeper into our home, I found my mom sitting at the kitchen table. Her chair was facing out into the family room. When she saw me, she sat up straight, her face red, her eyes out of tears. Marcus had left the house already—likely to walk Texas's serpentine drainage ditches alone and in quiet anger, a habit that would become increasingly common moving forward. I did what I still do when there's trouble: I took a closer look. I knelt down in front of my mom and gazed into her eyes. But I was unable to recognize her pain. Although I was best at being silent, in this moment I needed words. "What's wrong?" I asked her.

She looked back with more love than I'd ever seen, and said, "My baby . . ." Then she took a breath, steeling herself so that what came out next might not sound like the end of our world. "Your daddy has gone away."

The thing is, he was always going away for work, so what the heck was all the drama about? "Where did he go now?" I asked.

"I don't know." That was new. Now I worried. "Someplace else," she added. Then finally: "He's not coming back this time, Lancer."

She was in incredible pain. I could feel it like it was my own. This family she had wanted more than her education, more than becoming a doctor, more than staying close to the mother and siblings she loved had just been ripped in two without warning.

I had to protect her. No one had ever told me that was my job; I'd just known it by instinct since the day I was born. So I said what I

thought might help fix things: "He'll come home . . . I *promise* you."
I was already well aware that a promise was a very big deal in our
home. My mom and our church had both taught me that "a promise
is sacred," something I still believe today. And right there, at the age
of six, I had just made a whopper of a promise.

My mom didn't have the heart to argue or a clue how to explain
what had happened, so she just held me. I didn't have time for that.
I wrestled free and ran into the room that held her craft box and a
rocking chair piled high with homemade pillows. I knelt down in
front of that chair that only a few years earlier had rocked me to
sleep, and I folded my arms, bowed my head, and prayed the way
I'd been taught to by all the kind, white-haired Mormon men in our
church.

"Dear Heavenly Father," I said as I began to shake with tears.
"Please bring my daddy back home. I *promise* I will be a good boy.
I'll do my chores. I'll listen. I'll do as I'm told. I *promise* I'll be the best
boy ever if You bring him back to me, and Marcus, and Todd, and my
mom. In the name of Jesus Christ, amen."

I let my tears dry and waited for the trembling to stop. Then I made
myself get tough. I'd just made promises to my mother and God that
were far too weighty for a six-year-old. Only as I look back now can
I say with certainty that when I left that room to face my mother in
her chair again, I left my childhood behind for good. I was now one
of three small boys abandoned by their father with a paralyzed mom.
For survival's sake, it was time to man up.

Weeks later, I was putting warm, freshly washed sheets on my bed
when I heard my mom shout for me to grab Todd and run out into
the backyard. I could hear a shiver of fear in her voice. That lit up
whatever fledgling paternal instincts I had: I grabbed Todd and hit
the gas. When I passed our mom in the front hallway, it was clear she
was covering up real panic.

"Lancer, whatever happens, no matter what, I don't want you to
come back inside until I've come out to tell you it's safe. Okay?"

I nodded.

"Say 'okay.' "

"Okay."

She kissed my head and Todd's, and I ran out back, closing the door behind me. Marcus was already out there. With Todd in my arms, the three of us tucked ourselves into a corner beside the glass door so we could just see inside. We watched our mom walk to the front door on her crutches. Soon we could hear screaming, back and forth, but I didn't recognize the voice of the man outside. It sounded sick, deranged.

Marcus told me to stay where I was, then ran as fast as he could, jumping the back fence. I sat frozen. Marcus was the eldest, and he knew that came with some responsibility. So I'd like to believe that he wasn't running away, that he was trying to find help. And I bet that was true, but I never got the chance to see help arrive.

Seconds later, *boom! boom! boom!* echoed from inside. My ears rang with the frightful sound. My mom began screaming but even that didn't satiate the monster outside. Then again: *Boom! Boom! Boom!* Now she started moving away from the door, quickly. With one last colossal *boom!* the lock burst free in a shower of splinters and the door flew open, smashing into our mother's steel-braced back and sending her crashing to the floor inside.

And there stood Raul, his eyes blazing. Beneath him, my mother, splayed out on the floor, afraid for her life. But she didn't scream for help; instead, she screamed for me to run. And I did, Todd gripped in my trembling arms.

That was the last time I would see my father for decades.

Many years later, I found out that my mom had walked in on Raul "laying on top of" my "aunt" Louise the night after our trip to the zoo. Propositions had been made for my mom to join their incestuous dalliance, and when she had denied her good Mormon husband's desires, he had left a note saying that he was leaving her for good.

Raul would never write us a single letter, call to see if we were alive, send any gifts at Christmas or birthdays—or the child-support checks he would soon be ordered to pay by judges. He never again acknowledged that we existed. As my uncle James had feared but never voiced to my mom, she had likely been Raul's ticket out of Vietnam. Now that threat was long gone, and so was he. We had no idea where he'd gone, and when I eventually tried to track him down, I couldn't find him. Decades later, with the help of a private investigator, I finally learned that soon after abandoning us, Raul wed Louise, his first cousin, in Colorado, one of the few states that would allow such a marriage. Step-by-step, he was creeping dangerously close to fundamentalist LDS culture: an officially long-disavowed, slippery slope into incest and polygamy.

Gauging by their reaction to Raul's misbehaviors, it began to seem to me as if even our mainstream version of the LDS Church blamed only the women for any troubles at home. When my mom had begun to suspect that my father was interested in more than genealogical study with his cousin Louise, she had gone to our church's bishop for help and guidance. She had hoped he would talk some sense into Raul, or at least play marriage counselor. Instead, he told my mom that in our religion, it was the wife's responsibility to create a home suitable for her "priesthood holder," the designation used for the husband or dad. The whole cousin-as-possible-mistress thing didn't seem to raise the bishop's alarm. Not yet, at least. For now, he worried more that if Raul was showing interest in other women, there was something my mother was doing wrong, and she'd be wise to change her home environment to suit her priesthood holder.

Hopeful (if not a bit excited), my mom had taken the bishop's words to heart, and in her floor-length Mormon dress, she'd braved an adult bookstore to purchase *The Joy of Sex*. It was filled with graphic illustrations of men and women doing all kinds of things with each other's bodies. But when that book's lessons didn't help matters either, she quietly blamed her twisted-up body for Raul's lack of interest. I wouldn't learn most of this for many years, but what I could see then was that my mom's once inextinguishable flame was beginning to dim.

My aunt Josie stayed with us for a time. My mom was especially vulnerable now. It had only been a few years since my grandma Cokie had failed to get to the pills in her heart-shaped locket in time and her real heart had given out for good. Her death still affected my mom deeply. My mom would break into tears when certain songs came on the radio. I would hold her, and she would tell me colorful stories about the strong-willed mother she loved and missed so much. Josie worried that this double loss might permanently break my mom. So Josie took on the role of de facto matriarch of our family. She was a good bit older than my mom, and she became like a grandmother for my brothers and me. I loved Josie then, and I treasure her even more now that I realize what her larger fear was: that the state might swoop in and take her little sister's boys away if they deemed her physically and emotionally unfit to raise us alone.

Marcus was by far the most injured by Raul's vanishing act. He would soon fall in with a group of feral neighborhood boys who called the drainage ditches their refuge. And soon he began disappearing too, his new clan discovering cigarettes, shoplifting, and worse. His search for an escape, any escape, had begun, and it would lead my kindhearted big brother down a tragic path of self-destruction.

Me? I had made promises to God and to my mother, and now I was determined to keep them—even if God didn't seem all that interested in holding up His end of the bargain. With Marcus mostly missing, and my mom out looking for work, I was tasked with caring for Todd, who was still too young to do much but fall down. I loved this new role, and I set out to play it to perfection as well, so that God might finally give a damn and force my father to return in a hailstorm of apologies. But aspirations toward perfection come with endless lists of responsibilities. My chores would never be done now. There'd be little time left for play, or to paint red gorillas black, because at the age of six, when Josie returned to her own home, I became the undisputed man of our house.

I I I

In the months that followed our familial upheaval, I started finding small envelopes in the mail hidden among the overdue bills. No stamps, no return addresses. My mom opened the first with caution. Inside was a stack of cash, just enough to pay for our mortgage and food for the month, enough so we didn't have to apply for the government assistance that would have alerted the authorities that three boys were living in perilous circumstances with a paralyzed single mom who'd never driven a car or held a job. We later figured out that those envelopes had been placed in our mailbox by the same bishop who had failed to intervene months before. To his credit, since Raul's incestuous affair had been confirmed, this bishop had worked to ensure that Raul was excommunicated from the mainstream Mormon Church. Now that same church would quietly protect us from government intrusion until we could get on our feet.

Many of my friends who grew up outside of our Southern corner of the country, my arguably more progressive friends, are quick to dismiss organized religion as purely repressive or entirely outdated. But the honest-to-God truth is that despite its faults and blind spots, our church was the only family we had in San Antonio after Raul left. In the months and years to come, in ways big and small, the Christian values, tight-knit community, and care of our mainstream LDS Church were what we depended on.

When danger drew near for my Mormon forefathers, crossing the American frontier in the 1800s, they'd circle their wagons for strength and safety. Over a century later, when the rank and file of our congregation learned that our family was in danger, they "circled their wagons" around us. Without them, my mom likely would have lost us three boys to foster care. That would have killed her. And our family isn't unique in this respect. Putting arguments of scripture aside for a moment, there are many places in our world where a church isn't just the house of the Lord, but also the power center of community. To be barred from the chapel is to be excluded from society's protections; to be allowed in is an earthly kind of deliverance. We were lucky to still be in our church's embrace.

The Mormon Church's aid also helped buy us time so that Aunt Josie's daughter, my cousin Debbie, could source hand controls for the goliath Malibu Classic that Raul had abandoned in our driveway. Debbie was just a bit younger than my mom and tough as nails. She came to town and rounded up ten-year-old Marcus. "Grab yer screwdrivers, Marco, 'n get yer tail out to the driveway."

Marcus knew better than to disobey Debbie. He climbed down onto the Malibu's floorboards to help secure clamps to the gas pedal and brake. Then he and Debbie twisted, bolted, and secured chrome-and-black-rubber hand controls to the steering column. That day, Marcus discovered he loved working on cars. Debbie was convinced that these controls would allow my mom to become independently mobile. Like her father, James, Debbie didn't think there was anything she could do that Anne couldn't. She was determined to teach my mom how to use her new hand controls so she could get a license, and then a job.

Disability aside, my mom was a terrible driver. It didn't help that this car was far too big for her. It was like turning a cruise ship just to get out of the driveway, and Marcus had to stack up all of our rocking chair pillows on the driver's seat so she could see over the steering wheel. Beyond size challenges, it turns out our mom also had a lead hand and a surprising need for speed. So for the next week, Debbie and Marcus would come home from their amateur driving lessons with my mom looking like ghosts on life support.

Month after month, Anne failed her driving tests in epic fashion, returning home to hide her tears in a cup of hot chocolate in her lonely bedroom. Until that one miraculous day arrived when a single-mom driving instructor took pity on our mom and gave her a barely passing grade. In terms of wider public safety, it was decidedly irresponsible of the woman, but for us, it was family-saving.

From then on, we three boys buckled in tight, scared to death whenever it was our turn to sit up front with our mom and help navigate to church or a store. And with her confidence—if not her skill—quickly growing, we embarked on our first major road test: a Christmas trip to our aunt Martha's house, 265 miles away in Fort Worth, Texas. My mom was sure she could make it in record time.

Having spent too many of her own Christmases strapped to a hospital bed or in cut-rate hotel rooms with her mom and Martha, my mom had always made certain that the holidays in our home were more extravagant than we could possibly afford. Baking and handcrafting all of the youthful magic she felt robbed of, my mom declared Christmas the one day of the year the other 364 had been created for. Constructing and shopping for decorations and presents were yearlong tasks. The moment the Thanksgiving turkey's bones hit the trash, lights went up on the house and pine trees were cut down, hauled home, and set up—a main tree now bearing a decade's worth of ornaments personalized for us boys, and a little tree in our bedroom covered in homemade aluminum-foil decorations. There were lists of treats to be made: Tom Thumb cookie bars, coconut cherry bars, my grandmother Cokie's chocolate fudge, and sugar cookies rolled out with Cokie's red-handled rolling pin, then cut out with cookie cutters far older than I was. The dinner table was covered in newspaper, icing and decorations were laid out, and half a day quickly vanished as we frosted those cookies.

That year, there was no father in sight to help cut down and put up our Christmas tree, so we went to a tree lot by the gas station, where we discovered that our mom couldn't afford a tree nearly as tall as the ones we were used to. And each time Marcus and I broke a bulb hanging lights on the diminutive tree we'd dragged home, my mom choked back tears. Then "Silent Night" came on the radio, and my mom had to leave the room so she could cry out of our sight. Evidently, it was her and our grandma Cokie's favorite carol. We were doing our best to keep Christmas alive, but our family and our treasured traditions were in real peril.

Over the next day or two, the decision was made that we'd spend Christmas with Martha. Marcus loved this idea as much as he hated going to church. For him, this sounded like a "get out of jail free" card. As converts, we were the only Mormons in my mom's family, so none of her siblings would be dragging us to services. Marcus helped put the few wrapped gifts our mom could afford into the trunk of the Malibu, and we got on with the four-hour drive through the heart of San Antonio, Austin, and Dallas. My mom perched atop the tower of pillows on the driver's seat and worked her hand controls. Marcus proved a master with the map, and somehow we never got into the twenty-car pileup I had anticipated, or got pulled over, or even lost—a little Christmas miracle.

Aunt Martha met my mom at the curb, and one by one our other aunts and uncles emerged. They enveloped my mom. I watched her turn into a little girl, exhausted and afraid, but in their arms, seemingly safe from the storm. I had never seen her look so young and frail. It gave me real pause. They quickly got her inside.

It was Marcus's idea for us to bring in all the bags from the trunk. I didn't disagree. Who else was going to do it? So we pulled out our mom's baby-blue suitcase, the same one she'd cheerfully packed to take to college so long ago. Our own clothes followed, neatly folded into paper grocery bags, my Texan snakeskin cowboy boots sticking out of one. Next we unloaded the few wrapped presents that had made the journey. I carried each into the house and put them under Martha's towering tree with its bubbling oil lights, all perched atop her bright red shag carpet. Her house was a sight to behold, an honest-to-God '70s playground.

I emerged with a face-splitting grin, and shared the news with Marcus: "She has a hanging egg chair you can sit inside of and swing in, and a red carpet like on *Mork and Mindy*."

Marcus didn't react. He wasn't listening. He was staring down into the trunk. I followed his gaze. Just below where the wrapped gifts and clothes had been was our baby blanket, spread out the width of the trunk, clearly placed to conceal something. Curious, Marcus had pulled it back to expose what lay beneath: a brand-new, unwrapped Lego kit, a puzzle for a two-year-old, and the candy-apple-red plastic-and-steel Mustang I had begged Santa for all year long.

There's no telling how late my mom had stayed up in order to sneak those gifts out to the car without us knowing, or how she'd managed to even carry them all without our help. But to be clear, these weren't "mom gifts": these were gifts we'd asked Santa for, because we knew they were far too expensive for our mom. So either she was trying to one-up Santa, or at only six years old, the jig was already up, and Santa was dead.

Without a word between us, Marcus and I understood that we had to pretend we'd never seen these gifts and hope they didn't turn up addressed to us from Santa Claus come Christmas morning.

This pressure atop the months of mounting responsibilities and confusion finally broke my scrawny six-year-old body. Within twenty-four hours, I was in the hospital with a blinding fever, unable to breathe. Any of my mom's personal worries instantly turned to my care. I can only imagine how this late-night emergency-room visit with her seriously ill child echoed her own childhood experiences and deeply frightened her. The doctors took X-rays of my chest and diagnosed me with a dangerous case of pneumonia. They loaded me up with antibiotics, and after what felt like days, they finally released me with instructions to rest.

My mom slept beside me on a makeshift bed on the floor of Aunt Martha's spare bedroom, each night counting down to Christmas with her drawn-out version of "A Visit from St. Nicholas."

"'Twas the night before . . . the night before . . . the night before . . . the night before Christmas, and all through the house, not a creature was stirring, not even a mouse . . .'" She stroked my eyebrows to distract me from the pain and encouraged me to dream of a brighter future. It would be years before I understood how many nights she had dared to dream of untouchable, bright futures in brutal hospital wards in order to survive her own childhood, but without anyone there to stroke her brow.

On my second night back in the house, my sweet aunt Martha joined her in the recitation, and then Aunt Josie joined them both, then another relative, and another. My memories of those nights are mostly blurred by fevers, but I can clearly recall that by Christmas Eve, I was surrounded by strong Southern women willing me to recover with their soft drawls and warm eyes.

By Christmas morning my fever had dipped below one hundred degrees, and I could open my burning eyes again. I was awake before anyone else, so I slipped my cowboy boots on at 5:30 a.m. and snuck to the window to take a peek outside. We'd been given a rule: we weren't to wake any of the adults until the sky was blue. As I opened the curtains, Marcus snuck up behind me. He'd been awake since 5:00 a.m., waiting. Now, as quietly as we could, we watched the sky turn from pitch-black to a deep plum. But well before it became blue, Aunt Martha poked her head into the room carrying a steaming mug of coffee—a strictly forbidden beverage in our own Mormon home. We looked to our mom, who was slowly sitting up in bed. I wondered if she was worried that her sister was clearly going to hell for drinking the devil's caffeinated brew, but I let that go. Marcus and I had more existential St. Nick concerns on our minds.

Over the next hour, the entire family slowly rose, gathered around Martha's tree, and opened presents, starting with the wrapped gifts from Santa that had magically appeared overnight.

Todd went first, and got . . . a stuffed animal, not the puzzle from the trunk as we'd feared. So far, so good. Marcus followed. I could hardly watch as he pulled back the wrapping paper and opened his box . . . revealing two *Star Wars* action figures, not the trunk's Lego kit. *Santa might pull through,* I thought. But then my mom wagged her index finger, pointing out another gift hiding deeper under the tree. Marcus retrieved it. He read the tag: "To Marcus, from Santa." And he pulled back the paper, exposing the Lego kit. Our mom beamed, my heart sank, and Marcus and I dared not make eye contact. Our Santa had just stepped on his last rattler.

I'm well aware that most everyone has their "Santa's not real" moment, but I was quite young, and this was particularly tough timing. With the loss of Santa came that of another paternal figure and confirmation that parents are myth-feeders if not liars. And if Santa was a lie, well, what about God? Which of the untouchable ideas we'd been fed so far were lies? We'd already been worried that we were standing on quicksand; now we knew for certain that we were.

But Marcus and I had little choice but to get to work treading sand, because our kid brains feared that if our mom knew we knew, it might bury her. She couldn't take another heartbreak now. So I opened my long-desired candy-apple-red Mustang next, and I put on a spectacular show of gratitude . . . for Santa. It wasn't entirely an act. I knew my mom couldn't afford it, so I appreciated it in a whole different way. Besides, by now I had already guessed that my childhood was toast. In my mind, I'd been the man of the house for months, so in a way, I was now off the childhood hook. I no longer had to suspend any disbelief. I could get on with the necessary grown-up business of survival.

Later that night, drugged out of my mind on decongestants, sipping from a mug of hot lemon water, I received the real gift of Christmas 1980: an epiphany.

Sitting at Martha's breakfast bar, I watched my mom and her sisters make my grandmother's fruit salad together. They laughed and cried and told the story of Grandma Cokie and her burgundy bowl. And in that moment, I began to understand that there was another foundation just below the ones that were quickly crumbling beneath me. There was a history that I was a part of. I might not have understood it fully then, but I could feel it—that the real gift of this Christmas had come during the previous nights of blinding fevers as my aunts circled around me. I had thought our family was on its death march. Little did I know that my mom's entire extended family was lying in wait—sisters who'd been forged Southern-strong by the fires of poverty, tragedy, and ingenuity. They seemed inseparable, unbreakable, and invulnerable. And I was left with a growing sense of what "family comes first" really looked like and meant for us—it wasn't just the stuff of greeting cards and church testimonies; it was a promise that spoke to responsibility, endurance, and survival.

You see, in the corner of the world my mom grew up in, there weren't many folks with rainy-day bank accounts or good insurance policies. If something went haywire, lenders didn't leap to help her kind out. Why would they? Few among them had any credit. So all wrapped up into one, "family" was our brood's good credit, our rainy-day fund, and our most trusted insurance policy.

Sure, we fought among ourselves. My mom might call her siblings sinners for drinking Jack Daniel's and espresso, and they might call her brainwashed for her floor-length dresses and Mormon undergarments, but the moment anything threatened any one of us, we'd lock arms. Because husbands might come and go, and Santa might drop dead, but here in my mom's neck of the woods, I now understood that the family I'd been born into, the one she had fought through surgeries and comas to keep, could be counted on. They were my foundation now too.

That's why you don't mess with the institution called "family" where we come from. It's just too powerful and necessary to tinker with. I would have fervently argued the same that night. With a gun or worse, I would have chased anyone who tried to mess with its definition. And now I feel sure that if I had been able to tell my six-year-old self that thirty years later I would be called on to confront this foundational institution's definitions and do battle with its most devoted defenders and proponents, I would have called me crazy. Such a battle was unimaginable, incomprehensible, and far too dangerous. But that battle would come, and, not surprisingly, it would indeed turn my life on its head.

CHAPTER 6

Grand Theft Auto

I

By the time we got back from Christmas in Forth Worth, the bank had jabbed a "For Sale" sign in our front lawn. We'd been living in San Antonio for less than a year at that point. So with no family nearby and few friends, we dedicated any time away from school and Mom's fruitless job search to church. Our congregation wasn't just our faith anymore: it was our community, our second family, and our hope.

I was still quite small at six years old, easily mistaken for five or younger. Still, I'll never forget the details of that special Sunday when the LDS Church pushed the limits of technology to broadcast Spencer W. Kimball—the prophet, seer, revelator, and unquestioned head of the modern Mormon Church—live from Salt Lake City to every church that could install a satellite dish. The buildup was legendary. As if our prophet might see us all in return, everyone bought a new suit or dress for the occasion. The pews were jammed. Our ward even set up overflow rooms with television sets for the sudden revival of Latter Day Saints religious fervor. And come the blessed hour, projected onto a massive screen in the main chapel, Spencer W. Kimball's image was beamed in, clear, colossal, and exalted.

Marcus was doodling in a pad hidden in his hymnbook, but I paid careful attention to President Kimball's every word. I've always been curious about words. How they work together. Where they come from. Their many shades and connotations. Our prophet often used words I had never heard before. That was always exciting. And on this special Sunday, he used one in particular that caught my full attention. It was a spectacular new word, spoken slowly, gently, and with ample pauses. He used it like this: "Next to the sin of murder . . . comes the sin . . . of physical impurity . . . *ho-mo-sex-u-ality.*"

I was well versed in our Mormon history. I loved the big, brave, muscled warrior characters dripping with gold and clutching spears. I loved the idea that a mere boy named Joseph Smith had walked into New York's woods in 1820 and been visited by God and Jesus, who shared all the secrets of heaven with him. Each time I wandered into the woods by the lake near our home, I slowed in the hope that God might choose me as the recipient of His next set of revelations.

But of course, I'd never heard of any tribe called "homosexuality." I wondered if they had been neighbors with what the *Book of Mormon* taught were "good, light-skinned Nephites" or "evil, dark-skinned Lamanites." Not that I knew the details at the time, but until a "revelation" in 1978, skin color actually determined one's closeness to God in the LDS faith. Black people couldn't even receive the priesthood. No joke. But at six years old, already vaguely aware that our stories were made up of tribes of relative sinfulness, I wondered if this "homosexuality" tribe had been around when Jesus came to visit the Americas after rising up from his crucifixion unpleasantness in the Middle East. And if these "homosexuals" were around then, why hadn't Jesus saved them? Why were they akin to murderers? And how lucky was I to finally learn their name! With all of its syllables and its valuable *x*, I was sure to win a great many points with it in the next of our beloved Scrabble games back home.

My curiosity lasted for about a week—until the word slipped out of my mouth in earshot of a gaggle of my mom's pals from the Relief Society, the women's group in the LDS Church. I was quickly surrounded by women with long floral dresses and mouths pursed like cats' asses. They brought over a well-worn priesthood holder with droopy eyes and salt-and-pepper hair, and before I knew it, he began telling me the story of this mysterious tribe. No, not all of the details I was most curious about, but enough to get it.

There was something I recognized in this new idea of boys who "lay down on" boys or girls who "lay down on" girls. Thanks to my father, I had already learned that cousins "laying down on" cousins led to no good. I wondered if every form of "laying down on" someone was "akin to murder" the way our prophet said homosexuality was.

The salt-and-pepper-haired priesthood holder assured me, "No. Homosexuality is the worst kind. Anyone who 'lays down' with someone of the same gender will be barred from the Celestial Kingdom."

I already knew that the Celestial Kingdom was the highest and most glorified level in our church's stratified levels of heaven, so this meant one thing: anyone in the homosexuality tribe who was from a good Mormon family would be separated from their parents for all eternity. The idea of losing my mom forever scared the living daylights out of me. Then the priesthood holder added that anyone who darkened their door with such sin would also bring shame raining down on their family in this life. This was a threat worse than death. Death might bring salvation, and according to our beliefs, even my own planet. Losing my family to shame in this life meant isolation and starvation. So that was that: I wouldn't let this new word cross my lips again, or use it in any Scrabble game, regardless of its point value—at least not for many years to come. But that didn't mean this worrisome word wouldn't follow me, ever so quietly waiting until just the right moment to rear its head again, no matter how uninvited or unwelcome.

I I

Many months later, as my seventh birthday approached, I was still only three feet four inches tall, a full two inches shorter than the average boy in my Sunday school class, and far smaller than Marcus's ten-year-old pal who lived five houses down, the boy who would come around after school, dump out my hard-collected bucket of roly-poly bugs, and mercilessly murder them one by one. Sometimes he simply pinned me to the ground and thumped on my chest until he was bored by my tears. As luck would have it, he also admired Santa's candy-apple-red Mustang as much as I did, and so, like most of the things I cared for in childhood, it soon vanished.

It turned out that this bully of a neighbor was also a terrible painter. When he paraded his new black Mustang around the block, I could easily see the red peeking through his haphazardly applied spray paint. Marcus was no help. He was busy with his new family of leather-clad punks who valued ferocity, the Dead Milkmen's punk, and Megadeth's heavy metal over any sort of justice or kindness.

I convinced myself I couldn't tell my mom because her heart was still too fragile for a grand-theft-auto news flash. But truth be told, my hesitation to strike back wasn't because of my mom's heart, or because I was some sort of pacifist, or even because Marcus's friend was so much bigger than me. Yes, I was quiet, but I had picked fights with Marcus many a time and nearly won. Nevertheless, I merely watched as this car thief walked away with my prize, all the while wondering why I was standing so very still. And then it struck me—I didn't want to cause this boy any pain at all, no matter how justified . . . because that vise squeezing my heart wasn't anger; it was heartache. Yes, he was a bully. Yes, he had thumped my chest until I'd peed my pants a week earlier. But he was the bully with dark hair and light green eyes who I looked forward to being attacked by each afternoon. Sure, his chest thumps hurt, but my heart raced knowing that a boy with such startling eyes even noticed I was alive.

A wave of chemicals and feelings hit me like blue-hot lightning, and for the first time in my life, and for a few magical moments, I felt butterflies of love dancing in my stomach. Then all of the hair on my arms stood up as I suddenly realized that my heart wasn't breaking because I'd just been robbed; it was breaking because I'd just been robbed by my very first crush.

But for a kid like me on a hot sidewalk in Texas in 1981, that first blush of love lasted only seconds, because I already had a word for this kind of love. The Mormon prophet and his priesthood holder had defined it in no uncertain terms. In that moment, I understood that I was a member of a damned tribe called Homosexuality. And unlike the other kids my age experiencing their first crushes, I couldn't go on to dream of first kisses, dates, or future families. No, sir. My butterflies died then and there, and a deep and abiding terror took their place.

As a Mormon boy in a Texas military town, I had already heard a handful of other words for my new tribe: "faggot," "homo," "pansy," "cocksucker," "queer bait," and more. My freakishly crinkled, far-too-sensitive ears could hear those words rattling around inside my head, and in a whole new way. They were my words now, and none monikers the wise would wish for. I knew that if anyone found out, I'd bring great shame to my family and myself. I knew I was down there with all the murderers and rapists, that I could rightfully be beaten, bloodied, or worse. And these weren't overblown childhood fears. Where I lived, I was in real danger, and I knew it. The dark secret this crush had just revealed would most certainly kill my mom, prove my father's rejection justified, alienate me from my brothers, from my aunts and uncles—and that's if I survived the physical blows that were sure to land.

Standing there on that hundred-degree sidewalk, watching my first crush disappear into his house with my toy car, I understood with absolute clarity just how close I was to losing what little I had left in this world. My foundation. Sure, I was still my mom's man of the house—for now, for as long as I could hide this terrible secret—but I was also a dead man walking, a son with a fatal flaw who might take my whole family down with me if I couldn't hide my truth. That was the burden a prophet, a place, and a time put on my far-too-small shoulders. A brutal weight that would take many a toll, and one I'd have to shoulder for a damned long time in silence and shame.

Fag. Faggot. Homo. Pervert. Sodomite. Pansy. Queer. Mama's boy.

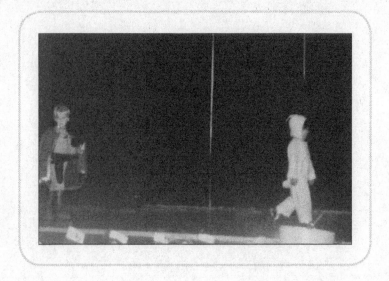

CHAPTER 7

Can't Walk, Can't Talk

My grandma Cokie's words about finishing college haunted my mom as she searched for work. Any work. It was my cousin Debbie who eventually suggested she look into military civil service jobs. San Antonio was jammed with bases: Randolph Air Force Base, Kelly Air Force Base, and Fort Sam Houston. The last option appealed the most. Fort Sam Houston was home to one of the army's best hospitals. Anne had dreamed of working in medicine before the promise of a family turned her wheels. So she applied for a job there. Any job. After all, beggars can't be choosers, and with the bank selling our home out from under us, she wasn't too proud to beg.

So just after my seventh birthday, my mom started her first job, working in a closet-sized room in the Brooke Army Medical Center's shipping and supply department. And with some help from the church and her first paychecks slowly trickling in, we moved into a small rental home in a San Antonio suburb called Live Oak. At the same time, I did what most devout Mormon boys did back then: I began my journey to becoming an Eagle Scout by signing up for the Cub Scouts. There I quickly confirmed my worst fear: my crushes on members of the same sex would not be isolated to that one lawless, green-eyed neighbor. They were no passing phase. There would be more crushes, and they would only grow more difficult to hide and deny.

To those who've said we ought to ban gay kids from Scouting for fear that the "queer" ones might treat the "normal" kids like a wanton boy buffet, I say they've forgotten what childhood crushes are like. For most kids, being anywhere near a crush is debilitating. You go splotchy-red, start to sweat, misplace half your vocabulary, and the harder you try to regain your composure, the more sweaty-bizarre-ignorant you become. Now imagine being surrounded by a handful of crushes all at once, or worse, being shipped off on a camping excursion where you can't get away from them for a week. Add in a dash of eternal damnation and a dime for every "faggot" slur over-heard, and you start to get why this supposed "buffet" felt a heck of a lot more like an obstacle course through hell. Gay kids shouldn't be kicked out of Scouts; they should receive a special merit badge for resiliency.

Until the LDS Church recently dissolved its century-old relation-ship with the Boy Scouts of America, for any Mormon boy, Scouting was a tacit requirement. Each church had its own troop made up of LDS kids. Together, Scouting and Mormonism reinforced a strict code of conduct. Add in my mom's new job with the U.S. Army, and our world grew increasingly black-and-white. There was good or bad, right or wrong, and moral or immoral.

Truth be told, I took comfort in our strictly defined boundaries. So did my mom. We knew the Lord's path and the devil's. Wiggle room would only have made life more complicated. We had enough on our plate already. Unlike my big brother, I had always been good at keep-ing to the "straight and narrow." But the newfound homosexual path carving through my heart felt inextricable, and the more I tried to step off it, the wider it seemed to grow. No amount of prayer would make it quit. Soon, my mind and heart were at war, and with that war came new dread and anxiety, fomenting my shyness and fueling panic attacks.

In response, I stopped talking completely.

For the next half a decade, I hardly said a word in public. I couldn't stand the sound of my own voice. I didn't want to be seen. I didn't want to excel or stick out. And I most certainly didn't want to stand up in front of our entire congregation dressed as Lieutenant Starbuck from the original *Battlestar Galactica* and perform with a musical instrument I had no clue how to play. But that's what my mom was insisting I do.

Come late summer in our church, all of the primary-age kids were encouraged to pull on a costume, pick out a musical instrument, and play along with a pianist in what our congregation called the Jingle Bell Band (despite Christmas being months away).

It should be noted that when I say the Mormon Church "encour-aged" something, this means participation was expected.

I had tinkered around on a piano and fiddled with my mother's clarinet, but my efforts had only proven that I had zero innate musical ability. My mom had witnessed this debility and knew my shyness challenges just as well, so she spent her last dime on the simplest instrument there is to play: two beautifully varnished percussion sticks. All I had to do was get up on that stage and knock those sticks together in as close to rhythm as possible. *Easy-breezy*, she thought.

My mom spent days sketching patterns of Lieutenant Starbuck's uniform before attempting to sew an exact replica for my costume. It's clear now that little of this effort was for me. She was trying to prove to her church friends that although she was a single mother, she could keep up with the best of them. And yes, the golden-haired lieutenant was my favorite character in my favorite TV show, but only for reasons I prayed my mom wouldn't figure out. Let's just say my admiration had nothing to do with his acting ability. Now my mom was going to "out" my keen interest in front of the entire church by dressing me up like him. For me, at seven years old, a shirt with a single stripe felt too bold. To dress me up in a gold-trimmed cape with a giant '70s leather belt cinching my tiny waist? To have my frail frame compared to that of such a fully formed hunk of a man? To brazenly hint at my darkest secret in front of five hundred of our nearest and dearest congregants? And to force me to attempt to keep rhythm in front of them as they were most certainly figuring out my sinful secret? It felt so brutal and blind of her. I begged her not to make me do this. I shed tears—some real, some counterfeit— but none proved effective. So I refocused my efforts on a full frontal, emotional blackmail assault.

I hid myself away in my mom's closet with her craft box's innards spread out and got to work on an epic construction paper, tape, and glue daisy. The head of the flower was as big as my own, petals three layers deep, with a large disk in the center that professed my undying love for my mom. Then I built a long stem that was as tall as she was and attached construction paper leaves to it. It was outstanding, by far my finest work to date. When I presented it to her, she seemed genuinely moved and impressed. I was certain it was my "get out of jail free" card.

I was wrong.

The fight that followed was epic. She told me that not only would I participate in the Jingle Bell Band, but I was to make her proud while doing it.

"You will get up on that stage, and you will stand up straight and tall like the man you are. Straight, and tall, and proud. Do you hear me, Lance?" She hadn't sat behind her sewing machine for hours on end after long days on the army base for nothing.

I absolutely lost it—or as Marcus so eloquently put it later that night: "You went balls-to-the-wall-shit-ball nuclear, man." He was right. And at some point during my nuclear meltdown, I shredded that construction-paper-daisy masterpiece into confetti right in front of my mom's face.

She shook, her eyes welled up, and my rage dissolved. My shameful secret had just provoked its first shameful act: I'd just purposefully and knowingly injured my own mother. I was supposed to be her protector. So stacking shame on top of shame, I died inside.

My mom ordered me to my room. I gathered the remnants of her slain daisy, hung my head low, and did as I was told.

When it came time for my song on that terrible Tuesday night, five hundred sets of curious eyes were indeed watching. I stepped up onto the stage with a dozen other kids, my percussion sticks hidden inside the gold-trimmed cape of my perfectly re-created Lieutenant Starbuck uniform. I hit my mark just fine, but that's all I managed to do right.

I couldn't look into the crowd to find my mom's face. I couldn't meet her eyes. I was sure that my trembling body would soon release my bladder and I would die from all the combined humiliations. And when the music began, I didn't stand up straight and tall at all. Slowly and steadily I slumped down deeper and deeper into myself, praying to become a snail, wishing I could vanish. My percussion sticks never touched each other. Not once. I was no man. I was no strong Mormon. I was no proud Southerner. I was a failure. A freak. The great shame of my family line.

My mom never said a word about it.

II

Marcus was eleven when I melted down in front of our congregation. Mercifully, at the time, he was away on a Boy Scout camping trip. There, he would test his once-fragile preemie lungs with his first few puffs of weed. Thanks to his absence, my mom asked me to take on a new responsibility that had always been Marcus's—to go shopping with her at the local mall.

Second grade was looming for me, Marcus was headed into sixth, and Todd was growing fast. We all needed new clothes. What I didn't think to consider was that I'd never been out in public with my mom before, not outside of the safety and familiarity of family or church. So with no awareness of the minefield ahead, I buckled up, and my mom bulleted us toward the J. C. Penney in the Windsor Park Mall.

Whenever I rode up front with my mom, I clicked myself into the middle of the big bench seat. I wanted to be close to her. And now I took the opportunity to rest my head on her shoulder. She was so little that my head reached her neck and fit perfectly into the groove between it and her collarbone. I remember noting what an exact shape it was for my head, as if it had been made especially for me.

I wondered if she was still upset about the destroyed daisy, still disheartened by my pathetic performance in the Jingle Bell Band. I worried what my world might become if she ever gave up on me, lost faith in me. She was my most important thing in the world.

The mall's lot was nearly full. My mom pulled her massive Malibu into a regular parking spot way at the back. A year earlier, when the charitable woman at the DMV had offered my mom a handicap license, my mom had shot back, "And what exactly is it you think I'm incapable of?" This left the startled DMV woman in a terrible state of silence. My mom let her words linger, then put the woman out of her misery with: "I will have a regular driver's license . . . thank you *very* much."

After a few failed attempts, my mom squeezed our tank of a car into the tiny spot. I jumped out, grabbed her crutches from the backseat, ran them around to the driver's side, and opened her door like a good Southern gentleman ought to. She tucked her crutches under her arms, grabbed their handles, and we were on our way. Clockwork.

There were only days left before school would start, so the mall was teeming with parents and children. I put on my best vanishing act: I looked down, made myself as small as possible, and slowed my breathing, as if that might somehow make me invisible.

Click-clack, click-clack, click-clack. It was the sound my mom always made as she walked, and now she was moving through the mall with grace, speed, and determination. I did my best to keep up.

Once we were well inside J. C. Penney's boys' department, digging through a pile of clearance denim, I got up the nerve to lift my head to make sure no one was looking at me. Unfortunately, I discovered the opposite. More than a few shoppers' eyes were on us, and not just gazing our way, they were staring. It was a worst-case scenario. Had I been identified as an introvert? An antisocial child? A weirdo? The giveaways seemed too clear: the crinkled ears, the bowed head, the too-small size. Perhaps some were even deducing my other hidden difference: that I was a Mormon queer.

But when I met their eyes, it quickly became clear they weren't looking at me at all. They were staring at my mom. But why? I was the misfit. Why were they staring at my mom like they'd just seen a car wreck? Within our family or church, no one had ever treated my mom as if she were different. Now, with every new stranger's worried gaze, I grew more baffled and bothered.

Done with the clearance table, my mom walked to the stacks of poorly folded Levi's 501 jeans that she knew Marcus and I wanted but that she couldn't afford. That's when I watched the gawkers dissect her swinging body. I watched my mom ignore their looks, her head held high and proud, just the way she had tried to teach me to hold mine. And for the first time, I really saw how she planted her crutches in front of her and swung her body forward again and again. I saw her spine through strangers' eyes, with all of its twists and turns. I looked at all the other mothers with their straight spines and nimble legs, and for the first time, I understood that my mother was different, perhaps too different, and that no one saw her difference as a good thing. They stared like she was a carnival freak, and the few who bothered to notice I was alive offered only pity.

My blood boiled. I wanted to wad up their pity and shove it down their holier-than-thou windpipes. My breath got hot, my palms began to sweat, and the edges of my eyelids burned. What I didn't realize until much later was that I was no longer looking at the ground. I was no longer hiding behind my mom. I was staring every single gawker right in the eye, daring them to keep judging.

I knew my own sins. I was sure I deserved these gawkers' scrutiny. But what had my mother done to deserve any? This was unjust.

So when a boy, maybe one year my senior, refused to stop staring, I waited for him to get just close enough, then grabbed hold of the fleshy back side of his arm with my thumb and index finger. And just how Marcus had taught me, I pinched and twisted the living heck out of his skin. He reacted, but when he met my eyes, he knew full well that he would be the one in trouble if he squealed, so he wisely didn't alert his mother. I stared him down until he was well out of sight, making sure he would never look at my mom that way again.

That afternoon, I realized I wasn't the only freak living under our roof. I already knew ours wasn't a land that celebrated differences. I knew it was best to keep mine hidden, so I didn't need words to know that my mom wouldn't want hers openly acknowledged either. It would take many years before we'd both learn that our differences demanded to be seen, understood, and perhaps even celebrated.

When we got home, I excused myself to my room. My ears were ringing. It's a sound that springs from pain-filled silence. I still hear it whenever I feel anything deeply. On this day, I finally, truly understood my familial duty. I wasn't just there to make perfect vacuum lines in the family room; I was there to stand guard for my mom against an unjust world.

But I also knew that weeks earlier, I had done the opposite. I had broken her heart with a construction-paper-confetti fit that she didn't deserve. I understood now that I needed to make amends for that. So

I got on my knees and asked God for His best advice. This time I thought I felt an answer.

I snuck into my mom's room and raided her craft box, looking for Scotch tape. An hour or two later, I found my mom in the kitchen, and I presented the paper daisy to her for the second time. It wasn't a new daisy. That would have been a copout. This was the same daisy I had ripped to bits and pieces, meticulously reconstructed with tape and glue. It had demanded saving.

My mom took the flower and let out a little breath. I can so clearly remember her looking down into my eyes with a rather somber expression and asking, "You think you could put the whole world back together again with tape and glue, don't you, Lancer?"

This wasn't the reaction I had hoped for, so I thought hard on her question. I remember imagining the world splitting in two, all the lava threatening to flow out, people being knocked from their huts and homes, oceans pouring into space. Then I thought about what I might do if that really did happen, and after some sober seven-year-old calculations, I confidently answered: "Yes . . . if I had enough tape."

There it was. Despite all of our tall challenges, I seemed to believe that none were insurmountable, at least with enough tape. My mom laughed loud and hard for the first time in a good long while. She hugged me, shed a couple of joyful tears, and then stuck that flower to the fridge with a magnet.

It turns out I was very much my mother's son, and I was growing into a foolish little optimist, just like her. Perhaps she saw a glimmer of her indomitable old childhood self in my earnest eyes that day, and it gave her some hope back. What I know for sure is that we both felt a bit less alone in the world from then on, and her dimmed light began to flicker back to life. And boy, how we both needed that company and light like we needed oxygen.

The paper daisy came down from the fridge when we finally moved out of that musty rental, but years later I would discover she'd given it a home with her hospital autograph book and her golden book of boys. It was the very first thing I ever made that earned its place as a sacred object.

CHAPTER 8

Bull by the Horns

By 1982, Anne's stellar performance reviews at Fort Sam Houston came with modest pay raises that made putting enough food on the table increasingly possible. Occasionally she even splurged, surprising us with a box of Fruity Pebbles or Cap'n Crunch cereal that vanished into our faces in minutes. Her three boys were healthy and showed up for Sunday services in well-ironed navy blue or brown suits with matching clip-on ties. Enchanted by the easy access to weapons and heaps of praise for killing animals, twelve-year-old Marcus was thriving in the Boy Scouts. I had placed into a set of high-IQ-nerd-fest classes that sealed the deal on my friendlessness but left my mom proud. Todd was walking upright, and we'd begun having in-depth, markedly normal kid conversations about things like *Star Wars* versus G.I. Joe action-figure joint designs. He had no memory of Raul or his vanishing act.

But my eighth birthday loomed. Eight is the age when good Mormon boys become men, become responsible for their own sins moving forward, and need to be baptized to rinse away any previous no-nos. Worried that my fantasies might count as celestial demerits, I was understandably eager for this righteous rinse. But usually it's a boy's father who has the honor of performing this full submersion in front of a gaggle of LDS nearest and dearest, in a font hidden behind an accordion divider in the center of the church. Raul was still around when Marcus required dunking, but we hadn't heard a peep from old Pops for years now.

So as my birthday drew closer, Anne realized that she needed a man, and quick. One who was blessed with the holy priesthood, could baptize her middle boy, and get us all into the highest level of heaven together. One who was into paralyzed, divorced women with three raucous boys. Any man like that would do. She didn't have time to be too picky.

A candidate soon presented himself. Merrill was a divorced staff sergeant now stationed at Randolph Air Force Base in San Antonio. His two young daughters occasionally came to visit and could be spotted next to him in the pews on Sundays. The trio stuck out in the same way our little family did. They were well-behaved, but it was rare not to see two parents per family. Divorce was allowed but frowned upon, a last resort. Everyone knew my mom had been abandoned by Raul in favor of a fundamentalist-style marriage to his first cousin, so no one judged her too harshly. But no one seemed to know why Merrill's temple-blessed marriage hadn't worked out. Perhaps because he wasn't very handsome, I thought. At least not according to my standards, which increasingly seemed to match my mom's—we often turned our heads in unison, gazing at this fella or that, and snapped them back in perfect time before being caught by the other. Merrill hadn't drawn a head turn from either of us. He smelled a little like moldy bread, and he wore government-issue glasses ripped from *Revenge of the Nerds*. But he was nice enough and tall enough, and he seemed strong. He certainly wouldn't have a problem holding my little body underwater until my first eight years' worth of sins were washed away.

Upon his arrival, the leadership of our ward moved quickly to get Merrill involved in church activities. He soon rose to be the leader of Boy Scout Troop 624, our church's very own troop, and thus became Marcus's new Scoutmaster. Merrill liked going to church dances and could be seen spinning and dipping various children on special Saturday nights. And Merrill tended to wear a smile—although it was always a bit crooked, a lot like our old neighbor's smile after her second stroke.

Last, but certainly not least, Merrill's curly hair reminded me of a Brillo pad, and I thought for sure its inky color had inspired his last name: Black. His last name was by far the coolest thing about him. The second coolest was that he didn't mind spending time with my mom.

What I wouldn't understand for several more years was that according to our church's deepest beliefs, a person could get to the highest level of heaven only if he or she were married. Single people are sent to lower, less valuable real estate—celestial suburbs with a few more fences and a little more crime. And it's not that the church arranges marriages, not exactly, but concerned that these two "unmarriageable" members might not make it to heaven's A-list, our bishop played matchmaker. Trouble is, as I've said before, when a leader in the Mormon Church "encourages" a member do anything, the understanding is that the request has come from heaven itself and ought to be honored.

When Merrill finally got up the nerve to ask Anne on a date, her heart didn't leap. She knew Raul had been her one and only chance at having it all, and she'd grown to accept that perhaps he'd married her only for a draft deferment—or worse, that he'd loved her and she'd screwed it up. Regardless, such happiness wasn't in the cards anymore, not for someone in her condition, at her age, saddled with three young, mud-loving boys. She was lucky to have been asked at all. And if she ever wanted that perfect body she'd been promised, she needed heaven's top floor. Merrill held that ticket. So she plugged her nose and said yes.

Marcus was blunt about the situation. He told me he saw Merrill as a paycheck and a way out of poverty. I didn't feel our poverty like Marcus did. I ate like a bird, so I was rarely hungry at night like he was. I had only ever known the free lunch line at school, and I liked the plain nature of the clearance-rack clothes. They drew less attention. At four years old, Todd didn't care how tattered his clothes were. Catching tadpoles by my side was all he knew, and that seemed to be enough for him. Still, I saw the wisdom in having a set of working grown-up legs around. And how cool would it be to have the Scoutmaster as our stepdad? That would surely win me a friend or two, right? So I followed Marcus's lead and put on my best-behavior show whenever Merrill came around.

Mere months after our mom's first date with Merrill came that very special night when all of our mortal and celestial concerns found themselves an answer. My mom's hair was perfect. She'd put on a Sunday dress despite it being Tuesday. She took her place on our tattered, faux-leather living room couch, and when Merrill arrived, he took his place next to her. Marcus, Todd, and I gathered before them. It looked like a community college theater production of a family drama, and it felt worse. In the end, Merrill was too nervous to share the big news himself, so my mom did it: "Guys, Merrill has asked me something. . . . He's asked me to marry him." Silence. We weren't stunned—we'd seen this coming—it was just that it felt exactly like what it really was: a solution to a problem, not a cause for celebration. She added, "What do you guys think about that?"

Marcus grinned bigger than he'd ever naturally done, so I echoed his fake smile and added a nod or two. Todd didn't know what to make of it all and didn't seem to care much. Our mom finally added, "Well, I told Merrill yes . . . as long as you guys think it's okay."

Marcus nodded, I vocalized a weird "Yes," and Todd said nothing. She then laid out what would come next: "We're going to plan a trip to a temple in Utah. No big ceremony. And children aren't allowed in the temple, so it'll just be us. But when we get back, we'll be a family. What do you guys think of that?"

Playing his part to perfection, Marcus outright hugged Merrill. Like most of the other "stoner" kids, Marcus had chosen drama class as an alternative to PE and had grown into a rather good little actor. His performance on this night was stellar, and I admired that.

But I remember looking my mom in the eyes that night, telling her how much I loved her, and giving her a kiss. I'll never forget the long look she gave me in return. She wasn't in love. The only joy in her eyes was that which springs from putting your children's needs before your own. I'd seen it many times before. I just never thought I'd see it on the day she told me she was going to get married—much less the whisper of terror that lived just behind it.

On September 4, 1982, Roseanna Garrison became Roseanna Black in an LDS ceremony that took place behind a Mormon temple's closed doors. Upon her and Merrill's return, it was time for me to turn over my role as man of the house to our family's new "priesthood holder." And then, as quickly as we could arrange it, Merrill Black baptized me in the font behind the accordion screen in the middle of our church. I was now a man in the eyes of our Heavenly Father, responsible for any and all of my sins moving forward. As relieved as I was to be free from punishment for my few convenience-store baseball-card heists, I was equally aware that if I ever acted on the "homo thing" now, there was no escaping the devil's hot spot. From here on out, I had to be on my very best behavior, and for me that included chasing away any impure thoughts.

Beyond concerns of heaven and hell, Merrill's arrival provided one other opportunity to help cleanse the past. Raul's last name was a daily reminder of his abandonment. Despite my mom's assurances that his leaving had nothing to do with me, hearing his last name increasingly led to self-loathing. I wanted a new name, and the courts in Texas seemed willing to hear that wish in the form of a legal adoption proceeding by Merrill. I led the name-change charge, and Marcus and Todd happily followed. I even helped my mom put the court-required ad in the newspaper to notify the world just in case Raul wanted to fight it. I'll never forget the day my mom came home from work, opened up the mail, and showed us a copy of the court order that made our adoption official. It was on long, legal, baby-blue and white paper. And from that moment on, I was Dustin Lance Black. I loved the ring of it then, and still do today. But Merrill's last name would prove the only good thing this monster-in-waiting would ever provide.

I I

The next many months get fuzzy. My memory has mercifully blurred some of the oft-recurring dark episodes. But other moments were so distinct that their details stuck.

Within weeks of their temple wedding, Merrill moved into our little rental house in Live Oak. It turned out I hadn't cleaned my room to the standards of an LDS staff sergeant Scoutmaster, and I was getting a good tongue lashing for it. I had always considered myself the tidiest of our trio, so I stood in the doorway of my room protecting it from the intrusion of his standards, my eight-year-old mind reasoning that this man was only our stepfather, and a brand-new one at that. Concessions and compromises would have to be made. Then, rather sure of my argument, I told Merrill just that.

In a split second, this "nice enough" man we had known for over a year stopped breathing. His face turned a deep blue-red, his forehead wrinkled like a bulldog's, and the bags under his eyes began to quiver. This was a man I'd never met before. And when he moved again, he did so with the full strength of a six-foot-something military man's fist crashing squarely into my eight-year-old face.

Getting punched in the face isn't what the movies make it out to be. It made a loud *smack*, not some dull thud. My thin neck whipped back, and my body followed, slamming onto the hard linoleum floor of our bedroom and into my latest Lego creation. *Bang!* I vanished for a moment or two. I don't know if he knocked me out cold or if the pain was just too terrible to record. When I came to, I didn't cry. I may have been the quiet, shy future "homo," but I was no fool or chickenshit. I knew I couldn't show any weakness right then. Instead, I shouted at the top of my lungs to Marcus, "Call Mom!" But she was at work, a forty-minute drive away. So I stood back up, as tall and strong as I could, and stared into Merrill's suddenly hollow face, daring him to punch me again, to finish the job. I didn't bother wiping away the blood that was now dripping from my nose onto the white floor. I made him see it. Because I was a Texas boy before all else.

My mother raced home and crashed through the door. The blood from my nose was now crusted onto my top lip; my eyes were already turning black and swelling shut. But I wasn't the most alarming sight. That title belonged to Merrill, who had turned into a sobbing child, hunched in a corner of the room, already begging for my mother's mercy as snot dripped from his nose. As I look back now, his performance made it clear that this had happened before, likely with his previous family, and he knew exactly how to play the moment. I remember hearing my little mom laying into this big sobbing soldier: "If you ever lay a hand on my son again, I. Will. Kill. You. You son of a bitch."

He had no answer for that, just more snot and tears.

Who's the pansy now? I thought.

I didn't have to go back to school for a while, not until my eyes no longer looked like a raccoon's. Merrill had to go to meetings with our bishop and my mom each week. Only then did my mom find out that Merrill's first marriage had ended thanks to similar violence that a church report had labeled an attempted murder. Merrill had asked for forgiveness and sought treatment through the church, and evidently that was enough to make our own bishop leave this detail out during his matchmaking.

A week or two later, we all donned our Sunday finest and our best fake smiles and snapped our annual family portrait at Olan Mills Portrait Studio. And as the jolly photographer positioned us just so, I could still feel my mother's gentle brushstrokes where she'd painted flesh-colored makeup over the fading black in the corners of my eyes. Somehow the previous pain all seemed worth it for this moment. My mom's care and attention is what I lived for. And I'd always wanted to experiment with her makeup but never dared. Now I thought, *With her at my side, I can make it through anything. I can survive this.*

Unfortunately, all the counseling in the world from the Mormon Church couldn't help Merrill control his temper. He would lash out again and again over the next few years, in ways big and small. Such as the time my mom accompanied him to pick up his mother from the airport. Everything had been going great; the house was spotless, some discount meat was in the Crock-Pot, and everyone was excited. Then my mom said something Merrill didn't like, and he backhanded her hard across the face. Her eyes turned black like mine had, and she told everyone she'd fallen. It was the same lie I'd been coached to tell, so Marcus and I didn't buy it, and our protective instincts began to kick into high gear.

But here's how our situation was different from that of others in similarly precarious positions: we weren't allowed to turn to traditional avenues for protection. Even after Merrill blackened my mom's eyes, the church still didn't want the police involved. They considered ours a domestic dilemma of eternal consequence that should remain in the hands of the church.

This was my first up-close look at a deep division between two tribes most imagine would be well aligned—a rift between two powerful, conservative institutions: our church and our state's law enforcement. It's a divide whose roots date back to the origins of the LDS Church. You see, Mormons were a brand-new minority in the early 1800s, and just too different for most other Christian folks. So in an effort to get Mormons out of town, their homes were burned, their cattle killed; my forefathers were tarred, feathered, and senselessly slaughtered by militias, and our first prophet, Joseph Smith, was murdered by a government that refused to protect him and his "peculiar people." The church's second prophet, Brigham Young, even threatened war against the U.S. government if it didn't stop harassing his faithful.

Conveniently leaving out our church's uncomfortable polygamist history, these stories of government-sanctioned persecution were still being shared in Sunday school lessons when I was a boy. And although we were encouraged to run for public office or sign up for the military, a general distrust for the U.S. government lingered— a feeling that at any moment, no matter how virtuous a citizen or soldier we were, our government might come for us again. This further explains the money from the Mormon Church in our mailbox after Raul's vanishing act. The church would rather we take care of our own and not lean on the government for help. So now, again, we were forced to lean on our church's instruction during Merrill's latest reign of terror. We were told to never call the cops.

I dreamed of calling 911, of the brave Texas police officers who would quickly arrive. Tough and grizzled, they wouldn't let it stand if they discovered a paralyzed wife and her children were being beaten by a man who smelled like old bread. They believed in right and wrong, not some LDS mumbo-jumbo about who Heavenly Father had blessed with "priesthood authority" in the home. "Bullshit," they'd bark. And I would ask God to forgive them for the curse word. I dreamed of seeing these cowboy hat–wearing cops bust down the front door, tackle Merrill to the ground, and press his face to the cold linoleum he'd knocked me down onto. A few kicks in the ribs, and they'd read him his rights and drag him away for good.

Instead, we caved to the fear of eternal damnation, obeyed the church, and lied our asses off at school and in our neighborhood. We must have seemed like the clumsiest kids in San Antonio. My home-room teacher even chided me when I showed up with a new shiner under my right eye. "Maybe if you kept your head out of the clouds, you could keep your feet on the ground, Dustin." I didn't bother telling her that the people I actually cared for called me Lance. I was raging inside: against Merrill, against a world that was set up to allow this. But for now, all I could do was look for ways to make myself scarce at home.

• • •

I increasingly spent my afternoons with Todd, whom I tried my best to shield from the terrible truth of our home life. We would go on long bike rides through San Antonio's flash-flood drainage ditches turned tween bicycle superhighways—anything to keep Todd from landing in Merrill's crosshairs. Todd was my responsibility, my pride and joy, and I wanted to protect his innocence. Most often we'd end up at Farmers Lake to gather worms, lizards, snakes, and every other sort of witches' brew ingredient. That lake was my respite. Dappled Texas sunlight under tall trees, cool waters teeming with fish, cutoff-jean swim trunks, knotted-up rope swings, and an endless supply of tadpoles. This was the life I loved. The America I loved. The South I still treasure and hunger for.

One Saturday afternoon in 1984, Todd and I had just returned from Farmers Lake with a heavy bucket of tadpoles. The most sociable and good-looking of us three boys, Todd coolly crossed the street to chat up two cute girls jumping through their mom's sprinkler, and I got busy hiding our bucket of tadpoles in the bushes near our front door so I could steal glances over the next few weeks as they grew legs and arms and turned into frogs. Soon there would be a chorus of frogs every night. I was lost in the thrill of the day's haul when I heard the most memorable sound of my first decade of life coming from inside our house. There were no words; it was more primal than words: it was my mother's voice buried somewhere deep inside a terrible, ear-splitting scream.

My adrenaline surged. I rushed through the front door just in time to see my mom racing up the hallway, her arms pulling her torso and legs up and forward with all her might, then thrusting her crutches forward as far as she could, again and again, running for her life as she tried to reach her bedroom door and lock it behind her. In her scream, I heard a plea for me to run, but it was all too nightmarish to believe, and I froze. Then Merrill came charging out of the kitchen after my mom, gripping a knife. This was no nightmare. This was real. My mom disappeared from view up the hallway, but there was no way she could outrun a grown man with two working legs. As Merrill disappeared around the same corner, I remained motionless, waiting for the most precious thing in the world to be ripped away from me like all precious things had. This beast, whose name I had just taken, was about to murder my mom.

Then, like some miniature mob-boss vigilante, Marcus came flying in through the back door. He had an aluminum baseball bat gripped in his right hand, his face raging with a lifetime of hell and rejection. He vanished down the same hallway, and a second later I heard the first terrible *Bing!* As it rang out, I came unstuck. Taking two steps forward I could now see down the hall. *Bing! Bing! Bing!* Thirteen-year-old Marcus was beating the living daylights out of Merrill. *Bing! Bing! Bing!* Fast, brutal, effective. Merrill ducked into the bathroom to escape the blows and locked himself inside.

My mom made it to her bedroom, locked the door, and started screaming that she was calling the police this time. Marcus didn't retreat. He beat on the bathroom door, screaming for Merrill to come out and face him like a man. I had absolutely no clue until that day—in fact, I had never suspected it in the least—but my increasingly distant big brother, the one who was so busy breaking all of the rules, was secretly a motherfucking superhero (excuse my language).

The police never arrived. Our brand-new bishop did. Even with her life at stake, my mom still couldn't bring herself to break the "Lord's rules." And much like the former bishop had when my biological father dipped his crane into his first cousin's oil well, this spongy new bishop blamed my mother for Merrill's misbehavior, prescribing the same softball solutions for this new, life-threatening situation. I can still hear that bishop's seemingly requisite sedate LDS tone—like I'd imagine water torture sounding—as he asked my mom, "What . . . is it . . . that you . . . say . . . or do . . . that triggers this . . . reaction . . . in your husband . . . Sister Black?"

But there was no way to answer that question. Merrill's anger was like lightning. It struck when, where, and how it liked. And now this new sponge of a man was not only "strongly encouraging" us not to seek refuge in the law but also blaming my mom for Merrill's latest attempted murder. And if that wasn't enough fun for one blessed afternoon, he told my mom she couldn't leave Merrill. "This was . . . the choice . . . you made. . . . Heavenly Father . . . has blessed your

union . . . in a temple . . . and now . . . it is *youuuur* . . . responsibility . . . to make this work."

The bishop's flaccid tone and tempo were as maddening as his ultimately dangerous message. But Marcus and I now understood what
this man refused to acknowledge: that our lives were truly in danger.
We knew we could no longer depend on our church for help. But we'd
also bought into the idea that the law couldn't be trusted. So without
a church or state to save us, we began privately planning a show of
our own—an old-fashioned show of Texan justice.

I I I

Rule number one in our state: don't mess with Texas. And as
far as my brothers and I were concerned, we were Texans,
and that meant outsiders shouldn't mess with us. Despite
being smaller than most boys my age, by 1984, under my mother's
loving guidance and tough example, I had grown Texas strong.
Where I grew up, a man might employ physical punishment in an
attempt to make his boys stronger but never to weaken them. A belt
to the butt to teach a child a lesson was commonplace, but to blacken
a wife's or son's eye because you couldn't hold your booze or control
your own temper was beyond the pale. We felt sure that Merrill was
an imposter of a man, and certain that he was an invader, an outsider.
And because our church wasn't going to bring Merrill to justice, and
because they wouldn't let us call the cops, "Fuck it," sixteen-year-old
Marcus said, holding a sawed-off .22 rifle in one hand and a pump-
action pellet gun in the other, "we'll do it our own fuckin' selves."

Hidden among the white plastic barrels of wheat the Mormon
Church "encouraged" us to stock up on in order to prepare for the
forthcoming apocalypse, Marcus and I tried Merrill in absentia. One
by one, we reviewed his crimes: the black eyes, the bloodied noses,
his terrible glasses, the time he told me what constipation meant,
the humiliation he subjected us to when he cheaped out and bought

an avocado-green hatchback, the way he slurped his hot beverages. Guilty. On all counts. Marcus handed down Merrill's sentence: "Death." That seemed a bit harsh to me. Marcus looked me in the eyes. "If we only injure him, he'll come back from the hospital even angrier and kill us all. It's him or us." He was right. This was the only way. Death it was.

Like most of the other kids who wore all black, Marcus was in auto shop class in high school. That meant he knew most every way there was to smoke dope, and a bit more each day about what made cars work. He would grow increasingly fascinated with both subjects. So that night, after Merrill got home and we'd wolfed down our mom's meat loaf and green beans, Marcus and I snuck out to the garage. I stood guard. He crawled under Merrill's hideous green car with a pair of metal clippers. I heard a *ping* of metal snapping, which I prayed only my sensitive ears could discern. Then, before my heart had a chance to quicken, Marcus was done. He cleaned his fingerprints off the clippers with a rag, and we went to bed.

Neither of us slept. By this time the next day, we would be murderers. Now the question was whether anyone would find out it was us, and if they did, whether we would face electrocution, lethal injection, or a firing squad. Despite those concerns, Marcus and I took honest-to-God comfort that night in knowing Todd would never get hit, and that our mom would soon be safe again.

The next morning, Merrill sat with us at breakfast and sipped on his hot lemon water. A long *slurp* followed by a loud *gulp* and a vocal "Ahhh." Merrill was an infuriating noise-making machine. *Slurp. Gulp.* "Ahhhh!" Again and again. A rage boiled up in me every time I heard it. A few more sips and "ahhhh"s and all doubts were erased. Merrill Black had to perish.

After breakfast, we heard the electric garage door open. We heard Merrill reverse his old clunker out and the garage door close. I looked at Marcus, who suddenly seemed a bit concerned. He steeled himself. "Might take a while for the brake fluid to drain out. Might happen now. Might happen on his way home. But it's gonna happen."

That night, Merrill got home just fine and right on time. He never once mentioned a problem with his car. He was even in a rare manic good mood—his good-mood days being the only thing more terrifying than his bad-mood ones. He wanted attention, lots of it. He put on faces and voices and did the most idiotic dances to try to get it. This made his unexpected survival all the more annoying. What had gone wrong? Had Marcus clipped something completely unnecessary? Or had Merrill found the snipped line and fixed it, and this was all an act? Marcus convinced me of the latter theory: "He found where I cut the brakes, and now he's pretending to be in a good mood so no one thinks it's him when he kills us all." He took a breath. "We have to do it again. But we have to do it right this time. A direct hit." I was already complicit. I had no choice but to agree.

After a round of particularly puffed up slurps, gulps, and "ahhh"s the next morning, Merrill revealed he was going into work a little later than usual because he had a "big meeting" with his commanding officer that day. Marcus worried that Merrill was setting a trap. We said our goodbyes earlier than usual, pulled on our backpacks, and walked out the door. But instead of joining the huddle at the bus stop down the block, we hid between a pair of massive bushes to see if Merrill would pull out of the garage. He didn't.

The school bus arrived, a few kids got on, and the driver waited for a suspiciously long time before pulling away. My heart was racing now. Marcus was stone cold. Mimicking every Green Beret, FBI, CIA, or James Bond film we'd ever seen, Marcus and I snuck along the sides of houses, hopped fences, and made our way back to our own backyard, sight unseen.

My mom had once told me that the narrow, foot-deep trench between our fence and the surface of our lawn was a precaution in case of flash floods, but when Marcus dipped his hand down into it, he pulled up his .22 rifle and a pump-action pellet gun. He'd planned ahead. Now he chose the pellet gun because it was quieter. "Five pumps hurt like hell. Ten pumps and it's lethal."

We crept up to the wooden side gate and waited. After what felt like hours, we heard the garage door begin to open. Marcus pumped the pellet gun until it was filled with so much air it couldn't be pumped again. Then he held his breath to steady his aim, just as he'd been taught in Boy Scouts. The garage door started to close, and through a gap between a fence post and the gate's hinges, we could just see Merrill pulling his green car into the street. Marcus took aim at Merrill's head but chickened out. It turned out he was incapable of out-right murder, so he aimed at the car's gas tank instead and took his first shot. *Pow!* The shot was so loud in my ears, I was sure the cops would be blazing our way any second. But I'd heard no impact. Marcus looked at me. I shook my head. He had missed. He pumped like mad: 1, 2, 3, 4, 5, 6, 7, 8, 9, 10. He aimed at the gas tank again, then *pow! Plink!* This time I heard the impact of metal on metal, but there was no explosion like when movie bullets met movie gas tanks. 1, 2, 3, 4, 5, 6, 7, 8, 9, 10. The car was quickly pulling away now. So out of desperation, Marcus took aim at a rear tire. *Pow!* But the car vanished down the street, seemingly unharmed. We sat there together, breathless.

When Marcus finally spoke, an unfamiliar resignation had re-placed his rage. "Maybe a tire blows going up the street, maybe it blows on the freeway when he's going sixty miles an hour and he crashes into a retaining wall and dies in a fireball, or . . . maybe it's us who God wants dead." That hit home. That very thought had crossed my mind many a time. "This is in His hands now," Marcus finished. Marcus was so cool—so tough, so dramatic, brave, and butch. Re-gardless of how this turned out, I already felt I owed him my life. I knew we owed him my mom's. And as I watched him rebury his weapons, I wondered if I might ever grow up to be anything like him.

My mom came home from work first that night and got right to making dinner: Hamburger Helper with canned creamed corn on the side. I knew how to brown the ground beef, so I volunteered to help. Feeling the guilt of our second attempted murder in as many days, I was putting on my best angelic act. Marcus was locked in his room blaring "Bitchin' Camaro" off the Dead Milkmen album my mom hated, and watching his window for Merrill's return. It was already well past the hour Merrill usually walked in and there was no sign of him. When dinner was ready, he still wasn't home. Marcus could hardly believe it. We'd done it. The monster was dead. Now we just had to wait for the gory details to hit the newspapers and pray we wouldn't be fingered for his demise.

We sat around the table together, a little family of four again, enjoying our Hamburger Helper and sweet creamed corn without the monster's slurping, without fear of physical attack. Yes, we were destined for poverty again, but we were happy to pay that price for peace.

Then we heard it: the garage door opening and Merrill's car pulling in. Our hearts sank as one. Panicked, Marcus tried to split to his room, but my mom stopped him. It was his turn to do the dishes. The chores sheet clearly said so. Then Merrill walked in. In his dress blues, he looked taller than ever and far too alive. His head wasn't bloody; there had been no car crash. His hands weren't dirty; he hadn't changed a tire. If our fate was truly up to God now, God had turned His back on us. There would be no deliverance.

I sat frozen. Merrill took the chair across from me and did the same. I looked up, dared to survey him. Physically he was fine, but something didn't seem right. When he finally spoke, he tried his best to force his whining voice into a monotone akin to our bishop's— a uniquely Mormon attempt to convey composure and fortitude. "Guys . . . I'm afraid that . . . well . . . I have bad news."

He couldn't make eye contact. "I didn't get it . . . I didn't get the promotion."

My mom tried her best to act surprised, but it was a piss-poor performance. Who could blame her? Merrill was in the computer-programming department of the air force, but, not yet out of elementary school, I could already do laps around him on our Commodore 64. Aside from being abusive, Merrill was also an imbecile. Still, my mom offered him a sincere "I'm really sorry, honey." Then, perhaps as disappointed as we were that he'd interrupted our one peaceful dinner in three years, she sharpened her invisible dagger and asked, "And when is your next review?"

That stung, and she knew it. Everyone knew she had gotten a promotion and a raise at every single one of her reviews. So Merrill didn't answer that question. He couldn't. He was too busy counting to ten, the way the bishop had taught him to when he thought he might punch one of us in the teeth. "One, two, three, four, five, six . . ."

Marcus finished rinsing the dishes at lightning speed, started the dishwasher, and began creeping his way out of the kitchen as casually as possible. He was halfway to the safety of his bedroom when we all heard it—the oh-so-magical strand of words that came tumbling out of Merrill's terrible lips like summer honey:

"My commanding officer is . . . sending me . . . for six months . . . to an air force base in Seoul, Korea."

Marcus stopped in his tracks. Anne took a breath. The hair on my arms stood up.

Perhaps God didn't want us all to die after all.

CHAPTER 9

Hungry Devils

Marcus may have seemed impenetrably tough to most, but he had at least one soft spot that I knew of, and it was as tender as soft spots come: our mom. She, in turn, treasured Marcus's care, and seemed incapable of seeing his faults: his poor school performance, his pyromania, his smoking and drug use. The rest of us warned and worried as he nearly burned our house down time and again, but blinded by the good in her firstborn, she couldn't see or smell any of the tough stuff.

I treasured my big brother too. I wanted (though most often failed) to win his approval. I often wished I shared his best qualities: his creativity, his strength, and his fearlessness. So I perked up when he crawled into the comforter-constructed tent I'd built between Todd's and my beds in our shared bedroom.

"Come with me," he said.

"I'm busy," I replied, embarrassed to have been caught still building tents at eleven years old.

"Playing house?" It was an accusation, not a question, and I knew better than to answer it too directly.

"It's a fort, not a house."

Normally he would have harassed me for playing housewife, but he wanted something, so he went easy. "Come on. I need your help." This was new. I liked it.

Wildly out of character, Marcus wanted to ace a homework assignment for his Judson High School biology class. This was the same punk kid who'd only ever labored enough to get Cs and Ds so the school would pass him up another grade with his long-haired cohorts. He didn't "give two shits" about his future. He was a self-defined loser, rocker, stoner whose only long-term goal was to get a job at McDonald's so he could buy weed and put enough gas in Merrill's crappy green car to drive as far from responsibility as possible.

But Marcus's latest homework assignment was a bug collection. He was supposed to capture, then freeze-to-kill every species he could find, shove a pin through the bodies, tack them into a provided cardboard display box, and label them accurately. Done and dusted. Marcus wasn't on the hunt for the ladybugs and butterflies the rest of his classmates were, though; he was after the most frightening bugs central Texas had to offer—the prize devils—and let me tell you, central Texas is home to some of the scariest six-, eight-, and hundred-legged monsters there are. Now he'd recruited Todd and me to be his soldiers on this mission.

Each afternoon for the next week, we ventured down to the edge of Farmers Lake, crawled into forbidden storm-drain pipes, and walked out into the cow fields. If there was an abandoned barn or shed, we trespassed, always armed with a small green fish-tank net and several empty margarine containers with lids—our version of bug prisons. *No problem,* I thought. I loved bugs. Except for spiders. And unfortunately we soon came across plenty of those—some furry, others glossy black with splashes of yellow and red across the bulbs of their backs. And now Marcus demanded I catch them all alive. He didn't want their bodies crushed before they were frozen and preserved. And though these spiders scared me, I dared not run. The shame of being called a chickenshit would have been worse than venom. That's how Texas boys think.

So when we found a massive black, red, and yellow monster perched in the center of a giant web between a wooden fence and an old tin shed, my job was to hold a margarine container's lid in front of it while Marcus snuck up from behind and pushed the container through the web, around the eight-legged creature, and then hopefully right into the lid in my hand. But if he missed my lid, I knew full well that the spider would be on my face.

Trembling inside, I stayed tough as Texas outside. Todd watched with a grin, not nearly as afraid as I was but too short to hold the lid high enough. I slowly moved my lid toward the spider, and that's when all of us realized how much bigger this thing was than we'd guessed from afar. It was barely going to fit in our container. Marcus talked in a steady, quiet tone to keep me calm as he coached me into place, and then, wisely, he didn't hesitate. He pushed the container hard toward the spider and me, and before I could leap out of their way, the container was around the beast's body, and both met my lid. Marcus pushed the container hard against my hand until it snapped shut. I stood there holding the sealed plastic prison, the spider flailing inside. It felt more like a crab than a bug. Marcus coolly took the container from me and walked it home, proud, victorious, the conqueror of monsters.

Marcus popped his specimens in their respective containers into the freezer to die. Then one by one, he drove pins through their shells and guts, and down into the big cardboard display box the school had provided. A scientist herself, our mom reveled in his newfound curiosity, so she helped him make all of the proper labels. His was a collection straight out of hell, but inarguably a masterpiece. As with anything Marcus actually put his mind to, he aced it. When he'd learned to draw, he'd proven himself the best artist in school. When he'd taken drama to get out of gym class, he'd won every leading role and genuine applause. But the second Marcus aced anything, he also immediately judged it to be "pansy shit" and quit it. So now he decided one giant spider wasn't enough of a crowning achievement. He wanted something even bigger. That prize arrived the night before his project was due. Signaling its arrival was a shriek from our kitchen.

Marcus ran into the kitchen, where he began chasing a big brown blur from under one cabinet to the next, my mom pleading, "Just smash it, Marcus! Smash it!" But Marcus wanted this beast intact. So using his own shoe as a trap, he caught that twitching, flying, three-inch Texas cockroach from hell. He wound plastic wrap around his shoe, popped it all in the freezer, and a few hours later, the roach was as stiff as ice. He drove a pin through its guts, my mom typed up the label, and he had it: the most terrifying bug collection Judson High would ever see. He popped the lid on his display, and despite my mom begging him to move it off her dining room table, he left it there in its place of honor, ready for its trip to school the next morning.

That night, Marcus marched about the house with an expression of pride I'd never seen on him.

But the next morning, when I shuffled into the kitchen, I was met with a more familiar sight. My mom was upset, and Marcus had gone stone cold again. "Fuck 'em. Fuck 'em all. Fuck the world." He left the room. The lid was off his display. I crept forward and peeked into the box. Almost every bug was gone, some half-gone, and the rest had no legs or eyes left. Only the giant cockroach was still intact, the needle still through its guts, but very much alive as it clawed its way around the box looking for more to munch on. Overnight, it had thawed out, woken up, and made a meal of every other bug in Marcus's once spectacular, hard-won collection.

But that morning's true heartbreak had little to do with the bad grade Marcus would now surely receive; the tragedy here was that he'd just learned a terrible lesson. No, not that he shouldn't have included an apocalypse-ready cockroach; it was that he felt he'd once again made the mistake of giving a damn. Because once again, when he'd dared to care, a monster had arrived, and taken away what he loved.

A few months later, Marcus got that job at McDonald's, and soon after, he got third-degree burns up and down his forearms from a grease fire. With the pittance of cash his injury earned him, he bought gas for Merrill's car and weed for himself and his friends, and he spent less and less time in our home. On the increasingly rare occasions I saw him, I couldn't help but notice the letters *FTW* tattooed on his arm where the burn scars were. He'd done it himself with guitar string and pen ink. It stood for "Fuck the World." He was finished with trying and caring.

When I think back on that morning, what sticks out most is that when Marcus looked down into his bug box for the last time, he paused and then picked up that roach, pulled the needle out of its gut, and let it go. Most sixteen-year-old boys would have pounded it flat in revenge, and frankly, my mom would have preferred that. But Marcus didn't. He had been ten when Raul took off, old enough to understand that his father knew him well. So Raul's abandonment felt personal. Marcus grew to believe that something was so inherently monstrous about him that he was worthy of being left with two little brothers and a paralyzed mom who couldn't feed them. He had in fact been left for dead. So Marcus wouldn't blame this latest disaster on a bug. Capturing it was simply one decision in a long chain of bad decisions Marcus felt he'd made in life. The fault must have been his own. He now believed that he himself was the true monster. So on this day, he likely added "too fuckin' stupid" to his long list of faults as he let that bug run free.

I was six when Raul flew the coop. Yes, it took a terrible toll on my self-esteem, but unlike Marcus, I didn't think I was inherently a monster. I was a bit more hopeful than that. I believed that I was filled to the brim with monsters and devils: my crippling shyness, my crushes on boys, my sensitivity, and my big temper at tiny injustices. My hope lived in a belief that I might one day conquer my demons and be worthy of love again. So unlike Marcus, who was off indulging his demons, I often leaned in to take a closer look at what I felt were my worst qualities, to see which needed changing or concealing the most.

I had long ago proven myself no natural performer in the Jingle Bell Band, but the same year that Marcus tattooed FTW on his forearm, an advanced-placement history teacher at Kitty Hawk Junior High, who was concerned about my asocial behavior, referred me to the debate club. It was a club for nerds, and I fit that mold well, but as it happened, the head of that debate club had also been Marcus's drama teacher. Hoping that some of his talent was in our blood, she set her sights on having me replace him. Picking up on my weakness, she explained that debate club meant I'd be up in front of audiences all by myself, coming up with lines on the fly, but drama class was more of an ensemble, and the words were provided.

Drama class did me no favors. Unlike my butch big brother, who had chosen to avoid PE, I was actually on the junior high football team. I liked being pushed to my limits. I liked the anonymity a football helmet provided. I liked it when all the boys took off their clothes right in front of me in the locker room after practice. Even so, I now wanted to address my abject shyness, and so I chose to make drama my sixth-period class. The first requirement was to participate in a series of one-act plays that toured the local high school theater competitions. I was assigned *Adam & Eve,* and my Eve would be none other than the drama teacher's popular, impossibly cute daughter. She had brown hair, light eyes, and a bashful smile that made most boys melt.

I won't dive too deep into the details of our performances. She was great, I remembered my lines, and we won an honorable mention in two competitions. And when our forward-looking theater teacher chose to stage a production of *Sometimes I Wake Up in the Middle of the Night,* a collection of monologues and scenes about adolescent drug use, love, sex, and suicide, our principal must have failed to read the script before approving it. I was given a role in the play with that same drama teacher's daughter. It seemed she and her mom thought I had some talent. But here's the thing: these performances didn't help my self-esteem. They were performances stacked on top of performances. The only achievement here was that I had succeeded in fooling them into believing I wasn't terrified of being in front of an audience. I did take a little pride in this ability. *If nothing else*, I thought, *I might survive my truly monstrous, unlovable self as a passable fraud.* A fraud. That's what I would aim to be in this life, and for now, that was fine by me.

I began making lists of other things I might acquire to fool people: name-brand clothes (namely, a collection of Izod polo shirts), a new haircut and products that might tame my cowlick, a flip comb like Eric Peterson had in his pocket in case of emergencies, and perhaps some actual muscles to boot. My list continued to grow, but I knew my mom couldn't afford any of the material things on it, so I looked for substitutes and begged her to scour the discount racks for fake polos while I counted down the days until the junior high dance of 1986. There I would attempt the ultimate fraud: I would ask that drama teacher's daughter to dance with me . . . with the entire student body bearing witness . . . and to a slow song. If I was successful, this would prove to be my most spectacular fraud to date.

The night of the dance arrived, and I pulled on the baby-blue Izod polo shirt my mom had found on a defectives rack at Ross Dress for Less. It had a bleach stain on it, but low enough that it would mostly be hidden if I tucked the shirt in, and my mom said it made my eyes look like gemstones. Done and dusted. Then I squirted out a handful of Marcus's green hair gel and tried my best to smash down my cowlick with it. I let it dry, and repeated the process.

My mom offered to drive me, but I said I'd prefer to ride my bike, thinking that was what a cool kid would do. But when I arrived at the school, sticky hair gel sweating down my face, I realized that every well-adjusted kid had let their parents drive them. The bike rack was completely empty. So instead of ruining my performance in the first act by locking my bike to an otherwise empty rack, I ditched it between two landscaped hills out front—nothing to lock it to, just the hope that it wouldn't be stolen.

I made it inside and found a gaggle of boys from the debate, math, and drama clubs all dancing together. Not one-on-one, of course—they were in a big, no-girls-allowed but decidedly heterosexual circle. No one was facing each other: all of them were side by side, grooving out of rhythm and with little style to Boy George's "Karma Chameleon," then Bon Jovi's "Living on a Prayer" and UB40's "Red Red Wine." I wouldn't describe this circle as fun, but I did manage to shuffle from side to side just enough not to stick out as terrified.

At least three slow songs came and went, and during each, our circle of dorks broke apart and I looked out across the auditorium for my drama teacher's daughter. She was nowhere to be seen. I was running out of time. Soon I worried that I might have wasted all of my efforts, Marcus's hair gel, and my mom's money. But then Madonna's "Live to Tell" took over the auditorium. In it lived a treasured lyric:

> Hope I live to tell the secret I have learned, till then, it will burn
> inside of me.

My good gay God, it was the perfect song for this charade. A song about secrets with a music video featuring an impossibly cute young actor named Sean Penn. I had leaned my head against the school bus window many a time when it had come on the radio in the morning, letting my tween heart beat faster, dreaming of my own secrets and forbidden loves. Now I would ask a girl to dance to it in my greatest performance yet. If only I could find her.

I told two of the boys near me that I was going to ask the drama teacher's daughter to dance. I needed witnesses. That was the whole point. I made my way from the front of the auditorium to the middle, but I still couldn't find her. Then I dared to step toward the back of the room, even though a good teacher's daughter surely wouldn't be there. The back was for kids with black clothes and jackets that smelled like smoke, kids like my big brother. But as I crossed into this no-man's-land, there she was: cute as can be, wearing a lovely pink dress, standing on her tiptoes, her chin tilted up . . . carving a circle with a tall, strong, thirteen-year-old Latin boy who looked like he already had to shave. His strong arms were around her back, pulling her body up next to his. She was consumed by it.

I stood there, quite still, knowing full well I had no chance of pulling them apart, that all of my preparation, sweat, and terror had been for nothing. Though minutes earlier I would have thought it impossible, I now felt even less like a man. And then that muscly Latin boy's lips touched hers, and my heart broke. Even if my plan had worked, I would never have experienced what they were—young though it was, right there in front of me, in the plain sight of others, and with no fear of judgment . . . was love.

I raced back to the front of the auditorium, to the land of kids from proper academic clubs, and found the boys I'd been dancing in a circle with, now assembled in an uncomfortably loose clump, none speaking to one another, all looking at the floor. And then, without a thought, with only the aim of burying my pain, I turned to one of the math club kids who absolutely wasn't my type. I suppose that was why I thought it was less than insane to ask him . . .

"Do you wanna dance?"

It wasn't a romantic invitation. It was a miscalculation of epic proportions. He looked at me like I'd just asked to eat his pet gerbil. Only then did I realize that "Live to Tell" was still playing.

"It's a slow song," he pointed out with disgust.

I raced to recover. "It's not that slow."

I've just listened to the song again thirty-plus years later, and honestly it's not the most romantic slow song, but he was right, it's slow.

Then a kind of angry laugh came vomiting out of him, and with it, "What kind of faggot are you?!" He was genuinely asking, and loud enough to make sure that everyone heard him say it, so that no one doubted his manhood in our exchange.

I don't remember what kind of shit-poor lie I might have spun. All I recall is a sickening panic rising up inside of me—my monster suddenly laid bare.

The next thing I remember is searching through the rolling hills in front of the school for a bike I would never find, tears streaming down my face. I was a failure even at being a fraud. I walked all the way home. It must have taken over an hour, but that was a gift. The long walk got me to my front door right when I should have arrived if I'd actually enjoyed the whole dance, and by then, my tears had had time to dry. Walking in and past my mom, I gave a decent performance. She said something about how sweaty I was, and I lied about how much I'd danced. She seemed happy for me.

That night in bed, I thought back to the play we'd put on in drama class, back to the series of monologues about kids who had considered hurting themselves in this way or that, and how they'd managed to reach out for help when those thoughts arrived. But as hard as I tried, I couldn't think of a single person who might help me. I was a sinner in my church, a criminal to the law and my community, and a pervert and a freak to everyone else. And so, that was the first of many nights I would lie in bed contemplating taking my life. I thought about how I might do it in a way that no one would know I'd been a coward. I thought about how I might make it painless and quick. But then I thought about how my death would hurt my mom, and honestly, even thirty years later, I can say that's likely the only reason I didn't do it. I was ready to hurt myself, but I couldn't bear to hurt her.

So that night I made a pact with myself. If my mother ever died, or was taken away, yes, that pain would surely be unbearable, but it wouldn't be my last. My final pain would come soon after, the price of ending my own life, and with it all of the horrible, hungry monsters and demons I'd been taught lived inside of me—by a father's rejection, by a state's laws, by a military culture, and by my own church. All those devils would finally go. But until that day of great sadness and relief, I would have to watch my big brother try and prove to the world what a monster he really was—despite the truth of his tender heart, and I would have to survive all of my own devilish monsters slowly eating me alive from the inside.

And so starting that night, I stopped making lists of lies I might sell, I stopped trying to achieve much of anything, I stopped putting on my little fraud shows, and I got down to the soul-swallowing business of disappearing.

CHAPTER 10

Deliverance

In the five years since she'd started at Fort Sam Houston's Brooke Army Medical Center as a government service employee, Anne had quickly moved up the ranks from a part-time GS4 (General Schedule 4) working out of a broom-closet-sized shipping office to a GS7 working directly with doctors as a microbiology lab tech, helping diagnose sick soldiers and vets. A GS7 was as high as this hospital would let her rise without the college degree her mother had tried in vain to convince her to complete. Still, the hospital's most senior doctors often slipped past higher-ranking lab techs to find her, their secret weapon: my powerhouse of a mom.

My mother was determined to never again be a patient in a hospital, but she was equally passionate about working in one—helping doctors get ailing soldiers and their spouses and children back home as soon as possible. She understood the trauma of being a patient better than most. The doctors respected her for that and more. When she moved down the long, slick hospital hallways, she often did so gripping heavy metal test tube racks with two fingers, her remaining eight digits holding her swinging crutches. Hoping to be heroes, new doctors would leap to her aid, only to be shot down. "I've got it, sir," she'd tell them. She'd then give a disarming, flirty wink. "I've been doing this dance a long time. Haven't lost one yet." She'd smile, then swing her way to the next lab, unaided, independent, and with one more doctor's admiration in her lab coat pocket. Second only to her sons, her work was her pride and purpose. And in these five years, us boys and her work had made for a full enough life.

But when Merrill was shipped off to South Korea, our home began to thaw, and things began to break up and shift beneath us. You couldn't see it yet, but I could feel it.

Sitting on her queen-size bed, her legs folded beneath her and a map of San Antonio spread out on her floral comforter, my mother held a well-sharpened pencil between her teeth as she traced a finger along a road leading out of Fort Sam to a public park beyond it. She considered the location, drew a circle around it, then hunted for another. When her finger found a far smaller park, she compared the distance of the two drives, and drew a circle around it too. Four other parks were already circled—all of them just off the base but much closer to her work than our rented home in Live Oak or our Mormon church in the Randolph Ward.

When she heard the front door burst open and her boys' messy racket, she quickly but carefully folded up the map and slid it into a bedside drawer. At nearly forty years old, my tough Rose of a mom was planning a new, illicit, top-secret mission.

My first clue came that same day, when she asked me to bring her the biggest encyclopedia volume from the bookcase. It was an odd request. In our collection, the *A* volume was the thickest, so I brought it to her, but as it often still does, my curiosity got the best of me.

"What are you looking for?" I asked.

"I just need something heavy."

"What if I need to find something that starts with *A*?"

"Then I'll let you look it up."

"Well, why an encyclopedia?"

"Because it's stiffer than the phone book," she said casually, as if that should have been obvious. And she gripped all those *A* words by their spine with her right hand and started doing curls with them. Actual bicep curls.

"What are you doing?" I asked.

"Exercise. What does it look like, Lancer?" As if that too should have been obvious.

I was twelve years old now and still rattled by her unwelcome explanation of the miracle of menses a few months earlier when I'd demanded we call an ambulance for her "tummy cramps." Fearing another such truth-telling debacle, I decided it was best to stop my line of questioning right there, but I knew something was up.

Months earlier, a group of U.S. Army paratroopers was thousands of feet above us on a routine training jump when a reckless soldier started goofing off. He was carving wide circles in the air, paying no attention to what was beneath him, and his feet hit something. He'd inadvertently stepped into the parachute of a soldier below. When the chute began twisting around this soldier's legs, he panicked and began trying to kick free. Only when he'd succeeded did he realize that he'd done so at the expense of the soldier below.

The chute below collapsed, and now the unfortunate soldier hanging from it began falling through the air, the ground racing up toward him. This soldier's name was Jeff. Jeff quickly began working to get air back into his chute, but when it was clear that wasn't going to happen, he deployed his reserve. But it was too late. *Boom!*

He blacked out when he hit the ground, so he didn't feel it when he bounced and hit it all over again. Broken ribs, a dislocated shoulder, a busted knee, and a fractured hip—he looked like a cartoon character in traction for many weeks, but he felt very lucky to be alive. The real despair came when the doctors determined that he could no longer jump. He was already a decorated Special Forces soldier at twenty-one, and this should have been the beginning of a heroic military career. Instead that dream was over.

Jeff's commanding officers promised to reassign him wherever he wanted to go in the military. Jeff looked around his hospital room and said, "Maybe I should just stay here."

Once he was well enough to walk again, that's exactly what he got: orders to report to the headquarters of the U.S. Army laboratory division.

On his first day of work at the army medical center, Jeff carefully pressed and pulled on his white dress uniform, then his Special Forces beret. Free of a helmet, bandages, and bruises, Jeff was an honest-to-God U.S. military hottie, with a perfectly fit body topped with a handsome baby face and a thin hipster-style mustache he could hardly grow but that said loud and clear, "I'm a little bit of trouble." He drove to the hospital and parked his crappy car at the end of the lot so as not to injure his playboy reputation. As he walked toward the hospital's front doors, he surveyed his new haunt, catching sight of a blonde with perfectly set curls sitting in a car putting the finishing touches on her blue eye shadow and peach lips. There were a lot more women here than on a Special Forces obstacle course. Nurses galore. Maybe this wasn't the end of the world after all.

Jeff was at the hospital that day to discuss his experience with the lab's sergeant major, who explained that this base housed a large laboratory made up of several divisions and specialties. Jeff thought about it and asked, "What about microbiology?" Jeff knew that in microbiology, most everything had to be done by hand. He thought that sounded like a better time than feeding machines.

The microbiology department was all as one might expect—full of test tubes, beakers, and petri dishes—until the very last room. There, a cluster of doctors was hovering around something that clearly fascinated them. But whatever it was, it was small enough to be blocked from Jeff's view. As the sergeant major completed the tour, Jeff kept glancing back at the huddle until it finally broke apart in a burst of laughter. At the heart of it was that same hot blonde with the blue eye shadow from the parking lot out front, now perched atop a lab stool like a little mouse. Jeff looked at her and smiled. That hot blonde, well, she smiled right back at this tall, handsome, and much younger soldier with the troublemaker mustache.

The hot blonde, of course, was my enduringly well-behaved, nearly forty-year-old, and most certainly married Mormon mom.

The sergeant major decided it was only right to give Jeff every advantage and team him up with the lab's best and brightest. So Roseanna Black's new job was to show Jeffrey Scott Bisch the ropes.

The micro section was made up of many different benches: one where lab techs received specimens, and others for reviewing respiratory, urinary, wound care cases, and so on. Over the next few months, Jeff had to learn how to care for each bench's specimens and cultures, with Anne by his side to show him all the proper procedures. In that time, in little ways, things began to get flirty. But Anne was a good Southern woman and a devout Mormon, so any temptation was quickly sublimated into setting Jeff up on dates with women his own age who liked to do twentysomething things. The thing is, Jeff had left home at seventeen. He'd been to war. He'd seen and done things most men would pray never to see or do in their lifetimes. It was hard for him to connect with twentysomethings. And Jeff loved that Anne could actually relate to his stories, hopes, and concerns.

Of course, Anne wasn't half as young as she looked—or as Jeff assumed. She had conveniently failed to tell him her true age, that she was married, or that she had three boys at home. It all must have slipped her mind . . . in the same way her wedding band had starting slipping off into her lab coat pocket each morning, starting back on that very first day Jeff walked in.

But Anne knew from the start that she wouldn't be seated on her stool forever, that he'd watch her swing in and out of the lab on her crutches day in and day out and take note of her twisting back. Then whatever crush he'd had would fade. For now, she was simply going to enjoy what she could of his attention while it lasted.

The trouble is, the first time Jeff remembers seeing Anne walk around was when a new girl who was just starting at the front desk rang the lab and said, "Mrs. Black, could you please come up to the front desk to pick up a specimen for your area? I sprained my ankle and I'm on crutches and can't bring it back to you." When Jeff passed Anne in the hallway that day, she had a devilish grin on her face as she swung up to the front desk on her hip-high braces and crutches and asked that girl with the sprained ankle for the specimen. It was a big container filled with twenty-four hours' worth of collected urine—heavy as a gallon of milk. And before the girl could apologize, Anne grabbed it up and swung it all the way back down the hall to her lab. Jeff saw the pride on Anne's face when she came in and set it down on her bench. That kind of moxie was sexier to Jeff than any pair of working legs.

Then one day, near break time, Anne dipped her hand into her lab coat pocket and felt around for something. Two things, actually. She checked the time, looked over at Jeff, and got up off her stool. Gripping her crutches a little tighter, she made her way to the laboratory door via Jeff's bench. It was far from a direct route. She leaned in, and as if offering some sort of illicit drug, she quietly asked, "Hey, why don't you go on break with me? I've got some hot chocolate."

Her heart was racing. She knew exactly what line she was crossing. She hadn't felt like this since her days flirting with the young priests and push-boys in the children's hospitals, or since her first moments with Don or Raul. It felt dangerous and impossible.

"Okay," he said. Once they were alone in the break room, she pulled the instant hot chocolate packets out of her pocket, ripped them open, poured the powder into two mugs, and added hot water. The deed was done. As if that transgression weren't enough, on their walk back to the lab, she mentioned the one thing that made her heart race even faster than hot chocolate: McDonald's apple pies. Devilish little vixen.

That Sunday night, instead of going drinking with his barracks buddies, Jeff drove through McDonald's for dinner and added an apple pie to his order. On Monday, when he and Anne dared go on another break together, he said, "I got something for you." Her heart leapt. He pulled the pie from his pocket and gave it to her. A confectionary line had been crossed. Now Anne began bringing him Froot Loops, Rice Krispies, an actual container of sugar, and a little bowl. She even bought him a plant for his window in the barracks. She was incrementally stepping away from all she knew to be true and moral in her church, the promises she'd made her "priesthood holder" husband in a temple. She was leaning back into her Southern roots, not quite taking the bull by the horns but damn sure looking it in the eye.

Then one sunny weekend, Jeff's planned trip to see some old army pals out at Fort Leavenworth in Kansas was unexpectedly canceled. Over the phone, Anne could tell that he was down about it. She suggested, "Why don't I come pick you up and we'll go get some ice cream?" He thought that sounded nice. She spent the next hour making herself perfect, and struggling to find civilian clothes that didn't look too Mormon. She told us three boys that there was a work emergency and she had to go in to the lab. Her performance was so believable that I have no distinct memory of this moment. Later, of course, I got all of the details.

She picked Jeff up at his barracks in her Malibu, they found an ice cream joint, and they slowly ate their dripping cones. Then she drove him back to his barracks. But this wasn't a work break. It wasn't even a lunch break. They had no rules for this. So they just sat there, parked in front of his barracks, talking until they realized the sun had long since set. Jeff was still a little down about not seeing his old Kansas pals, and was working that little nugget for all it was worth. And Anne knew full well what she was doing when she said, "Oh come on, give me a hug."

He did, and they held each other in the front seat of her car for a good long time, then slowly broke apart, looked at each other, and kissed. The game was over.

They kissed again and again until she finally stopped him with "I've gotta get going now." Jeff tried to act cool. He got out of the car, made his way up the stairs to the barracks, and walked smack-dab into one of the glass doors leading inside. Anne quickly looked away, pretending she hadn't just seen it happen. She pressed her gas-pedal hand control down and pulled away. A few blocks up, she found herself sitting at a stop sign, not moving, knowing full well that Jeff's collision with that glass door meant he was as wrapped up in what had just happened as she was. And she thought, *What have I done?*

Anne got her three boys all dressed up for church on Sunday and tortured herself all the way through services. Sitting in the familiar pews, she thought, *I was once a righteous Mormon woman, head of the Relief Society, and now Heavenly Father can plainly see I'm unworthy. The shame this will bring to my family, to my children. There is no happy ending in this.* She knew this had to stop.

Come Monday, things were awkward at work. When Anne and Jeff saw each other, they didn't know what to say. Anne suggested they wait until lunch to talk. He agreed. She drove them to a park just off the base where they wouldn't be seen together, where she could apologize for her part in this recklessness and end it. They got out of the car, sat at a picnic table, and didn't eat a bite. By this point, Jeff knew that Anne had been married once, but now she told him what he had also suspected, that she had children—three sons. But even that late-breaking news didn't seem to throw him, and before she could recite the rest of the affair-stopping monologue she'd practiced over and over again in her head, they were making out again.

After that voracious lunch, Anne bought herself that map of San Antonio and began staking out other public parks.

Sure, Heavenly Father knew what she was up to, but she would be damned if her congregation or Jeff's fellow soldiers would figure it out. However, not having quite finished her big breakup speech, Anne still hadn't told Jeff her boys' ages or even her own, and she'd failed to mention that she was still married to their air force staff sergeant stepfather who far outranked Jeff. It all could get very messy, very fast.

One night, following the pattern of the preceding few weeks, Anne picked Jeff up at his barracks. They had dinner, then drove to yet another darkened public park she had staked out and got down to business. This time, though, a car pulled up behind them and police lights flickered on. Terror hit them both. The cop walked over to the driver's side, put a flashlight in Anne's face, then looked at Jeff, at his obvious military haircut, and said, "Get out of the car, son. I need to talk to you."

Jeff did as he was told, leaving Anne alone with her thoughts in the car. As the cop questioned Jeff, her mind spun out of control. This was the end. She would be humiliated and cast out of her church. Merrill would return and take Jeff to some military tribunal and have him court-martialed. Merrill's punishment at home would be even more severe, his violent rebuke spilling over onto her three boys, her treasures.

Finally, Jeff returned to the car, and they waited in silence for the cop to pull away.

"What did he say?" she asked.

Jeff said, "He, uh, gave me a warning."

"Did he take your ID? He has my license plate number."

"No, he, uh . . . he just told me to be careful."

"Of what?"

Jeff stifled a grin and finally let it out: "He thought you were a prostitute."

Anne whacked him hard against the chest with the back of her hand. He laughed, but it was true! She was relieved, flattered, and offended all at once. From then on, she wore a bit less blue eye shadow and toned down her lip color, but she knew this was a real wake-up call. She and Jeff could no longer risk public encounters. Problem was, he lived in the barracks, and her home was filled with three boys who would give away her age and pictures of a husband that would reveal her current marital status. So Anne checked her credit-card balances and put together a plan only a lovesick mind might find sane.

After work one Friday, she sat us boys down and said, "Wouldn't it be fun if you guys had your own time together, sort of like a campout, but here in the city, near the mall? Marcus could take you to a movie, and shopping, and then you could have your own hotel room for the whole weekend and eat anything you want."

Her plan was and still is one of the more bizarre affair plots of all time. Why on earth didn't she just get her own hotel room? Isn't that how affairs are supposed to go? Why make this so oddly complicated? At the time, I hadn't yet sniffed out any affair, but I knew that what she was proposing was very, very weird.

A testament to how my mom and I had sheltered Todd, not a whole lot ever worried him, so he thought it sounded like a great idea. I voiced a concern: "What about church?" Marcus slowly ground his elbow into my ribs as punishment for asking such a stupid question.

With just a dash of hesitation, our mom replied, "Well . . . this will be a little vacation from that. It'll be guys' time. Man time. Doesn't that sound like fun?"

Maybe if the men were the Dallas Cowboys and the hotel was a locker room, I thought, but this was a hotel with my brothers, whom I spent every moment with anyhow, and an anxiety-provoking shopping mall filled with looky strangers. Was this a joke? A trap set by priesthood holders to block us from the pearly gates? But Todd loved the idea of skipping church and said so with a giant grin that showed off more than a few gaps where the tooth fairy had made collections. One more look in my mom's eyes and I knew this was no joke, no vacation, and no diversion from heaven. Our by-the-books Mormon mother with her closet full of floral dresses was going to start sending us away to discount hotels on the weekends because she was holding on to some big new secret.

I wanted more than anything to find out what it was, but Marcus silenced my curiosity. He'd turned sixteen and gotten his driver's license. With Merrill away and the brakes checked on his old green car, Marcus was loving his newfound freedom. He insisted that this was a portal into countless fantastic new adventures . . . if only I didn't ruin it with all my "stupid fucking questions." So I never inquired about the lingering smell of home-cooked food upon our Sunday-evening returns, or about the new little teddy bear by her bedside that smelled of men's cologne.

Instead, Marcus turned me and Todd into his accomplices again, this time training us how to help him shoplift from every store we walked into during those strange weekends.

Our job was to stand at the end of aisles, look innocent, and say, "Hey, have you read this," as a signal that someone was coming. By our fourth cheap hotel weekend, we owned every G.I. Joe, Transformer, and Atari and Commodore computer game we'd ever dreamed of. Sure, we'd gone from picture-perfect church children to expert criminals in the course of one month, but for the first time since Raul had abandoned us, we had what other kids did: new clothes, toys, and even a full-size Commodore 128 for me to hone my programming skills on. Marcus had just picked up that computer and walked right out of the store's front doors with it like it was nothing. That theft in particular gave him a great deal of confidence. Perhaps too much.

It didn't take a genius to know that my mother's affair and Marcus's heists were short-term solutions to long-term problems. Eventually Merrill would return. And eventually Target would install video cameras inside mirrored bubbles in their ceilings and record Marcus shoving a Summer Olympics computer game down the front of his pants. On that day, he was restrained by a security guard as he walked out of Target's front doors with the game against his manhood. Todd and I were pulled aside, sat down, and watched in the snack bar area. The security guard called our home to find out who these juvenile delinquents' rotten parents were. And when Anne refused to answer the incessantly ringing phone, real cops came knocking.

Anne had just served Jeff a spectacular spaghetti dinner complete with marinara sauce made from scratch. This was why she wanted the house and not a hotel room. She knew that Jeff had signed up for the army at seventeen because he hadn't had the best childhood growing up in Philly. She wanted him to feel the warmth of a home, not the illicit vibe of a hotel room. And she was expert at warmth, not so much at anything too illicit. Her plan now seemed rather clever when considered from the home-cooked-meal perspective. But just as they'd sat down to eat this candlelit marinara masterpiece, the doorbell rang. Her first thought was that Merrill had somehow figured out what she was up to, and all the way from South Korea had called the police to intervene. She convinced Jeff to blow out the candles and wait for the cops to go.

Yes, police were at the door, but not for the reason she feared. Still, Jeff waited for half an hour before finally sneaking outside. Thankfully, he'd parked his car on the street so as not to draw the attention of any curious LDS congregant neighbors.

When Anne finally checked our answering machine and returned the calls from Target, the store's security chief explained what Marcus had done but said they had let him leave with only a warning when they couldn't locate his parents. In a way, my mom's affair had just saved my big brother from having a rap sheet, from then on making it even harder for Marcus to believe her when she said, "Two wrongs don't make a right." Needless to say, Anne was now certain that she was the worst mother in the universe.

Anne hated that she couldn't even acknowledge Marcus's crime, much less punish him for it. Problem was, he was old enough to suspect what she was up to; the hotel freedom and unlimited use of Merrill's car were his rewards for turning a blind eye. Now that unspoken agreement was compromising her ability to parent.

But love can make the most reasonable people keep right on doing the most ludicrous things. So instead of calling the adulterous weekends off, Anne devised a new plan to break up our little crime syndicate. No more hotels. From here on out, we were each to spend our Saturday nights apart, at different friends' houses. *Easy enough for Todd and Marcus,* I thought; they had friends and went on sleepovers. I didn't. I was now the odd man out.

I I

By this time, puberty had begun to circle, amping up my crushes into what felt like undying love, and making me all the more motivated to kiss a boy, but failing to deliver a single inch in height or a strand of hair where it actually mattered.

I begged my mom to buy me a Hawaiian button-down shirt like the "cool kids" all had. But this shirt wasn't for some fraud-show sequel. I genuinely wanted to look good for an impossibly cute boy named Jason, a new kid from New Jersey who had great style, who all the girls swooned over, and who (for reasons I couldn't yet detect) actually wanted to be my friend.

Mobs of girls would literally chase Jason around the schoolyard at lunchtime. He'd eventually take refuge in the gym toilets, where I most often hid during any social hour. But instead of ignoring me or making fun of me, he actually struck up conversations: about Garbage Pail Kids, the Challenger space shuttle explosion, or Michael Jackson's burning hair. He even invited me to his house to do homework one afternoon. There I discovered that his father had ditched him too. There I met his struggling mom and his siblings. And there he popped the biggest sixth-grade question of them all—he asked to play a game of "I'll show you mine if you show me yours."

I nearly suffered a twelve-year-old coronary, but this time I didn't completely screw things. Instead, I quickly came up with a plan. "Isn't that more like a sleepover thing?" I asked. And bingo, like Todd and Marcus had with their own friends, I secured a sleepover invite. I now had a place to stay come our first Saturday away from home and out of hotels. But unlike Todd and Marcus, I wasn't just staying with a friend; I would be with the man of my dreams. All night. And guess what? My mom even agreed to buy me the Hawaiian shirt that would make my dream complete.

When that special night arrived, I put on my new shirt and kissed my mom goodbye. I rode my bike to Jason's house and dropped my things in his room, but before we settled in for what should have been the best night of my life, Jason suggested we visit our girlfriends. It's true: we had girlfriends. Not that either of us had ever actually spoken to them, but notes had been passed in class, and Jason had agreed to couple up with a cute brunette if her friend would agree to couple up with me. She mercifully acquiesced. And that was that, my first girlfriend, whom I never said a single word to. Because on our bike ride to meet up with them, Jason suggested, "Hey, let's take Suicide Hill."

It was years before I'd meet the hills of San Francisco, so at the time, Suicide Hill seemed to me to be the steepest there was. It had a four-way stop at the intersection at the bottom, so the skater punks and freestyle BMX anarchists loved to jam down it at top speed, ignore the stop sign, and tempt fate. Technically that made it more like Russian roulette than suicide, but parsing such things while pedaling for my life to keep up with Jason on the secondhand (if not thirdhand) bike my mom had picked up for ten bucks to replace the one I'd lost somewhere in the hills around my junior high school, I soon realized I was only halfway down the hill and already going deadly fast considering the junker beneath me.

I stopped pedaling, but that didn't help. Likely appalled by my devilish intentions toward Jason, God must have told gravity to suck me down that hill and toward that intersection with as much force as possible. So as gently as my panicking hands could manage (about as gently as a vise grip), I squeezed the bike's brake. My bike stopped on a dime. Bravo! Except that the good Lord's momentum now shot me into the air like a rocket. It was a classic rookie move. I had hit the front brake, the front tire had locked up, and I was now flying over handlebars I refused to let go of, sending my bike into a flip in the air above me. I soon lost my grip, and *bang!* I hit the ground hard, chin first. Just enough time passed for me to feel the excruciating bolts of pain race up my face and down my spine before the bike came crashing down like a holy reprimand on top of my head, slamming my skull, chin, and jaw even deeper into the angry Texas asphalt.

Thankfully, I'd been hit in the head more than a few times at this point, so I didn't completely freak out. I got up and sat down on the curb to let the pain fade like it always had before. The first thing I found different about this head injury, though, was that a chunk of my left front tooth was gone. My heart sank. As if I weren't ugly enough already. The second thing I noticed was the river of blood flowing down the gutter below me. I looked at my hands, which had been cradling my jaw. They were covered in blood, and even more was pouring down. I ran to the door of a house and started banging on it and screaming, leaving bloody handprints up and down it like in some over-the-top B-movie crime scene.

When Jason heard my screams, he turned around and pedaled back. I didn't need to see my reflection. I could tell from Jason's expression that whatever small dose of cuteness God had given me was now gone for good. And my new Hawaiian button-down? Soaked in blood. Ruined. The fates, the universe, and God Himself had just canceled my night of amorous discovery in epic horror film fashion.

A white-haired woman came running out of the house across the street. She shoved me into her Lincoln Town Car and asked where I lived. That was a toughie. I wasn't allowed home on Saturday nights. But surely this situation was worthy of rule bending, right? I was too rattled to unravel that, but when the woman raised her voice and demanded an answer, Jason gave it to her. At least now it wouldn't be my fault when we invaded my mom's top-secret weekend.

When my mom finally answered the door, the house smelled of perfume and home-baked bread. The look on her face was about as alarmed as the one on Jason's had been. She thanked our good neighbor, told Jason to go home, and got a clean cloth, which she had me press to my chin. "Put pressure on it, Lancer. It's going to be okay." That was an order, not reassurance. I had to press it hard because I had to be okay.

She went to the phone, took a deep breath to calm herself, and called Jeff. "Hey. I have to cancel."

"What's wrong?" Jeff asked.

"Nothing." It was clearly a lie. "Do you have Rick's number? From the lab? He lives out here in Live Oak, right?"

Jeff gave her the number, but he didn't like doing it.

My mom hung up and called Rick, then came back to comfort me as we waited for him to arrive. My mom understood childhood trauma all too well and proved so expert at comforting it, I was soon more worried about my Hawaiian shirt than what had happened to my chin, my tooth, or my jaw.

Rick finally arrived and drove as my mom held me on our way to the hospital she worked at. As the military doctors rushed to stitch up my face and x-ray my jaw, a beautiful young nurse appeared, holding my blood-soaked Hawaiian button-down. She seemed to know my mom, and she could tell from when I'd demanded the doctors not cut off my shirt that it must have meant the world to me.

"Do you wanna see a magic trick?"

I couldn't move my jaw with all the doctors tugging on it, so I just nodded.

She pulled out some sort of chemical, poured it into a big glass bowl, and plunged my shirt into it. My eyes went wide as the liquid fizzed and bubbled. When she pulled the shirt back up, the blood was magically gone. Life could go on! Perhaps, like one of the characters in all of those miniseries my mom and I loved to watch, after years of plastic surgery and rehabilitation, Jason might find me attractive again and we could start over. Perhaps there was some gay God in heaven doing battle with our straight God and sending me this guardian angel army nurse to save the flamboyant Hawaiian-print shirt Jason had actually thought was "pretty cool."

No. One look at my mom and I saw the same expression she'd worn when "Aunt" Louise had bought me that red wax gorilla.

It turned out that this nurse had once worked at Fort Leavenworth with someone named Jeff whom my mom now worked with, and every time the nurse waxed poetic about Jeff, my mom got more and more annoyed with her. And as it came to light that this Jeff guy often visited this nurse up in the ICU, and that he had chosen her over his commanding officer to swear him in during his initiation here, my mom lost it on both this nurse and the doctor who had been tugging on my jaw for ages now. "Aren't you done with that test?"

"We're trying to determine if his jaw is broken or displaced."

"Well, it looks like you're hurting him. Are they hurting you, Lancer?"

I nodded. They really were hurting me, and my jaw *was* broken, so the doctor was actually making things worse.

My mom's eyes met the doctor's, and all five foot nothing of her demanded, "Stop pulling on his jaw until you know if it's broken or not." She left the word "moron" out of this sentence, but we all heard it.

"I'm not some kind of an idiot, ma'am."

"No? Have you been tested for that? I want a specialist."

The offending nurse split, and the doctor followed. Alone with my mother for a moment, now with dozens of black wormy stitches squirming out of my chin, I managed to open my jaw just enough to ask the question she would have known was coming if she'd had her wits about her. "Who's Jeff?"

But she'd lost her wits amid my trauma and her jealousy. She was completely caught off guard and now rather embarrassed. "Oh. Oh, just . . . someone I work with. I'm sorry, baby."

Her hesitation exposed her lie. So I smiled.

"What?" she asked.

I shook my head to say "nothing," but she knew I smelled a rat. At some point during the long silence that followed, the reality of my injury began to settle in, and with it, a little fear.

"Mom?"

"What, baby?"

"Thank you for being with me."

She melted, stroking my white-blond hair. She could be so tough one minute and so soft and sweet the next. "I'll always be right here with you, my Lancer. Forever. I *promise* you that."

That gave me real comfort—and now I knew I had her right where I needed her. "Mom, if they can fix my tooth, will you make sure they make it look as normal as they can?"

God, I wanted to be normal so badly. She knew the feeling well. Recognizing that same fear in me now, lying in a bed that must have looked a lot like her childhood home, tears came.

"Baby, when this is all over, you're going to look perfect. I won't let them put a metal tooth in there. No matter how much it costs. I *promise* you that too."

Promises were sacred to us, so I could relax now.

We sat there together in silence for most of the rest of that night.

. . .

The next morning, my mom got into an epic fight with Jeff. She demanded to know the nature of his relationship with the chatty nurse. He demanded to know why she hadn't asked him to help bring her son to the hospital. What was clear now was that their secrets were destined to end their love affair just as surely as their truths might. So after agreeing to meet for a late-night ice cream, Anne finally came clean about her boys' ages, her own age, and the fact that she wasn't yet divorced from Merrill. Jeff told her that he wasn't interested in anyone but her, not even that nurse, no matter Anne's age or marital status. He loved her for who she was.

Looking back now, it's clear that Jeffrey Scott Bisch was the first and only man besides me, Todd, and Marcus who truly loved my mom . . . and who was also devoted enough to shoulder the responsibilities that came with loving her.

My birthday was coming up in a few weeks, and now Jeff knew how old I would be. We had never met, but on his next free weekend, he went down to a hobby store and bought a World War II SB2C Helldiver model airplane with wings that folded up. He brought it to work on Monday, handed it to Anne, and asked her to give it to me as a birthday present. He was handing her a challenge: a loving way to say it was time to take their affection out of the shadows and share it with the three other precious men in her life.

When my mom got home, she put the gift on the dining room table. "Lancer, that's a birthday present . . . from Jeff." She knew damn well that I hadn't forgotten Jeff's name. She tried and failed to suppress a grin. The puzzle of the past months was quickly coming together in my mind. Lucky for my mom, my jaw was locked shut, so I couldn't ask my usual probing questions. Instead, I quietly set to work turning that model into a masterpiece. If there was a new man in town who made my mom grin like an idiot, I damn sure wanted to make a stellar first impression.

I I I

Ayoung, single, enlisted soldier rarely calls the same city home for much more than two years. He or she is always on to another tour of one sort or another. It's a migrant life. By 1987, Jeff had already been in San Antonio for well over a year, and so it shouldn't have come as a surprise when his commanding officer informed him that it was time to pack up again.

Anne didn't receive Jeff's orders with the same delight we'd all felt when Merrill was punted off to South Korea. Jeff's orders turned what had felt like a lovely fantasy into something far too real. Anne understood that the decisions Jeff's imminent departure forced would have far-reaching earthly, heavenly, and familial consequences.

So with the clock ticking on Merrill's return, and me slowly figuring out what Marcus already knew but wouldn't say, my mom joined me in front of the sliding glass door, where, for the thousandth time, I'd spread out the contents of her craft box. That morning I had decided to sew an entire cast of sock puppet characters who had lived in my head for some time but had suddenly demanded physical forms. Marcus was in the backyard. He'd been out there all morning shooting arrows into the wall of our "tree house"—a shipping crate on stilts secured to a pair of thick Texas palm trees. Whenever Marcus became too focused on anything, destruction in particular, I knew something was amiss.

My mom began helping me sort through the spare buttons and colored felt to find options for noses, eyes, and hair. In a similar quiet time together, she had taught me how to sew. It wasn't the most butch activity for a Texas boy, but in a home filled with men, she was happy to seize an opportunity to pass down one of her own mother's skills. Now I loved that I was threading a needle the same way Cokie had to tailor my mom's beautiful blue prom dress.

My mom broke our companionable silence. "I think you know I have something to talk to you about . . ."

My mind whirled and raced. There were always a thousand things I wanted to talk about.

"Do you remember Jeff? Who I work with? Who got you the model airplane?"

Right. That conversation. I looked up at her. She was forcing her brow into a serious expression but her eyes were watery—filled with nerves atop a joy that made her shiver. This was the very first time I had ever seen true love in my mother's eyes. That image of her face will forever live in the top treasure drawer of my mind's memories. It was an absolute miracle. One of the greatest gifts I'll ever receive. But I wasn't ready to let her know that yet. So I composed myself and let out a trademark, understated "Sure."

"Well, he wants to meet you guys." She was terrified to say the next words. I could see it. And without meaning to, I neutralized her fear with the biggest grin she'd gotten out of me in a good long while. But because my yet-to-be-repaired, half-missing front tooth was giving her a salute, I quickly hid it again.

She tried to stifle her own smile. "So you wouldn't mind meeting him?" she asked me.

A yes or no answer would have been a total cop-out, like some bad mother-son conversation from those movies of the week we both loved and hated. So I cut to the chase: "You love him, don't you?"

My candor sent her heart tumbling, but it shouldn't have been a surprise. She knew I could read her mind. And although I'd never seen real love in person, I'd seen it plenty on big screens and small. My mom and I had cried together through *Doctor Zhivago*, *The Winds of War*, and *The Karate Kid*.

It all spilled out now, the entire story with all the details a mom could share with a twelve-year-old son. How she'd learned to cook spaghetti sauce from scratch for the dinners she'd made for Jeff on those hotel room weekends, how she called him her "bear," how he sprayed the little teddy bear he'd given her with his cologne each time he came by, how he called her his "mouse" because of her pint size, and how she thought the only right thing to do now was to divorce Merrill before he returned.

As happy as I was for her, my reaction to this last bit of news was similar to Marcus's. It was likely the reason he was out back poking our tree house full of holes. Divorce meant returning to poverty. And Merrill would surely exact revenge. I thought of the beatings we'd have to endure, and I was scared. But unlike Marcus, I understood that my mom was stuck between love and real life. It was where I'd been stuck since I'd realized at age six that I liked boys. And though my romantic desires dared not find a voice yet, hers just had.

So, understanding her dilemma far more than she knew, I said, "Well, we should probably meet him, then."

That was that.

Anne invited Jeff over to the house for dinner a week or two later. This time my brothers and I weren't hiding in a hotel or at a friend's house; we were hiding in Marcus's room, a bit terrified that our latest potential man of the house was on his way over. As an offering, I'd left the completed Helldiver model in the center of the kitchen table. I had never built a model so perfect. I still believe it looked better than the picture on the front of the box. And when Jeff walked in, he immediately began examining my detail work: the plane's microscopic, impeccably painted rivets, its historically accurate sulfur-yellow nose and propeller tips.

One by one, my brothers and I emerged to face this new man in our lives. Marcus went first. Hardly ten minutes later, he came back to his room without a word, just a tough-guy look in his eye. Then it was my turn. I handed Todd my last surviving G.I. Joe from our mostly finished battle, stepped out of the bedroom, and walked down the hall.

I wasn't at all prepared for what awaited me in the kitchen. There was Jeff, inspecting my Helldiver, an honest-to-God, beefcake U.S. Army soldier. Jeff was more handsome than Raul, and far better looking than Merrill, but it was that troublemaking mustache that was just too much for my adolescent heart. I blushed, choked, and sat down in petrified silence. Indeed, my mother and I shared the exact same taste in men.

It turns out that despite his military credentials, Jeff was also a bit shy, so we danced around the big subjects and talked about the airplane's paint job instead . . . then about the big, thick, ugly new scar across my chin. He told me about his own scars: from his battles in South America, from his parachute accident, and from a thousand other things gone wrong. Then he told me that my scars would all eventually fade, adding, "Even if you don't want them to." I liked hearing that. I showed him where the dentist had just fixed my front tooth. There was only a little seam now between what was real and what the dentist had bonded in. It took some trust to share that, and Jeff knew it.

Dinner was ready. Everyone came to the table, and Jeff told us a few stories about growing up in Philadelphia, about how often (or seldom) Catholics like him went to church, and about what it was like to jump out of airplanes.

After dinner, my mom and Jeff had planned on watching a movie together. Jeff had already rented a VCR from the grocery store up the road and picked up a few movies with it. We were now free to go play. Todd and Marcus ran off, but perhaps because I was the first kid he'd really heard about thanks to my epic face-plant, or because he'd heard I'd proven tough enough to survive my injuries without too much complaint, he stayed with me for a moment alone at the dinner table and popped his actual Special Forces airborne beret on top of my head. I think he could tell I was the most tuned in of us three boys, at least back then, and probably the most nervous too, so he cut right to it: "Your mom told me about your dad. About Merrill."

I quietly corrected him. "He's not actually my dad."

"Right. Right." There was a bit of silence. "You know, in the army, they taught me how to break a man's legs and arms with my own hands." He took the requisite dramatic pause, and then added, "It's not something I like doing, but it's something I've had to do before." Color me terrified and turned on. "And . . . your mom told me some of the things he did. How your dad acted with you guys."

"He's not my dad," I reminded him.

Jeff nodded. "I know. I get it. I was also raised by a man who wasn't my father." I liked that he understood. Then he leaned in and looked me dead in the eyes. "I want you to know that if this Merrill asshole ever steps foot in this house again, if he ever tries to hurt you, any of you, I'll break both of his legs and arms before he knows what hit him." He was dead serious.

My heart leapt from my chest. Who was this knight in "shimmering" armor—as my mom always put it—this man who had just extinguished so many of my worst fears with one sentence? With his Special Forces beret sitting atop my head, Jeff was the first man to ever offer me his full protection. No God or law would get in his way. I had never known what it was like to feel protected. And for the first time in six years, that angry, spinning ball of anxiety that told me over and over again that everything I loved would soon get ripped away . . . suddenly . . . stopped . . . spinning. For the first time I could remember, I slept safe and sound that night.

With the blessings of her sons, and only weeks to go before Merrill returned, Anne gripped those proverbial Texas bullhorns more firmly than she ever had and told Merrill she wanted a divorce. She offered what I thought were generous terms. She wouldn't share his physical abuse with the courts as long as he never showed his face around us again. Afraid of being excommunicated and court-martialed, he agreed. Once the divorce was under way, we quickly ran out of cash, so I gave my mom what little savings I had from my *San Antonio Light* newspaper delivery route so we could cover the mortgage. And although I wouldn't have minded seeing Merrill's legs snapped, my mom didn't want to risk the encounter, so we stopped attending church altogether.

Instead, we started going on little adventures with our mom and Jeff. Butch stuff. Sweaty Texas stuff. I loved it. Jeff also began spending more nights over. Then weeknights. Soon he moved in full-time. And when I got into an argument with my mom, and Jeff stepped in to check my language, and I pulled out the old "You're not my father" card, he didn't punch me in the face. Instead, in a calm, stern voice, he said, "I know. But you're not going to talk to the woman I love like that." Any fight drained out of me. He was protecting the woman we both loved. After that, I wished more than anything that someone like him had been my father my whole life. But I was rather attached to my last name now, so instead of changing it again, I named my new kitten after Jeff. I called him Airborne. And in a show of approval, Jeff took the airborne patch off his treasured beret and let me sew it onto Airborne's collar. Just like my grandma Cokie would have.

At the beginning of the summer, Jeff was given the details of his next tour of duty. He was being sent to a base in central California called Fort Ord. But the military doesn't pay to move girlfriends and their children, and we could never have afforded the move on our own. So as he and our mom sat in his brand-new pickup truck, Jeff made a little ring out of a silver paper gum wrapper and asked her if she would be his wife. This was the third time a man had asked her that, and arguably the first time she knew for sure that it was for all the right reasons, but she said she needed to talk to her boys first.

A pang of doubt hit him.

"Why me?" he asked her.

"What do you mean?"

"You probably could have had any doctor who worked at the hospital, and all the prestige that comes with being a doctor's wife, so why choose me?" He meant it.

Who is this knight in shimmering armor? she thought as her eyes welled up.

But she was conflicted. Saying yes meant leaving our church and her supportive family in the South for the unknown, and going against everything she'd taught us about family and eternity. But she was also more certain than ever that this was right—despite it being the most selfish thing she'd ever do to her boys, and she told me just that when she sat me down to look at a flyer about this faraway place called Fort Ord, perched along the central coast in California.

It was tough being Mormon in a place like Texas, and it was tough keeping my "homo-tribe" secret there, but I loved the rowdy, warm people. I loved the long summer nights at the community pool, the slushies, the lightning bugs, the thunderstorms, the drainage ditches, and the tadpoles. I loved that for better or worse, family was primary there. I loved that we Texans were taught to take life by the horns when necessary. And although I couldn't do it myself, I admired the tough men and women who stood up straight and tall and faced their rough circumstances with strength and pride. This was the America

I had been raised in, the South that I loved, and the land I would always consider home.

Besides, I had heard terrible stories coming out of California lately. From San Francisco to Los Angeles, men were dropping dead from a new cancer brought on by a mysterious disease called GRID and then AIDS. Even rich, famous men like Rock Hudson were dying from it. Working in a hospital laboratory, my mom knew more than most about this new disease, and she assured me that it was mostly only gay men who'd gotten it so far. Little did she know that this only complicated things further for me. And here she was, proposing that we leave the safety of our beloved corner of America for this very different land of dying homosexuals—another kind of America, one our church had warned us was filled with sinners. So she added, "Do you know who Clint Eastwood is?"

Of course I did. Dirty Harry. What kind of idiot did she think I was?

"Well, he's the mayor of a city called Carmel, right next to the army base out there. He would be like our mayor."

That did sound appealing. And I liked the photos of ocean-side cliffs, and the beaches free from all the oil globs we found along our Texas coastline. Plus, it wasn't as if I had any friends in San Antonio. Someone at school had called Jason a "fag," and he'd stopped returning my phone calls and gotten himself a tough blond girlfriend with the same short haircut as mine.

"Okay," I said. Somewhere deep in my heart I thought maybe I could start over in this new place, and boy, did I need a fresh start.

And so Anne and Jeff got married in August of 1987 in a courtroom. We three boys weren't invited. She didn't want to put us through too much of a roller-coaster ride in case this didn't work out the way she'd hoped. Jeff left for California ahead of us to try to find a place for us to live. A couple of our aunts showed up in his wake to help us hold a garage sale and try to convince my mom how foolish this was: "He's so young. Are you sure you're sure?" My mom got angrier every time they brought up his age or hers, his pay grade or hers, or how far she would be from family when something inevitably went wrong. She shot back, "I love you, but I am perfectly capable of managing just fine on my own, thank you *very* much." They knew to leave that alone.

We didn't tell anyone at church, at school, or in our neighborhood that we were leaving. My mom didn't want anyone else to try to convince us to stay. So we just jammed what little we had left in the world into the trunk of our car, shoved sedatives down Airborne's throat, and pushed him into a crate in the backseat with me and Todd. Marcus spread out a map in the front. My mom started the car and backed it out of our Texas driveway for the last time.

And that was it. So long to Texas. So long to the South, to the Mormons, the Baptists, and the Catholics. So long to the tadpoles and cicadas, and to this corner of America I knew and most often loved. We were now strapped into the Chevy Malibu that Raul had left behind when he abandoned us, blasting toward New Mexico, across Arizona, through Los Angeles, and over that winding Grapevine to a town John Steinbeck had aptly called East of Eden. Because there was Eden, where Dirty Harry reigned, and then there was the small farming town just *east* of it, in a place not nearly as nice—our soon-to-be home in a very different kind of America.

PART II

CHAPTER 11

West of Home and East of Eden

I

I was fourteen years old and hadn't grown an inch since leaving Texas, though there was now some peach fuzz emerging under my arms that I'd examine during my rare alone time in the early-morning hours locked in our tiny new apartment's windowless bathroom. It was 1988, one year into our coastal American adventure in Salinas, California, where John Steinbeck had seen an "Eden" to the west: Big Sur, Carmel (where Clint Eastwood was no longer mayor), and Monterey (where my mom and Jeff worked at the Fort Ord army base). But we'd settled east of all that beauty. It felt impossibly far for a teen with no hope for a car come sixteen.

Jeff was still in the early days of his career, and my mom had been forced to take a demotion in order to transfer to Fort Ord, so we were dead broke again. We could just barely afford to live in this agricultural town of ninety thousand souls where most of our neighbors were surviving well below the poverty line. But my mom felt that love was worth such adjustments. Even in our new claustrophobic abode—no backyard, no lake to be found, and all the little adaptations living in a mostly Spanish-speaking area called for—I agreed that a loving home was well worth any new challenges. Besides, I found learning to speak Spanish empowering, loved the refried-bean burritos at Rosita's café, and looked forward to looting the straw-berry and artichoke fields that surrounded our apartment once the sun had set and the agricultural workers had gone home.

San Antonio had been diverse, but our neighborhood and my junior high were primarily white. In my new school in Salinas, I was now the minority amid first-generation Latin American kids who were so busy handling their own challenges that they didn't seem to pay much attention to mine. I caught fewer stares aimed at my mom as she swung her way through the local mall or into a school meeting. I appreciated that. And hundreds of miles from our Southern traditions, fewer men rushed to hold doors open for women. Here, my mom would have to fend for herself a bit more, but she liked that people assumed she could. Feeling a touch more daring, I even asked my mom's new hairdresser in the local mall to cut my hair however she saw fit. She promptly gave me a flattop, but as she approached my Texas mullet, I stopped her. I wasn't quite ready to let everything from home go. Not just yet.

On special weekends, we drove a handful of miles west to Monterey to gaze at the piles of blubbery seals sunning themselves on warm rocks as Pacific waves lapped over them. We fed the silky-furred squirrels who'd eat right out of my mom's outstretched hand, or ventured farther down to Carmel or Pacific Grove along the seventeen-mile drive where the photographer Ansel Adams captured his iconic images of lone cypress trees swept landward by the sea breeze. It really was a special kind of paradise. And back home at night, all tucked into bed, I occasionally dared to dream of a sunnier tomorrow, even if during my waking hours it still felt like a handful of miles out of my grasp.

But a year in, I would still slip up and say "y'all" in class, inviting choruses of laughter from my new classmates—this in a school where a teacher who stuck out too much for being "cool" had been shot by a student (the teacher survived). Add in my persistent shyness problem, and I had a grand total of zero friends at North Salinas High School.

Then one particularly warm day, I was walking toward the exit after the final bell had rung when I saw a gaggle of North High's most handsome boys holding court by a bank of lockers. Tony Graffanino was the first to catch my eye. He always did. He was taller than the rest, and at only sixteen, he already had a triangular patch of wispy brown hair on his chest that turned into a fuzzy trail leading all the way down his belly. He wore his shirts unbuttoned to his rippled stomach to show it all off. The one thing we had in common was that we were both on the struggling swim team coached by my biology teacher. She was desperate for athletes, and expert at social pressure, so she'd convinced me to join. Tony was her one star, a natural jock. So during practices and meets, I had to be extra careful not to look in his direction or my body might betray me.

But it was the off-season now, and Tony and I hadn't said a word to each other since our last crushing defeat. As I approached him in the hall, I had a choice to make: say nothing and cement my weirdo status with the one teammate who'd bothered to cheer me on during my hundred-meter backstroke humiliations, or work up the guts to say hello like a normal human being. It took every bit of courage I had, but as I passed, I looked at the ground and let a "hey" escape my lips. To my surprise (and great discomfort), Tony extended a long, strong arm, pulled me in by the shoulders, and introduced me to his assembled brood of boys. My heart raced, my head went light—this was too difficult to navigate. It had to be a dream. Correction: a nightmare.

At the center of these impossibly handsome boys was an aberration: Ryan Elizalde, a husky Latin eighteen-year-old with a thick, black, '70s Freddie Mercury pornstache that made him look thirty. I'm well aware that it's not politically correct to lean on stereotypes, but Ryan had a certain flare, a flamboyance I recognized, a swish he didn't seem to be trying hard enough to hide. Given my roots and this town's Latin-machismo leanings, I thought this Ryan fella must be an absolute lunatic not to try to dim his "burning flame."

But Ryan had one other thing few in his clique did: a job, and a job with some power. Ryan was the head of the personnel department at the local Toys "R" Us near the crumbling stucco shopping mall, and he used that mighty power to hire all of the best looking guys at our school. Every single one of them. North High lore was that on weekends, he'd buy gallons of beer and wine coolers and caravan North High's hottest to a series of natural caverns just outside the city limits for epic bonfire parties where all sorts of drunken, sweaty shirtlessness took place. During my sleepless nights in the room I shared with Todd, his growing legs shaking all night, keeping me and my sensitive ears wide awake, I often fantasized about those mystical cavern boy parties.

So yes, Ryan had a detectible swish in his step, but he also drove a motorcycle that roared when it came and went. Like me, he was a freak and a likely "homosexual," but unlike me, he was fearless— a wild-man rule breaker in a town where sticking out in any way could literally get you shot.

That warm afternoon, Ryan looked me up and down, and with an audience of North High's most popular, commanded me to spread my legs.

"What?" I asked. He couldn't possibly have just said what I thought I'd heard.

"Spread your legs."

Holy crap, he had.

I was surprised, but I was also a military, Southern boy, and did as my elders instructed. I shuffled my feet apart. He waited a moment for maximum humiliation to settle in. It did. Then he swung the rolled-up poster in his hand upward like a nightstick, connecting hard with my family jewels. I tried like hell to act as if it didn't hurt, but it was painfully apparent how much it did. Tony offered an arm around my shoulders to hold me up, but he was laughing like the rest. Throughout, Ryan maintained eye contact, his supremacy established.

Somewhere in the blur of the next few moments, I was invited to join Ryan's crew that night at Denny's, the only spot in Salinas open after sundown for kids our age. I debated not showing up, but I knew the value of an invite like this for a geek like me. So I changed clothes a dozen times (an impressive number given my collection of only four outfits). When I finally stepped out of our apartment's door, a wet, cold fog had snuck in and began biting my cheeks. But I stuck to my short-sleeve choice. I was already late. By the time I had walked the fifteen minutes to Denny's, I was shaking from both the cold and my nerves.

Right off, I saw Ryan and his friends, jammed into the big corner booth. Most of the boys from school now had girls with them—Tony had two, one under each arm. My trembling tripled. Then Ryan made everyone get up and move over to make a space for me right next to him. I foolishly mistook the gesture for kindness and accepted the position. After ignoring me for what felt like an eternity, he picked up a spoon and passed it to his left.

"Everyone contribute," he said.

One by one, they each added something to the spoon—food remnants, condiments, salt, pepper, hot sauce—until it made it all the way back around to me. It was a vile dripping mess. I added a drizzle of maple syrup and offered the gruesome spoon back to Ryan. He didn't take it. That's when I realized that the rest of the kids were staring at me with crooked grins and stifled laughter. The girls under Tony's arms offered pitying gazes.

"If you want to be here," Ryan said with flare, "you'll eat it."

My first instinct was to run, but I couldn't take the lonely walk of shame that not eating this concoction would surely result in. I felt certain that this was my first and only shot at ever leading a less than lonely existence, and looking back, I may have been right. So I opened my mouth, shoved the mess inside, and ate it. All of it. And then a little bit of my mom's toughness bubbled up in me, and I licked that damn spoon clean.

When I look in the rearview mirror now, it becomes increasingly clear that despite all of our ambitious efforts to effect change in our lives and our world, it's often the small, unplanned events that lead to cataclysms and triumphs. That late-night spoonful of rotten hell would come to alter the course of my life.

I I

There's a moment I can't shake, a time I could clearly see my footprints changing as I stepped from one kind of America into another. Texas and Salinas were both rather conservative areas. Strictly red or blue thinkers might not have guessed I'd find too many differences, but one had begun to affect me—a difference whose power I had missed, until this moment.

One afternoon in late January, I scrawled an X across the top of a cardboard moving box with a black permanent marker. I drew a hyphen beside it, and added "mas." Christmas had been over for weeks. It was well past time to pack it back into the many boxes we used to store our now massive decoration collection.

Jeff had proven even better than advertised—strong, playful, loving, handy, and, most important, safe. Bonus points: Jeff wasn't Mormon, so despite the relentless door knocks from two impossibly cute, celestially concerned Mormon missionaries who'd been assigned the task of saving us from eternal damnation, we stopped going to church on Sundays. Here lived a subtle difference between our new and old homes. In Salinas folks were faithful, but church wasn't the center of community like it had been in the South, and so it didn't form the core of conversations with classmates and neighbors. Missing church in Salinas didn't feel like missing out on life. I had hardly noticed the change, but our mom had.

When I dared to scrawl "Xmas" on that box, my mom looked up, saw it, and slowly and deliberately looked away.

I started filling the box: in went a macramé Santa Claus, a three-foot-tall Mr. and Mrs. Claus made of felt and cardboard, and an intricately beaded Advent calendar. All handmade, all testaments to my mom's years in the Relief Society, the women's group in the Mormon Church that she'd proudly presided over before our vanishing act. She hadn't been called to be its president out of sympathy. Not by a long shot. She knew every crafty skill there was, and our house at Christmastime was a testament to her LDS homemaking virtuosity.

The box was nearly filled when she looked back up and said, "Do you realize what you just did?"

I didn't, but from her tone it clearly leaned more toward naughty than nice. She wagged her index finger at my *X*.

"It's just less letters," I answered.

I could see her wheels spinning. This was likely the first time she had acknowledged the effect this move was having on her boys. Sure, Marcus was out tattooing FTW on his arm with a busted guitar string while under the influence of weed, Jack Daniel's, and Marlboro Reds, but that was like looking into the sun—far too hot for her to see. I had just taken the "Christ" out of Christmas as if it were no big deal.

My mom always treaded most lightly when she was most pissed off. So now she very quietly said: "I hope you know I still believe in the stories we shared when you were growing up. In Texas. Just because we don't live there, or go to church anymore, doesn't mean those stories aren't true."

Truth be told, I had little clue anymore if any of those stories held water, and I was growing increasingly certain some were outright make-believe. "Seer stones" dropped into a top hat to help decode a set of golden plates dug out of the ground in New York in the early 1800s by a horny teenager named Joe who wanted lots of wives—this, the discovery of the long-awaited sequel to the Old and New Testaments? Really?

But my mom missed the community and stability of our old church. She missed the promises of an eternal family and that perfect body she'd clung to for so long. She wasn't going to let go of all that overnight, not even for the healthy kind of love and family we now had.

I could read those concerns in her tone, so I chose not to voice my doubts. Instead, I carefully wrote "CHRISTmas Decorations" on the rest of the boxes, and I helped her wrap, pad, pack, and protect all of the individual ornaments she'd carefully selected for each of us boys every year of our lives to date. Crisis averted. For now.

Christmas in our family had always been and still remains the time when past meets present and whispers to us about our most hopeful futures. Marcus, Todd, and I understood that, and we knew well that nothing should ever get in the way of its promise. A quarter century later, my views on Mormonism, Christianity, and faith have changed and grown. But each year, far too late in January, I still write "CHRISTmas" on each of the ever-increasing number of boxes it takes to house our family's ornament collection, and I wrap, pad, pack, and protect those treasures with even more care than I did on that January day in 1989. Because, while we can debate the effects of taking Christ out of Christmas until we hate our own neighbors, we can't debate that Christmas in America is about family, and that the preservation of family merits our making some compromises and allowances.

But despite my giving in to her preferred CHRISTmas orthography, my mom concluded she needed to keep a closer eye on her sons' celestral futures in this new place—and thus on any outside influences that might threaten our salvation.

III

Ryan was from a family of immigrants from Mexico and the Philippines who had been in California for a couple of generations now but most often still spoke Spanish at home. They were Pentecostal, but I never once saw Ryan go to church. They drank caffeine and a little alcohol, worked on Sundays, sometimes smoked, and had very likely done the unthinkable: voted for Democrats. One of Ryan's brothers had even had a child out of wedlock. His family checked most of the boxes I'd long been taught to steer clear of.

But those contrasts aren't what worried my mom most. What lifted her brow was what was left unsaid.

Ryan and I shared an invisible bridge, that secret Oscar Wilde's lover Lord Alfred Douglas had rightly observed dared not speak its name—not in Europe a century before, and still not here in central California in the late 1980s. And so, despite our many differences, we were members of a secret family as old as the ages, and we felt that bond, even while refusing to acknowledge or confess it.

Despite this connection (or more likely because of it), Ryan never missed a chance to use me as a foil for his showmanship. He tortured me in public every opportunity he got. Secretly loving the attention, I gave him ample opportunities. I was the Jerry Lewis to his Dean Martin. As the only person in school who didn't need a fake ID to buy alcohol, and who had the power to employ classmates, Ryan had become North High's godfather. When I was by his side, I felt confident that if anyone attacked me, Ryan would use his power to destroy that aggressor. So I stuck close to him, and within months, Mr. Mustache and I had become inseparable. I could often be spotted zipping around Salinas, Monterey, or Santa Cruz on the back of his motorcycle.

We toured all over central California, often ditching my last two classes to catch a sunset over some solitary beach in Big Sur. Nature filled the space in our hearts that our peers filled with girls' affections.

Eventually, Ryan and I picked up cameras to capture her beauty and majesty.

In one of Ryan's shots, I'm sitting on a fallen tree that's sunken almost entirely into the sand of a beach in Big Sur—my favorite place in the world then and still today. My hands are covering my sensitive ears, my chin is tilted up to the sky, and my mouth is wide open as I scream out into the abyss. I appear bold, uninhibited, and unashamed—qualities I wouldn't dare touch publicly yet but could experiment with in the safety of Ryan's friendship. Yes, I ditched classes to do it, but as I look back, it's clear to me that these adventures were the early hours of a young man searching for the voice he would one day find. And in that era, when our hearts' desires spelled danger and death for our kind, Ryan and I found ample substitutes in Mother Nature—in whose embrace we never felt oppressed or afraid. And despite Ryan's cool act, I knew I wasn't the only one who felt lucky to have this friendship.

My mom wasn't so sure about Ryan. This was partly because I'd avoided letting them meet, but also because when they finally did, he'd shown up on his motorcycle wearing ripped jeans and a jacket covered in safety pins. He made George Michael's hoop earrings seem butch. Then, after assurances Ryan wasn't as old as he looked (it wasn't his fault that puberty had doubled its dose on him—or mine that it had skipped me altogether), I climbed on the back of his motorcycle, wrapped my arms around his waist, and we roared away as one. My poor mom's heart.

That night, Ryan finally brought me to the caverns of North High lore. I spent the entire ride quivering in anticipation of some orgiastic boy festival. But when we arrived, I found surprising communion. There was less booze and more hiking than I'd imagined. Finding our way deep into a ravine, Ryan and I came upon a dozen other youngsters—some I recognized, some I didn't—and we set about building a campfire on the sandy floor. Thanks to Texas and the Boy Scouts, I knew how to build a big, healthy campfire. Soon, everyone had gathered around its warmth, sitting together quietly. And I wasn't the only one finding comfort in this silence. This was the first hint that perhaps even the well-liked kids in school felt like outsiders in their own ways too.

Ryan's friendship was helping my confidence grow—not by a tall measure, not at first, but enough to get me to sign up for drama class again. Unlike my theater class in San Antonio, this one had two teachers: a white-haired librarian and a thin man with a harelip who wore snakeskin boots. I proposed we stage the same play we had at my junior high back in Texas, that collection of stories by and about real adolescents. But to my surprise, this California farm town's faculty wouldn't allow any content that got near themes like drugs, loneliness, shame, or suicide. It turned out California wasn't the monolithic, liberal place so many Texans feared it to be. In fact, in some ways, rural California was even more conservative than central Texas—a fact we would rediscover two decades later in the fight for marriage equality.

My new drama teachers preferred I put my efforts into a production of a tired old 1950s melodrama called *Egad, What a Cad!* Sharing stories that spoke some brand of truth is what had helped me feel a bit less alone for the first time back in Texas. *Egad, What a Cad!* had nothing to do with me, anyone in Salinas, or on the planet Earth, for that matter. At fourteen, I already knew that the teachers' suggestion was condescending, tone-deaf crap. So I abandoned their play and hid in the back row of their class from then on, disappointed, biding my time.

Just before the end of the school year, a local community theater put on a workshop for local high school drama classes, and our class was invited. I went along for the free snacks, but halfway through a day of group theater games, the company's dramaturge spotted me being my antisocial self in the back of their concrete amphitheater. She walked up, bent down to my level, her hands on her hips, and— talking to me like one might talk to a puppy in a shelter—asked if I was interested in auditioning for their summer apprentice program. I could spy condescension a mile away. Without a doubt, this was an offer born of pity, not perceived talent, and I knew it. But I also knew this was a chance to prove my worth. It turned out to be an act of mercy that set a career in motion—another small turn with enormous repercussions.

Now isn't the place for all of the details (those will come later), but that community theater, the Western Stage, saved my life. I ran lights on *Steel Magnolias* and *The Crucible*, worked set crew on *Cabaret* and *Babes in Arms*, toured the central coast in a musical called *Pola-roids*, in which I sang the Beach Boys' "Surfin' USA" in public librar-ies and senior homes. I studied under guest playwrights struggling to adapt Steinbeck to the stage and with directors who taught me to be a Renaissance artist—props, lighting, sets, directing, acting—and who eventually helped me land the role of John in *Peter Pan*, in which I actually flew.

And in subtle and not so subtle ways, I began to realize that Ryan and I weren't alone. More than a few of the men in this theater com-pany seemed to lean our way. We had a secret tribe—a tribe that still mostly lived in silence and had yet to find its full voice, but a tribe all the same. And for that reason, I began to feel that life might actually hold possibilities. I stopped trying to vanish, and started stepping out onto limbs.

I V

At some point during these school years, I discovered the "foreign film" section of our local video store. It wasn't well stocked, but it captured my imagination, though not due to the cinematic curiosity the store's manager likely hoped to inspire. Gazing out from the cover of one videotape was a cute boy under an alluring title, *The 400 Blows*. Mistaking François Truffaut's master-piece for an oral sex blowout, I smuggled our VCR and TV into my bedroom for the privacy I hoped the film called for. Instead, I found myself enraptured. I'd just stumbled into the French New Wave and was witnessing something I'd never known was possible—the abil-ity of cinema to shine light onto regular people's lives. This wasn't at all what I'd thought movies were. There were no Ninja Turtles or giant sharks. This was relatable, authentic, and undeniably human. So in place of arousal, I swelled with tears as young Antoine Doinel struggled to understand his challenging familial circumstances and uncompassionate authority figures. I knew those frustrations well. The film helped me feel less alone, and for a painfully shy kid, that felt like salvation. So I began to rent more films from the foreign section, and soon I began to dream beyond just the stage to a future making movies that spoke to my own experiences the way Truffaut had his.

By now it was 1991, and that fall President George H. W. Bush announced that he was shutting down Fort Ord, a decision that immediately put my mom's and Jeff's jobs on the endangered species list. Later that same month, I opened the mailbox and pulled out something few but my mom had ever seen in our family.

Months earlier I'd decided to try my luck, take the SATs, and apply to a handful of dream film schools. Certain that my casual relationship with school attendance would put me out of the running, I'd done so without telling a soul. *Why risk heaping disappointment on top of rejection?* I'd thought. Now, one by one, I threw out the rejection letters as they came in. Until one day, something unbelievable arrived: an acceptance letter to the University of Southern California—all the way down in that wicked city beneath all that light blue smog we'd survived passage through so many years earlier.

Up to now, this had been a pipe dream. Few in our family had even finished high school. Now I was both petrified and invigorated by the thought of calling Los Angeles my home, of one day walking with a cap and gown as a genuine college graduate, of studying storytelling in one of the best schools there was. It was only thanks to seventeen years of watching my mom's imprudent determination that I had even dared fill out the USC application. Now I knew I would need her approval, and whatever little financial support she might be able to offer, in order to make this dream real.

I stepped into her perennially floral bedroom and flopped down on the bed. Even after leaving the children's hospitals, she'd never let go of her beloved flowers. Now she was sitting atop a rose-print comforter, the month's bills spread out before her. As casually as I could, I handed her the college acceptance letter. She looked at me, curious, stopped what she was doing, and read it. I remember her taking a moment for herself before she looked up again. Then, with tears threatening, tears I couldn't quite read, she hugged me tight. She told me how proud she was of me, and how she had always loved watching USC football games on TV, with their white Trojan horse running across the field at halftime. And though I felt a shadow in her tone, she rushed to do what she wished her mom could have done decades before when she had been accepted to college: take the whole family out to dinner to celebrate. This never happened. We didn't have the money for nights out. But when we went to the local Sizzler restaurant that night, she even added the salad bar buffet to each of our meals. This felt overblown—reckless, even. And I began to surmise why she was putting on such a grand display.

In my mom's tight smile lived a devastation born of long-unspoken truths that this letter would now drag out into the open. We came from loving but poor Southern people. Folks like us just didn't get to go to college. My mom had been able to only thanks to a scholarship for polio survivors. I knew it long before she ever had to say the words. She couldn't afford to send me to college. To add insult to injury, I was now forcing my family to admit the truth of our station.

That night, once Todd was fast asleep in the twin bed near mine, I did what I still do all too often: I quietly blamed myself for bringing pain into our home. There was no such thing as a school counselor at North Salinas High who could teach us poor kids how to rise above our family histories and circumstances, but I felt I should have done that homework myself. I shoved my acceptance letter down between my bed's frame and the wall. A grave for dreams. Then I put a tape in my Walkman and quietly cried while listening to Joey McIntyre of New Kids on the Block sing me "Please Don't Go Girl." I didn't even like the boy band, but I had a crush on the blue-eyed kid crooner—another dream I was sure to never touch. No matter how far I stretched, it seemed life lived just beyond my fingertips.

But somewhere over the course of that sleepless night, I began to feel what my mom must have felt in her own childhood beds. My grief started spinning and churning into a rage that made my jaw grind and my head hurt, because as much as I loved our hard-won family, I heard a call from beyond it, from beyond our town and the black-and-white nature of military life. I started plotting insane ideas, and the next morning, I set out to share a brand-new plan with the one man I hoped was crazy enough to hear it out—Salinas's own Mercury-stache closet case: Ryan Elizalde.

"I'm leaving this place when I graduate," I told Ryan over a Sprite in the Toys "R" Us break room. I explained my plan: I would pack up and leave this small town before my mom was forced out of California by Bush, then I'd enroll in and ace community college down in Los Angeles before applying to UCLA's film school, where with the help of scholarships, the in-state public tuition might be within reach of a kid like me working a few retail jobs. "I'm doing this. I'm getting out of here. Whether you come with me or not." I tried to act like I didn't give two shits if he came along, but he could see through my piss-poor performance.

"Yeah? Where ya gonna live?" he said, acting like he didn't give two shits either.

"Guess I'll move in with whoever'll take me."

I was laying a trap. He didn't like the sound of "whoever," and he hated the sound of "take me." I saw it in his eyes. Platonically or not, I was his and his alone. So I added: "If I leave, and you don't come, where will you be in two years when I'm all done with community college? Who will you live with . . . or be with?"

That was as close as I could get to acknowledging our shared but still unspoken bond. He looked sick about it. Over nearly four years of high school, we'd become incredibly close, pushing all others away. Now we were each other's lifelines, and I was pointedly threatening that in pursuit of a pipe dream that was even more impossible than I knew at the time.

I was terrified he'd say no. The truth was, I wouldn't have been brave enough to go without him, but of course I couldn't let him know that. So it took weeks of heavy conversations, lofty pitches, buckets' worth of false confidence, and at least a dash of emotional blackmail before he agreed to leave his prized job at Toys "R" Us and his tight-knit family and move down to Los Angeles with me for two years. Two years. That's what he'd give me, and in that offer was a helluva lot of faith, so I ran with it. With no jobs lined up, no apartment, and only a few hundred bucks in savings between us—mine from nights and weekends working in Taco Bell's kitchen and at Target's refund desk, his from what little he had left after all his parties and adventures—we began scratching out plans to move south when I graduated.

Perhaps Ryan hoped that the big city might allow him to live more openly, or even to love. Perhaps he interpreted my ceaseless pleading as affection—not the kind our parents had, not the kind that could ever be spoken or fulfilled, but affection just the same. And wasn't that better than nothing? The truth is, I loved Ryan more than any other human being whom I didn't share blood with, but it was a brotherly love. I wasn't looking for romance. I was too dead set on achieving my silver-screen dreams, and far too naïve to know that a life without love would ultimately hinder my ability to tell decent stories.

A week after my graduation, Ryan and I loaded up the oxidized old Chrysler he'd bought off his dad. My mom watched from our driveway with Jeff as I put her powder-blue suitcase in the backseat—the same case she'd headed off to college with decades before. Her mom had shed tears on that day, but she'd felt certain her baby girl was making solid choices. I was headed off to a city my mom feared was wicked, with no college safety net to speak of, alongside a slightly older man she'd grown fond of (like Texan women do their hairdressers) but still feared was a "homosexual" who might lead her middle son astray.

My mom tried to get me to reconsider, to enroll in community college in Salinas, but we both knew that she and Jeff would soon have to find new jobs, possibly outside of California. So, in this sea of uncertainty, I gave Todd a big hug and told him to watch over our mom. Todd was quickly growing tall and strong, and given the responsible young man he was shaping up to be, I trusted that he could protect our mom now if anything happened in my absence. Then I looked around for Marcus, but he was nowhere to be found—an increasingly common occurrence in our home. Jeff gave me a few words of encouragement, telling me that he too had left home at seventeen—evidence that such an adventure, so young, wasn't necessarily doomed.

Then I kissed my mom goodbye and held her close. I was her first child to leave home, and this wasn't how she'd hoped it would go. It wasn't my dream come true either; this was a backup plan. So after she shed a river of fear-filled tears, and I shed just as many, Ryan and I loaded into his car, got onto the 101 Freeway and began the five-hour drive south to Los Angeles. I was sick to my stomach. Up to this point, I had been my mother's fierce and loyal protector; now I was the source of her greatest anxiety. Mile by mile, as Ryan and I got farther and farther from John Steinbeck's Eden, I grew less and less certain that I had made a wise decision.

CHAPTER 12

Secret Somethings

I

Within a week of arriving in L.A., I got a job working in J. C. Penney's boys' department. Turns out if you close the door on any small white room, little boys think it's time to drain their bladders. My task was to remove all traces of these "accidents" from our changing rooms. It wasn't glamorous work, but it was my only hope of making enough money to survive here. Ryan and I stayed in a cheap hotel with a loud, rusted mini fridge for the first two weeks before accepting the fact that the only place we could afford was a studio apartment in a rather dangerous corner of town.

Our tiny enclave of Section 8 housing was full of contradictions: it was where I learned to speak more Spanish with the neighbors who cooked us food when I looked *"demasiado flaco,"* but it was also where gunshots often woke us up at night, and where we heard a young man being stabbed to death outside our building's front gate on Halloween night.

Ryan and I agreed never to tell our mothers about the murder, or how often we went to bed hungry. I also never told my mom just how bad the car wreck was that sent my salvaged junker of a Honda CRX smashing into the side of a Del Taco drive-through, or that I couldn't afford a new car even with the insurance payout. Every morning for months, I walked nearly an hour on crutches to Pasadena City College, where I'd signed up for classes, on the busted kneecap that had gone through my Honda's dashboard. My mom couldn't know. Besides, who was I to complain to her about crutches?

The details of these years tended to cycle and repeat: I studied my tail off to earn all As, I worked any and every job I could to help pay rent, I avoided any situation that might lead to romance, I visited my family in Salinas as often as I could afford to, and I cried for a week after returning from each brief visit. The only big change in this time was that my tears lasted a month straight when my mom and Jeff officially lost their jobs at Fort Ord and could only find new ones at an army medical hospital in Washington, D.C. From now on, frequent visits home would also prove too expensive.

Looming over my head was what a PCC counselor had unceremoniously pointed out during my first week of classes. According to her, my "far-fetched" plan was "highly impractical" at best, because I wasn't the only kid who had figured out that UCLA's tuition was much cheaper than USC's. She didn't hesitate to share that UCLA's film school received thirty thousand applications a year and accepted only fifteen students annually from outside its own campus. Fifteen out of thousands upon thousands.

I'm not going to lie. Many a night, with the sounds of helicopters, gunshots, and the 110 Freeway outside our studio apartment's one small window, I worried that this adventure was a naïve miscalculation. And Ryan, who'd always provided inspiration, was losing his spark. Working at Macy's gave him no power or influence in a big city like this, and with few new friends, he rarely left our apartment outside of work and began putting on more weight.

So as my worries grew too large to hide, I chose to share a few during my brief long-distance calls with my mom. We talked at least once a day, me learning as she once had how to jam every bit of gossip into the handful of minutes we could afford. But even with my growing list of concerns, she could hear past my fears to what lived beneath: the passion for a dream others were branding "impossible," the sort of dream my mom knew best. I can almost hear her now, whispering in my ear from across the country, "Who am I to tell you any dream is too big, Lancer? I had a few 'impossible' ones once too. Their names were Marcus, Lance, and Todd."

So I followed her advice, put doubt to the side, and kept my shoulder to the wheel—our Mormon pioneer way of saying "work hard, and be diligent." That year, I sold more J. C. Penney catalogs than any other employee at our store and earned enough credits to buy my first video camera. I never imagined I would actually have one of my own, but I'd found a way.

With that camera, I shot stop-action animation films, then got up the guts to write scripts and convince actors to perform them. But as much as I enjoyed making these films, a classmate pointed out that my only genuine tales centered on parent-child relationships. Anything I wrote about love or romance came off as tired and derivative. It was a tough criticism, but I understood it. I had no experience with romance. I was a virgin. I'd never even been kissed. So I entered one of my father-son short films into our school's festival. Ryan attended the screening in my place when J. C. Penney wouldn't give me the night off. And when it was announced that my film had won, Ryan collected the prize. It was my first. But when I finally got home and saw it, I didn't feel pride, I felt like I'd gotten away with something. I knew full well that like my own life story thus far, my raconteur tool chest was sorely lacking.

Then one sunny afternoon, on the heels of my long walk home from school, I stopped to check our rusty mailbox with its busted lock—two familiar ex-cons watching my every move from behind their barred screen door, just like they always did. I waved. They looked away. Same as ever. But on this day, there was something unusual inside the box: a nine-by-twelve-inch envelope. I carefully pulled it out. My heart wobbled when I saw who it was from.

There are dozens of moments in my life that are still far too painful to fully recall or comprehend. There are four that still feel too magnificent to grasp. This was the first.

There's a photo of me on the day I received that envelope because Ryan quickly grabbed his camera to snap it. My nose and the edge of my eyelids are bright red from tears . . . and I'm holding up an acceptance letter to UCLA's film school. By some miracle, I had been chosen as one of those fifteen students out of thirty thousand. Like my mom, I'd proven the seemingly impossible possible, and to this day, I still can't believe it.

But this good news presented a new problem: I now needed Ryan to extend his promise and put his faith in me for two more years, despite the fact that the first two hadn't been easy on him. He had put on more than forty pounds since we'd moved to Southern California. His belly now lapped far over the belt of the cheap suit he wore to work at Macy's each day. At only twenty-four, he looked like a forty-year-old begging for a heart attack. Two more years of this might kill him, and I couldn't let that happen. I loved him. Despite all the challenges, he had kept me safe, sane, and hopeful on this adventure. But it was painfully evident that he was self-destructing.

I had a sneaking suspicion what was to blame: hunger—that hunger of the heart we couldn't sate, that secret "something" we had long since wordlessly agreed to never name.

I I

Before I go any further, I ought to come clean about what anyone's big differences (including my own) signaled to me growing up. To do that, I'll need to step back to 1982, when I was still a white-as-rice, eight-year-old Mormon closet case living in a household below the poverty line in San Antonio, Texas.

According to the census, well over half of all Texans in 1980 considered themselves religious, with Southern Baptists edging out Catholics with 18 and 16 percent of the population, respectively. Mormons made up less than half of 1 percent of all Texans, and at less than .25 percent each, finding a Hindu, Jewish, Muslim, or Buddhist neighbor was as rare as catching a golden sparrow, and just as tough to get your classmates to believe. Baptists and Catholics ruled the roost. The trouble for the rest of us wasn't so much religious intolerance (though that did rear its head) but that being a member of a religious minority meant being excluded from the centers of social life, business, politics, community, and the Baptists' heavenly deep-fried-everything.

Then there was the "homosexuality" thing. The census still doesn't ask that question. If it had back then, I can only imagine that few LGBTQ people in my home state would have dared divulge. It was still illegal to be gay there. Many still considered it a mental illness. If you answered, "Heck yes, I'm a gal who likes gals," you could legally be kicked out of your home and fired from your job. Truth is, you still can be today. So as far as I knew then, I was the only boy like me in the entire Lone Star State.

The studies that do ask the LGBTQ question today can only count those brave enough to come out to a complete stranger. According to Gallup, that number is 4.1 percent. God knows it would rise if they could count the gays who suddenly deepen their voices, pretended to lose service, or plead the Fifth. Bottom line: I was less alone than I feared, but that bit of life-saving data wouldn't find its way to my wrinkled-up ears for far too long.

I did tick one majority box, though—the race box. Texas was 78 percent white at the time. And although my family's income was below the median, I figured out that I could keep my second-hand clothes tidy (like the better-off kids), never bring up the Angel Moroni or my crushes on neighbor boys, and let people make their assumptions based on my pale skin. I could hide from the label of "too different"—a label I'd seen provoke alienation, harassment, scorn, and violence at school. At eight, I foolishly believed that my zipped-lip policy was a workable long-term strategy. I could not yet see, much less understand, the daily micro-injuries I was inflicting on my pint-sized soul with such denials of self and my cowardly reliance on our region's history of racism.

But those are mostly just the numbers, and as much as I enjoy statistics, I don't believe they do a whole lot of good when light needs shedding and hearts need opening. So here's how some of those numbers played out for me in 1982, on a bright spring day that already felt like July.

Without checking its fit, I loosened a snorkel's rubbery black head strap. My head was abnormally large for my age and looked downright massive atop my skinny frame. I spit into the mask, used a finger to rub the spit around, pressed the mask against my face, and pulled the snorkel into position. A big breath, and I kicked my way under the water. My heart slowed, my body relaxed. Down here, the world could no longer see or hear me. I was on my own, safe.

Colorful toys littered the bottom of the aboveground pool, the temporary type set up in the backyards of the slightly more fortunate when our summers got long and Texas-hot. To my left, a pair of thin, blinding-white legs on tiptoes met a pair of far-too-big trunks, then an outie belly button, a thousand ribs, and two hairless armpits. It was all reflection and distortion from there on up.

With my snorkel mask perfectly fogless, everything under water was in sharp focus. So I examined this other human being, wondering if I was just as awkward, and knowing full well I was worse. Its inward-leaning knees began to bend, and its feet suddenly pushed off the bottom. I turned away so as not to get busted scrutinizing this other boy's body.

I heard a deep thump, splashing, bubbles. I turned back to find a mass of writhing curls trying to wrestle free from the boy's mask. He went straight for the action figures on the pool floor. Action figure role-play wasn't really my jam, but this boy was the only person on the planet willing to call me a friend, so . . . His name was Timothy. I called him Tim.

From kindergarten to third grade, I had proven too skinny, too short, too big-headed, too often in the free lunch line, and far too quiet for the rest of the kids to be seen palling up with. Tim had a normal-sized head, but his mother had rendered him friendless by preemptively ironing patches on the outside of his trousers to protect them from wear and tear.

But there were qualities I truly valued in Tim: he didn't talk much, and he didn't ask me too many questions, so we could simply "be" together. And whether I realized it then or not, I needed Tim— because it's one thing to find a bit of safety in solitude, and quite another to be condemned to solitary confinement.

On this afternoon, Tim seemed to have lost his usual appetite for action figure warfare. Something was weighing on him, but we knew better than to give voice to our "somethings," so we retreated into our own thoughts, and I began plucking oak leaves off the water's surface— a blessedly endless task. But on this day, Tim interrupted my work with these words: "My mom says I need to talk to you about something."

No! I thought. I had mountains of "somethings," but I had long demonstrated the common Texan courtesy of keeping my mouth shut about them. Until now, Tim had shown similar good sense. My mind began looking for words to stop him, but all that came out was, "Oh, yeah?"

Tim began carving a circle around the edge of the pool. I planted myself at the farthest point from him—the pool's center. We both went silent for a time, but this afternoon would soon prove to be my very first "coming out" experience. No, not my own. This day was for Tim's difference. My memory of it is as crisp now as the day it happened—mostly because of how royally I screwed it.

Looking as far away from me as possible, Tim finally said: "My mom thinks I need to tell you that . . . she says I have to tell you that . . . that I'm Jewish."

My mind rummaged about, searching in vain for the meaning of this curious word I had never heard before. Was it a condition? Was a "Jewish" something he had done to someone, been accused of, found guilty of? Was he the only one or was it another tribe? And if it was a tribe, was it condemned to eternal separation from friends and family like my homo tribe? I was a very confused Texas boy. There just weren't many Jews in this part of Texas at this time, not that I knew of. So despite the warmth of the water, I froze.

"I'm getting cold," I said, and I climbed out of the pool. Tim stayed in.

My Southern upbringing had taught me better than to pry when things get uncomfortable, but as it tends to do, my curiosity got the best of me, and I began asking questions, piecing together what "Jewish" meant—that Jewish people believe in the Old Testament, but to Tim, the New Testament was like a bad game of telephone. Obviously this would have put him in an awkward position with our Baptist and Catholic classmates. But in a way, I could relate. Most everyone at school thought my church's latest addition to the Bible, the *Book of Mormon*, was baloney.

Luckily, I'd been armed with a secret weapon for this kind of religious debate: as different as Mormons are, we were still Christians. The elders at church had long "encouraged" us to remind our Baptist pals of that whenever they attacked us as cult members. This had proven to be valuable advice in the schoolyard. Now I just needed to arm Tim with this advice and we could put this "something" out of mind: "But you're a Christian."

With a glance up toward the sliding glass door of his house, Tim let out a quiet "No" before disappearing under the water. I looked back and caught his mom watching us.

When Tim finally surfaced, I got up the nerve to ask, "But what about Jesus?"

"I don't know," he said.

"You don't know who Jesus is?" Bingo. I got this.

"I've heard of him, but . . ." And he shook his head.

Now I was truly worried for my one friend. I'd been preached to time and again that I needed to be baptized in the Mormon Church and have a temple wedding in order to get to heaven. I was going to have trouble enough with the marrying a woman bit, but Tim was many more miles away if he didn't even tick the "believe in Jesus" box.

It was time for me to go full missionary.

A proper Mormon childhood is spent saving nickels, dimes, and quarters for the mission we pray to be called on when we turn eighteen. As missionaries, we might don the crisp white shirts and black slacks, receive name badges that called us "elder" despite our baby faces, and get shipped somewhere around the globe to convert more tithe payers. As a people who frequently believe themselves to be members of the only true church on the planet, we had a responsibility to spread the word of our young faith far and wide, so that no one would be inadvertently left out of heaven. I still had a decade before my turn came, but this mission before me couldn't wait.

"I know, Christ can be confusing," I said. "Like . . . why do you only get to go to heaven if you say Jesus is real if he only ever talked to people in one part of the world? What about the Indians? Do they all go to hell because Jesus never flew here or to Mexico?"

Tim looked baffled.

"Well, that's the thing about the *Book of Mormon*. It has the answers," I said. "A long time ago, a boy named Joseph Smith walked into the woods in New York, and a light came down, and he looked up, and there was God and Jesus." I paused for the first time, realizing that this story sounded a bit silly when said aloud to a non-Mormon, but Tim didn't seem to mind, so I carried on. "And Jesus and God told Joseph that they'd already answered all of Christianity's big questions. It's just that nobody knew how yet, but they would send another angel later on to tell Joseph how they'd done it."

"In New York City?" Tim asked, incredulous.

"The state, I think. But a long time ago." As if that somehow helped. "And one night, an angel named Moroni came to Joseph. He's the gold statue on top of our temples. And he told Joseph to dig up some buried gold plates that were in the woods. And he did. And he decoded them with a hat and special rocks so that everybody could understand what the plates said." I decided then and there that it was best to leave out the hat and rocks details the next time I told this story. "Do you know what was on those golden plates?"

"No," Tim said.

"The story of two tribes who lived here, from America on down. Good guys with light skin, called Israelites, and bad guys with dark skin, called Lamanites. And they had muscles and wore gold wristbands and had spears and fought each other and killed each other, and do you know what happened next?" *Too many details, too many details, Lance.*

"This is real?" Tim asked.

"There's proof." I was making that bit up, but I was so certain these stories were true that I felt sure there must have been proof. But unarmed with facts, I tried distracting Tim from his questions by amplifying the horror vibe. "See, after getting nailed to the cross, blood coming out of his hands, head, and side, Jesus rose from the dead like a zombie and came here!" I waited for Tim's reaction to this wonderful news, but there was none, so I put it together for him. "He came to America. That means the Indians knew about Jesus too. Everybody in the world got a chance to hear about him, and believe in him. They all got their chance. Get it?"

Tim didn't react to this good news the way I'd hoped he would. All I could hear now was the chorus of Texas cicadas growing louder as the sun got low. Tim finally cut to the chase: "Do you think I'm going to hell?"

Hearing that question from my one and only friend sent a shiver through me. I answered to the best of my eight-year-old LDS ability. "If you die right now . . . yes." Then I added, "Because only people baptized as Mormons go to the highest level of heaven . . . and I really want you on my level," I said. And I truly, deeply meant that.

I felt I had just been a great missionary. Tim's salvation was now up to him, but I couldn't imagine why he wouldn't jump right in and be by my side in heaven. Instead, I saw a flash of anger in him. Then a pang of guilt broadsided me. I didn't know what I'd just done, but I knew it was bad.

"It's dinnertime," he said.

If there was any question as to whether my proselytization had taken root, the way he climbed from the pool, wrapped himself in his towel up to his armpits, and shuffled back into his home made it clear that the seed I'd just tried to plant was dead on arrival. I'll never forget the proud, protective glare his mother aimed my way as her son vanished into their home. It was the same look I'd given all the gawkers at the San Antonio mall who'd dared judge my mother for her walk and spine.

That was the last time I ever heard from Tim, and for many years after, I would have a grand total of zero friends.

I wouldn't really understand what had happened that day for many years, when a week's worth of history lessons at North Salinas High School focused in on World War II, and Hitler's concentration camps. In our textbook was a picture of a handful of patches the Nazis had used to classify people's differences. Among them was a yellow Star of David and an upside-down pink triangle. Our teacher shared some of the atrocities that were committed against the Jewish people who were made to wear that star. And on that day, I asked questions and listened, finally learning something about Tim's heritage.

Having learned from my childhood church and state that many, if not most, human differences are best kept hidden, I had done to Tim what I'd been told would happen to me if anyone discovered my own secret difference—I'd found him guilty of being too unusual, and thus unworthy of respect. Now I couldn't shake the memory of his mother's proud, protective look. It turns out hers was the quiet lesson, taught by example, a seed pushed deep into the ground that would eventually grow to whisper in my ear that there was something about being an outsider that was worthy of love and worth fighting for. Tim and his mom had been the true missionaries that day.

But it would take many more years before I fully grasped their lessons, as there was at least one piece of information my history teacher left out of his World War II history. He never shared the story of the upside-down pink triangle that sat next to the yellow star. I couldn't know that it had been designed by those same Nazis to brand my tribe of homosexuals. Tim's people and mine had been tortured, murdered, and worked to death together in Hitler's concentration camps. Perhaps if I had known I had a people, a history, and a brotherhood with Tim's people—if I'd known enough to give Tim the embrace he deserved for his courage in sharing his difference, or if I'd had the courage to be equally honest about mine—then I might not have ended that hot spring day riding home on my cruddy bike, confused, tears streaming down my face, with new shame stacked on top of old. Perhaps I might have ended that day with a sturdier friendship and a new ally. But I didn't know. I had yet to learn our rich histories and the incalculable value of difference.

I I I

More than a decade later, in the summer of 1994, I would finally have a second chance at getting a coming-out right—this time with Ryan.

It was the June before I started UCLA's film school, and the night before I left Ryan behind in California, my sights set on my mom's new home in northern Virginia for the summer break. I had unilaterally decided it was time to take Ryan's deteriorating health situation by the horns. I couldn't ask him to dedicate two more years to this L.A. life if it would cost him his physical well-being. I hoped that by setting the stage for him (and perhaps even for me) to come clean about our shared secret, it might unburden him, perhaps even liberate him the way I had begun hearing some gays and lesbians felt when coming out. And if it went well for Ryan, then perhaps I might follow.

So with both of us perched atop his futon, I slowly but surely ventured into unfamiliar, forbidden territory. First I asked him about love in general, then about loneliness, about what or who he was attracted to, and why he never once brought a girl around. Ryan proved expert at avoiding my prodding, but I was equally determined.

Aiding my pursuit was the fact that Ryan and I were like brothers now. We were going to miss the hell out of each other that summer, and so we both wanted to stay up all night to milk every last moment together. As the clock neared 5:00 a.m., the lack of sleep took its toll, and left us both feeling a bit drunk. Defenses began to soften. And with the sun threatening, Ryan looked to a faraway wall. "It's what you think."

No. I wanted him to say those forbidden words plainly. So I played dumb. "What do you mean?" I asked.

"The guy with the goatee," he said. "You know . . . we did some things."

I knew who he meant. As he had with me for years, he'd taken a handsome young Latin man up into the mountains for a photo shoot. Ryan had been careful not to let our paths cross. I'd only ever seen this young man in negatives in the darkroom Ryan had set up in our small bathroom. Again, I played dumb: "What do you mean?"

An endless pause. No breaths taken. Then finally: "I'm a . . . I'm gay," he confessed.

A lifetime of silence had just given voice to the unspeakable.

His words hung in the air, and I let them hang as I searched for courage of my own. But as I did, I watched his brow lower, his eyes move to the floor, his hands clasp for safety, as if in prayer, and he shook as if he were ill. And in that dreadful silence, my hope turned to concern. His big reveal hadn't brought the relief I'd hoped for or read about. Instead, his words seemed like a poison fog, now eating him alive. This long-delayed acknowledgment was not the antidote I'd wished for him and, deep down, for myself. That frightened me. And so I didn't find the strength to follow his lead. Instead, I failed Ryan like I had Tim, and arguably worse.

With Tim, I'd been ignorant; with Ryan, I knowingly lied. "Well, I'm not sure I understand your choices. And it might take me a while to . . ." I went silent.

"To what?" he asked.

"I don't hate you or anything, but I'm just not sure if we can be friends in the same way when I get back." I hadn't damned Ryan to hell like I had Tim, but I'd offered him no acceptance, no love—only a hurtful lie told in the feeble, self-righteous hue called tolerance.

"I understand," he said, accepting the rejection he'd long anticipated.

I knew that the words I was employing were lies, delivered in exacting fashion, the way I feared straight people might use words against me if I ever came out. I was putting on my best "straight" act to ensure that my closet door stayed shut.

To put this into perspective, Ellen DeGeneres wouldn't come out for three years, *Will & Grace* for four. Pedro Zamora would come out later in 1994 on MTV's *The Real World*, but he would die of AIDS by November, just like so many of our brothers who were dying day after day. Ryan had been very brave to come out that night. I was a coward. And this night's denial would call for a web of new lies.

With both of us wobbly from lack of sleep, Ryan dropped me off at LAX the next morning, giving me a quick hug before he drove back home to Salinas for the summer. As I flew east toward Virginia, to where my mom, Jeff, and Todd were now living outside the nation's capital, I worried that I'd just seen my best friend for the last time. I worried what my pathetic charade might drive him to do now. And without Ryan in my life, what chance did I have of finding the courage and strength I knew my heart, my home, and my creative endeavors all needed to ever grow true and full?

I V

My mom and Jeff had both found civil service jobs at Walter Reed Army Medical Center in Washington, D.C., and this time they both had to take pay cuts. The upside was that Walter Reed was a highly esteemed hospital, "where the president sometimes goes for care," my mom often said with a twinkle of pride in her eye.

Todd started at a new high school, where he followed in my footsteps and joined the swim team. Increasingly lost in drugs and alcohol, Marcus had chosen to stay behind in Salinas with his equally high girlfriend in a house that reeked of weed, beer, and wet dogs, working his knuckles until they bled at the local Sears auto garage. We all missed "our Marco," and now in more ways than one. My mom's heart broke. We had been her impossible dreams, and with her return to the South, she was down to only one son in the same time zone.

When I landed at Dulles Airport after my strained farewell with Ryan, Jeff picked me up in his truck and drove me through the lush green woods of northern Virginia. We hung a right into a brand-new housing development atop the land where the bloody Civil War Battle of Bull Run was waged, and there it was, their new house. It felt like home the very first time I saw it. It was yellow and had a long porch we could sit out on all night and watch thunderstorms roll in and fireflies glow. Turns out it was a lot cheaper to live in northern Virginia than in California, particularly an hour's commute from D.C.

My mom seemed at home here too, relaxed for the first time since we'd left Texas. We stayed up talking late into many of that sticky summer's nights. She taught me how to make her chicken casserole with the crushed potato chips on top. I made her the star of my home movies, shot on that camcorder I'd earned at J. C. Penney. And this proved to be the summer she would call me into her room, open the bottom drawer of her dresser, and introduce me to her sacred objects—including her golden book of boys. Together, we flipped through her favorites, and once I left the room, she got up the courage to rip up that impossibly cute picture of my father I'd just pointed out on her book's final page.

Since moving to Virginia, Todd had begun driving my mom crazy with a brand-new bullheaded defiance. He refused to even answer when she called his name. With his boyish looks growing increasingly handsome, he reminded me more and more of that photo she had just torn up—of the father he had no memories of. And thanks in part to those good looks, soon there were more girls coming and going than my mom felt comfortable with. Sometimes he closed his bedroom door with them in there. Alone.

For one full week that summer, Todd and I woke up before sunrise to drive into D.C. with Jeff and our mom on their way in to work. As we neared the Washington Monument, Jeff would block traffic for a second so we could quickly leap out. Todd and I had decided we needed to see every exhibit in every Smithsonian museum on the National Mall in that one week. That's no small order. But on one of our brief lunch breaks, somewhere between NASA space capsules and what was left of "The Star-Spangled Banner," I took an extra moment to put on my old paternal hat and tried confronting my younger brother about his fresh rebellions.

"Mom's worked really hard to get us to where we are, you know? Where you are now. Maybe try being a little nicer to her? Or at least answer when she talks to you?"

Todd looked away from his food, but more specifically, from me. He was tough on the outside, but also the quickest to tears. I could tell my criticism had stung. But instead of an apology, he only let out a deep, chesty hum that landed in his gut: "Hmmmmph."

I'd never heard such a sound out of my baby brother. It was a man's sound, not a boy's. I was a bit stunned by it. "What do you think, Todd-o?"

Once he felt safe from tears, he looked back at his food, then back in my direction, and said firmly: "I think I don't wanna talk about it."

And that was that. He wasn't interested in my opinion anymore either.

That week we spent together in the Smithsonian's treasure-filled rooms left us both in awe of our nation: its many cultures, its terrible and triumphant histories, its failures and grand achievements—but it also left me feeling rather proud of my little brother's willfulness. I think I could see what my mom couldn't yet. Todd wasn't rebelling in self-destructive fashion like Marcus had, or trying to please everyone like I always did. Yes, Todd's behavior may have been abnormal for our home, but he was only doing it because we'd made sure he knew his home was strong. He was a bright, easy-to-laughter, quick-to-tears, opinionated teenage boy, asserting himself in ways Marcus and I had never felt safe doing as we danced for survival in the quicksand of our youth. Turns out our mom had nothing to worry about— Todd was her masterpiece, a pain in the ass because miraculously he'd turned out healthy and "normal."

Ryan checked in on the phone every now and then, and to my ear, his melancholy was fading. I was pleasantly surprised, if not a little envious, when he said he'd come out to his Pentecostal mother and she'd assured him that she loved him regardless. He told me that he missed me. I asked him to look out the window at the moon. He did. So did I. "How nice is it that we're looking at the same thing right now?" I asked. It was my way of saying I missed him terribly—that I wished in more ways than one we could be in the same place.

Still, Ryan's path wasn't an option for me. Seeing my mother's happiness taking root again—a loving husband, and back in the South she preferred—I knew I couldn't start kicking over beehives, not in her military, half–Jack Mormon, half-Catholic home. The vacuum left by Marcus's infrequent calls already threatened her sunny days, and I loved witnessing her blossoming contentment.

So that summer I made a conscious decision to go in the opposite direction, and just as my mother had taught me to do, I gave this new commitment my all. I signed up for lifeguarding classes and turned golden brown working at a pool with a few twisty water slides. And when a voluptuous, remarkably forward fellow lifeguard asked me if I'd like to get dinner with her and another couple, I took her up on the double date offer. She was kind and patient and had a Southern drawl and a smile to die for.

That weekend, I bought her a rose, which she held in her lap on our ride to a restaurant in D.C. I never told her this was my first-ever date. I simply tried my best to be a gentleman. I was nervous; in retrospect, it was incredibly sweet. Afterward came my first kiss. It was just as sweet but wetter. Then she let me know she had other designs, and revealed her breasts. I found them fascinating but far softer than I had anticipated or hoped. Then came sex. I didn't tell her that I'd never done it. Thankfully, she knew what she was doing. I did my best to keep up. All of this in a handful of hours that ended on an old industrial carpet in a basement next to a poorly tuned TV screaming sports headlines on the late-night local news . . . all the while knowing full well that I was exceedingly gay but just as determined not to be.

Putting Mormon logic to the task, I convinced myself that if I had a child or ten, this potential family of my making would bring me more happiness than any passion or romance ever could. I'd witnessed this with my mom and brothers. Now I dreamed of having lots of little ones of my own. After all, I had long heard folks say that romance fades. *So why waste time on it in the first place?* I thought.

And so using this logic time and time and time again, I tried my best to get this unsuspecting young woman pregnant. Condoms? Forget about it. Birth control? We never had the conversation. Go down there? No thank you. But no matter how hard I tried (and thanks to nineteen-year-old hormones, I actually could try hard), by summer's end I was convinced that my sperm must be just as defective as I was.

There would be no baby. No future family.

That summer of heterosexual sex wasn't all for naught, though. It made one thing abundantly clear: no amount of trying, no matter how beautiful, loving, or supportive the unsuspecting woman might be, would ever cure me of my "secret something." There was no escape route from my difference. And unlike Tim, or most racial minorities, I hadn't been born into a family that inherently understood my big difference. Like most LGBTQ people, I had been born to *heterosexual* parents who didn't know to, or even *how* to, instill in me the steely sense of self-worth an LGBTQ minority needs to survive and defend his or her differences. Sadly, it's all too often those very parents who prove to be their child's first attackers when they do find out. In this particular way, and like most of my kind in those days, I knew I had been born behind enemy lines.

CHAPTER 13

Allemande Left

*A*llemande left: A square dance move in which corners face each other, take left hands or forearms, walk around each other to the left, let go, and return to their original position.

I got back on an airplane in late September, a few weeks before I was set to start at UCLA's film school. As I looked out the window, we took to the air and headed west, over Virginia, over the rust belt and the Midwest, across the Rocky Mountains, and back to that Southern California style of America that still felt a bit too foreign, particularly now with no family for miles. A few weeks earlier, Ryan had enthusiastically agreed to spend two more years in L.A. and to pick me up at the airport—the former a big surprise and a huge relief, the latter a test of true friendship for any Angeleno.

When I saw Ryan again, I was gobsmacked. I hardly recognized him. He was now fit and trim. His mustache had vanished. His head was shaved too. There was even an aggressive, black tribal tattoo blazing down his forearm. In three short months, he had emerged from his chubby closet-cocoon as a butterfly. *What the holy living hell did I help unleash?* I thought. Ryan was no longer in SoCal for my dreams. This was a new Ryan, looking to fulfill his own ambitions in ways only a big city could provide in 1994.

We moved into an affordable apartment well south of the university, and Ryan got right to work. Over the summer, he had rediscovered the charm he'd once wielded at North High. His devilish grin was back and he was now using it to build a new circle of friends out of the brightest, wildest, and most attractive young men he could find—this time harvested from a vibrant, fast-growing gay ghetto just east of us called West Hollywood.

This wasn't the West Hollywood of today. Gay tourists and bachelorette parties from around the world weren't flying in to stuff Benjamins into go-go dancers' G-strings, or spilling out onto wide, well-lit sidewalks at last call in hopes of finding "the one"—or the one for the night. Boystown, as it were, was on the same Santa Monica Boulevard it is today, but it was only reliably gay between Robertson and Palm. It was dimly lit, with narrow sidewalks. Most bars' windows were covered to protect the identities of those inside, and patrons knew better than to walk back to their cars alone for fear of being bashed verbally or physically by the "straight" men out trolling "fags" for sport.

But for gay men at the time, Boystown was still a far safer place to be out than most any other neighborhood in Los Angeles, and it was certainly safer than most cities in the world, so bold college boys ventured to what we called "the strip," traveling in packs for the security even this sanctuary still required. Some packs had older leaders who showed their boys the ropes and kept them safe in exchange for companionship (if not occasional physical delight). Other packs were more like *Lord of the Flies*, led by the wildest boys among them, often in search of drugs, sex, or both. It was a combo that far too often led to HIV, AIDS, and an early death. In 1994, any hope for effective HIV treatment was still years away.

For Ryan, being the leader of a pack came naturally, and in West Hollywood, he was more successful than ever. He quickly stole away all of the most handsome young men from other pack leaders, because unlike them, Ryan was a true and loyal caretaker. He didn't offer his boys drugs or ask for sex in return for his protection. As he had with me, he genuinely loved taking care of those in need. And for better or for worse, home base for his operation was our little apartment between Sawtelle Boulevard and the 10 Freeway in West L.A.—wall-to-wall carpet, a new bed in Ryan's room, and our old futon in the living room for me.

On big nights out—most Wednesdays, Thursdays, and Saturdays—Ryan's boys flooded in. I would hide behind my homework and put on my best heterosexual impersonation when lured away. But I don't think a single one of them bought my cover story that I'd installed a detailed collage of Leonardo DiCaprio on the wall because I considered him to be the greatest actor of our generation. No. They rightfully suspected that I wanted to grab Leo by his long bangs and kiss him hard. I know this because they continually shared exactly that theory with Ryan whenever I left the room.

When I had pushed Ryan to come out earlier that year, I had mostly just hoped he would stop eating himself into an early grave. I had never imagined that he would turn our own home into a gay extravaganza, or that so many of his new clique would be so impossibly attractive. Worse, I could see myself in all of their eyes, countless new ones every week: gay refugees from all over the country, and from every background, religion, color, shape, and size, many running to Los Angeles after suffering rejection from their families and hometowns, now seeking freedom and safety here.

As much as I tried to avoid eye contact, I increasingly caught them seeing themselves in my eyes too, and I soon understood that a clock was ticking. I either had to move out of this apartment and leave my best friend behind in order to avoid being outed, or do the unthinkable: come out willingly. This dilemma came to dominate my thoughts, to keep me from my schoolwork, and to distract me from the dream that had brought me this far. That tugging (and my new, equally un-LDS all-nighters with Dr Pepper) left me physically ill. In search of guidance, I did something some might find surprising: I got down on my knees beside my futon to pray.

"Dear Heavenly Father, I'm so lost right now. If you can still hear me . . . can you please help me see where I should go?"

When I first realized I was gay, at the age of six, my choices were clear: I had to hide, or suffer the shameful personal and familial consequences of exposure. So I hid. By twelve, I had considered suicide to quiet the pain of isolation and shame. At nineteen, I'd tried to replace love with a family by getting a young woman pregnant. All of this because I'd been told by my church, our state, the news, and our neighbors that gay people lived horrific lives of indignity, sickness, and death, followed by eternal loneliness in a burning hell. Yes, I still treasure Texas and the South, and yes, our church kept my family alive in so many generous ways, but both had long been tearing me to pieces from the inside out.

Now I was bearing witness as Ryan rose like a phoenix, seeing firsthand that his friends didn't have horns hidden under their hair like our old Mormon prophet had suggested gay people did, and that they didn't seem sick or sad like so many shrinks on daytime talk shows claimed gay people were. In fact, they seemed as happy as, if not happier than, most straight people I knew—thriving *because* they'd come out, not in spite of doing so. I now had dozens of real-life examples of gay people that didn't match the terrible stories I'd heard and believed my entire life.

Still on my knees in prayer, I grew silent and listened, not for some actual voice like the prophets of our church had claimed to hear, but to my own heart. Because if there really was a God, I felt sure that He could speak to a far deeper place than my crinkled-up ears. And that night, I thought I felt some sort of God whisper to me, "I am love." And so . . . I chose love.

Instead of running further, hiding deeper, losing myself in work, piling more lies on top of old ones, more shame on top of shame, or coming up with new ways to end my life, I started writing my story in the margins of my class notes, documenting every moment I'd known who I was but hadn't been brave enough to accept it, and all of the anger I felt toward those who'd tried so hard to make me believe that I'd never love or be loved in return. Next, I transcribed or physically cut and pasted all those words into a seventeen-page "manifesto" and left it on our sad apartment's bathroom sink. Then I picked up Ryan's decidedly pink Oil of Olay moisturizing bath bar and scrawled on the mirror above it: "Read this. Do what you will with it. Carpe diem."

I ran off to my modern poetry class at UCLA knowing full well that my most steadfast ally in this life would soon find my manifesto, and that my deepest, darkest secret would finally . . . be out.

EXCERPTS FROM "THE MANIFESTO"
MARCH 6, 1995

Dear Ryan, my dearest and most beloved friend in the whole entirety of this world. You are the one person on this earth who God has sent for me. You are a blessing, a gift of unknown proportion . . . Oh Lord, how are you supposed to start a thing like this?

God, I'm suddenly feeling as if this is the most selfish thing I have ever done. In fact, perhaps there is not a single person on the face of this green and blue planet who will prosper from all of this, least of all myself. Several times my mother has told me that the most selfish thing she has ever done in her life was to marry Jeffrey Scott Bisch. In her case, it turned out to be her entire life, her joy, her love, and her happiness. I fear with all my soul that from this singularly selfish act will come not so forgiving a fate.

[On a page of its own, two pieces of paper (dime rolls from a bank) were stapled facedown with a note above each: "Turn if you dare." Under them "I am" and "gay" were spelled out.]

[Top of the following page:] "I'm shaking violently now. Oh GOD, it is over isn't it?

With this packet I have sealed something . . . and I fear it. I will lose everything because of it. Why has God cursed me? My mother and brothers will reject me. All I have ever wanted was a family. A little boy of my own. Oh God, how I have always wanted children! FUCK YOU! HOW CAN GOD DO THIS! BENEVOLENT MY ASS! All is lost. There is little reason to go on. I need you [Ryan], now more than ever. Please don't tell anyone of this, but keep it; it is ours, and when I wish it, it will be the world's, but not yet. I have "seized THIS day." It is all I can do for now.

Yes, it was arguably a bit theatrical, but that's how immense the stakes felt at that age, in that time. My budding drama-queen heart was beating hard and low in my chest on the ride home from UCLA that afternoon. I parked my car in its usual spot up a side street, took a deep breath, and started slowly walking home. As I turned the corner, I saw Ryan striding quickly toward me, head down, lost in thought. My heart sped up to a jackhammer flutter. When he looked up and saw me, relief rinsed his sullen expression. He didn't pick up his pace. He was too cool for that. When he reached me, he simply said, "I was coming to look for you. I thought maybe you went to hurt yourself."

Ryan's worry was not overblown. We were living in darker days, when suicide was a far too common way out of all the fear and shame that was being heaped upon gay kids. Studies at the time suggested that three out of four gay teens considered suicide. I had been one of those three. Ryan knew those feelings too. And years earlier, one of Ryan's high school friends had thrown a rope over the clothing rod in his bedroom closet, stepped up onto a chair, tied the rope around his neck, and, obeying the self-loathing that had been drilled into him, pushed the chair out from under his feet. His parents found his body hanging there hours later. They were as silent about his death as he had been about his troubles. No one ever named his reasons, but those of us with the ability to see ourselves in his eyes knew. Ryan had been this boy's friend, and thanks to what I can now see was a rather overdramatic "manifesto," he worried that a version of that tragic scenario might have been playing out with me. He had over-slept that morning. He was panic-stricken when he finally read my words and had grabbed his car keys and rushed out the door. That's when our paths crossed.

My manifesto was the opposite of a suicide note. It was meant as a declaration of my intention to live, and to live openly. But recognizing the fear in Ryan's eyes, I thought back to his high school friend and the path he'd chosen, perhaps the only path he could see, and I felt luckier than ever to have had Ryan in my life to light a different one.

"Happy birthday," he said.

But it was only March 6. My birthday was months away.

He clarified: "Today is your new birthday. You get to start again."

I I

It was a warm Los Angeles night in April when I pulled my favorite T-shirt over my skinny frame, let my blond bangs hang low and seductive over my brow, and handed Ryan his car keys. My hands were trembling in my pockets as he drove east, up Santa Monica Boulevard and into Boystown.

At a stoplight, Ryan handed me a small clear plastic baggy filled with a couple of condoms.

"What the heck is this?" I asked.

"Must I explain everything, kitten?"

"I'm not a kitten! And I'm not going to need these."

"Well, I didn't think you would. But *he* might, whoever *he* ends up being."

"Are you saying I'm a slut?"

"No. I'm calling you a catcher. A receiver. Likely passive. What I call a hungry little—"

I was not going to let him say "bottom," so I protested: "You know, unlike you, I have actually—"

"Done it with a woman."

"Yes!"

"That's your fault. Don't get pissy with me about it. But I can only guess that while you were 'doing it,' you were dreaming of the roles being reversed."

"That's a big assumption."

"But an accurate one, am I right?" I silently protested by examining the condoms. I'd seen one unrolled on a cucumber from afar in a sex ed class in high school, but I'd never actually handled one. Ryan took a sincere turn. "Just . . . if you ever actually land the opportunity, use them. And don't be too shy to insist."

It had been a while since I'd felt Ryan's protective embrace. Now I was one of the boys in his West Hollywood pack, and he'd be damned if I was going to get hurt out here. The truth was, sex at that time, particularly for gay men, was indeed deadly. The only treatments being

prescribed for AIDS either killed you faster or disfigured you while
you died slow and painfully.

Ryan parked his car, and I shoved the condoms in my pocket.

I might have been knocking at the door of my twenty-first birthday, but I looked far younger, so we were headed into Mickey's nightclub, one of the few with an eighteen and over night. For weeks I'd
waited for this outing. I suspected my life was about to be flipped
on its head, but I had no idea how many times I was about to be
smacked on the ass. This place was teeming with fit, mostly college-
age men taking full advantage of the lax age limit, some boys standing in tight, nervous circles, others swirling about, looking for a place
to land, or a pretty face (or whatnot) to call their own.

I'd never received a phone number from anyone in my life. Within
an hour, more than a few swirling types had scribbled their numbers
on matchbooks or mine onto napkins. Within a week, our answering
machine, which for me had only ever been home to my mom's voice,
was filled to capacity with potential suitors. It turned out that the
attributes that had made me too slight, young-looking, or hairless for
women earned me the oft-valued Boystown label of "twink."

I was too afraid to use most of the numbers I received that night.
Maybe it was all the AIDS and condoms talk, maybe it was the fact
that I was craving romance more than the sexed-up vibe I'd found in
WeHo; most likely it was a bit of both. But I did say yes to one invite:
a screening of *Doctor Zhivago* from a twenty-nine-year-old named
Bryan Singer who was sporting a goatee and a red flannel shirt that
should have died with grunge. He'd been quick to tell me that he'd just
finished principal photography on a film called *The Usual Suspects*.
I couldn't have cared less. *Doctor Zhivago* was the draw. It was one
of my and my mom's favorite films. When I was a kid, I'd spent my
last dime collected from delivering newspapers to buy her a music
box that played the film's memorable "Lara's Theme." I was thrilled to
learn that the film was going to be projected in an actual theater. This
was worth facing any social anxiety for.

The movie theater in Century City was mostly empty when I
arrived, but a few of the center rows were filled with young men.
Bryan saw me, waved me down, and proceeded to introduce me to
all the young, gay film buffs around him. Suddenly, I dared to believe

that I had found a tribe of my own. I began to imagine that these boys might become lifelong friends and collaborators, and twenty years later I can report that my optimism that night wasn't misplaced. I still know, love, and work with more than a few of those once-rosy-cheeked young men.

Then I saw him. The very first real-life man to grace my Cutest I'll Ever See in My Life list. He was polite. He stood up when it was his turn to be introduced. He was an inch shorter than me, a bit older, and I could tell he had to shave each morning and did so with precision. He had brown hair, a cute, self-conscious smile, and was wearing a conservative button-down. He didn't fit the mold of most of the other gay men I'd met. He seemed more like every boy I'd ever had a crush on at church or in school in Texas.

"Hi. I'm Jason."

Oh life, you funny devil, another Jason! I instantly fell for this brand-new Jason—I just prayed for a less bloody ending.

But of course, when I opened my mouth, something like this fell out: "Hi. Some people call me Dustin. That's my first name. But my friends and family call me Lance. You can call me . . . whatever you want."

I instantly resented my mom all over again for giving me such a mess of names, but I hated myself even more for how poorly I'd handled this explanation I'd had two decades to perfect. Why not just say my name was Lance? Why be such a moron? I'd lost my cool. I knew it, and Jason could see it.

He offered a curt "Nice to meet you" and sat back down. Bryan sat beside him.

Now I worried that they might be "together," but that made little sense to my naïve Southern mind. Bryan had clearly hit on me when we first met. How could they be "together"?

The film soon lit up the screen, turning Jason's neck into a long, lean, glowing curve. The lightly freckled skin of his cheek had clearly done its time in the sun. The few little hairs he'd missed when shaving sparkled in the film's light. This time I wasn't lost in Omar Sharif and Julie Christie's undying love; this time I was falling into my own. Three hours and twenty minutes later, when there had been no hand-holding between Jason and Bryan, I considered this conservative young man fair game and started a campaign to make him mine, but it was a campaign waged with very little know-how.

Months later, I had managed to sweat through dozens of stilted messages left on Jason's answering machine, and only succeeded in sharing one coffee with him, during a late-night "homework session" at the Abbey in West Hollywood. Jason had only agreed after making me repeat that we were only there to do homework across from each other. This wasn't a date. And this wasn't the bumping, sprawling Abbey bar and nightclub of today. In 1995, the Abbey was a coffee shop. A haven for the under-twenty-one crowd—at least those without fake IDs—with an espresso machine and a baked goods selection manned by a sweet Mexican American man who knew every one of his "children" by name.

At night, the Abbey was filled with students—some with books open and notepads out, others easing into a game of pool or dropping quarters into a brand-new machine in back that let you play chess with kids on similar machines in far-flung cities: the early days of the internet. Modeled after a Spanish church, the Abbey was our sanctuary, our new home away from our families' homes—homes that had rejected so many of us—a place where we could finally feel relatively safe, free, and normal.

But Jason didn't want to talk much during our coffee outing. Not with me at least. He was too busy talking to himself as he memorized script pages. He'd tried college for a time but left early to try his luck at becoming an actor. He'd already seen some success flinging a tortilla in a national Taco Bell commercial. I was so smitten that somehow this impressed me far more than Bryan's directing *The Usual Suspects*. So I tried to make a connection between Jason's Taco Bell work and my own, but he seemed less than impressed that I'd actually mixed beans for real customers back in Salinas. He was smart, confident but not cocky; his family was from Indiana, and he eventually came out to me about one other personal detail: he felt more Republican than Democrat. That last bit baffled most in West Hollywood, but it sounded like home to me. I wanted to kiss his Reagan-loving lips, but he only had interest in memorizing yet another page of lines for one of his many auditions the next day.

The reason for his lack of interest soon became clear: Jason's head turned only when men who looked to have spent ample time in the gym passed our table, often men with salt and pepper in their hair. I wasn't his type, and no amount of push-ups, sit-ups, or shaving my peach fuzz to encourage beard growth would prove helpful. I know because I tried all of those things, for months.

I lost sleep over my crush. My passions began to shift from work to romance, from a love of cinematic sentiment to a thirst for real love. I couldn't focus in school. And just like my mom's had during her heartbreak over Don, my grades suffered. I was lovesick for the very first time in my life, and eventually even Ryan got tired of my lamentations. He was now involved with a tattooed Greek man with muscular shoulders, and his new romance seemingly gave him the authority to tell me the truth about mine: "Girl, you're in lust."

"No!" I protested. "I'm not a 'girl,' and it goes far deeper than lust."

"Oh, does it?" He was genuinely asking.

"Yes. He's special."

Ryan thought on that for a second. "If he started giving you the time of day, you'd lose interest in a week."

"That's not true," I protested.

Ryan rolled his eyes. He'd been around the block a few times at this point. He'd seen many a newly out boy from his pack "fall in love" only to fall right back out of it after he'd gotten what he thought he wanted. "Just have sex with him; get it over with. And then maybe find someone who actually gives a damn about you."

Sex?! Are you kidding me? He knew me better than that. "I'm not that kind of gay," I said, and I honestly wasn't. You can take the kid out of the South and out of the Mormon Church, but you can't just rip those values out of the kid. Not that quickly, at least.

He let that stand for a moment; then, as he sat casually cleaning out his camera bag from what was becoming a second career taking actors' headshots, he offered: "You're so used to not being able to have the things you want, or love, that you've fallen for the one guy in all of West Hollywood who treats you how you think you deserve to be treated."

"What do you mean? I want him to be my boyfriend." The word

"boyfriend" felt so strange on my lips. I'd thought the word a thousand times, but this was the first time I'd ever uttered it. Then I added: "I think I . . . I deserve love."

"Not yet you don't." He knew this feeling all too well. "You think you deserve rejection. That's what you're used to. So that's what you're looking for, honey."

Of course he was right, but he was being too honest too soon. "Stop calling me 'girl' and 'honey'!"

"Whatever you like . . . sweet pea."

I fumed, and I convinced myself that he was either blind to the truth or simply jealous. I told myself I could no longer talk to my only confidant about matters of the heart, and because that's all I wanted to talk about anymore, the all-night conversations we held so dear ceased.

I pursued Jason harder, turning him into the producer of my student films, writing dreadful scripts with him late into the night. So yes, I was soon consistently physically closer to my "dream guy"—close enough to watch him date other men, including Bryan Singer, with his terrible flannel shirts, his now Academy Award–nominated film, and his endless bragging about his massive paychecks. How the heck could I compete with that?

Before I knew it, December was upon us, and Ryan left for Salinas to be with his family for the holidays. I felt his absence deeply that year. So close to love but still unable to touch it, a new kind of loneliness descended: just me and the hum of late-night traffic on the 10 Freeway outside the window of our one real bedroom as I curled up in Ryan's bed. I thought about what he'd said. He'd been right about my feelings for Jason. He'd been right so many times over the course of our friendship. In many ways, he'd taken on the role of father figure in my father's absence, of big brother when Marcus stopped returning anyone's calls, and I wondered then as I still do today what would have become of me if I'd never met him. I can tell you this for certain: I wouldn't have stepped out of my closet as soon as I did without him stepping into that unknown ahead of me.

In my coming-out "manifesto," I had asked and promised Ryan this: "Please don't tell anyone of this, but keep it; it is ours, and when I wish it, it will be the world's." I likely only meant that I'd one day come out to the rest of my world, meaning my own family. What I didn't and couldn't know that lonely night was that thanks to the foundation of our unlikely friendship, I would one day prove strong enough to confront my epic stage fright, literally come out to the entire world, demand our full equality in front of millions, and face down many of my country's most powerful forces of bigotry.

But if you'd told me that at the close of 1995, I would have called you a fool. My concern that night was that there was little chance I'd survive the Christmas ahead—a Christmas back in the South, where no one knew I'd begun to "start again," particularly not my good, headstrong, Southern mom. Out west, I'd begun stepping out; at her home in Virginia, I knew I'd have to climb back into that cage called silence or risk a whole lot of losing.

CHAPTER 14

Queen of the Ma'ams

I

Walter Reed was nearly an hour's commute from their home in rural Virginia, but the many hours on the road each week felt worthwhile—Jeff and Anne loved their new jobs. In her lab coat, her civil service military ID clipped to its top pocket, Anne would hold her chin a bit higher as they approached the hospital's gate.

Back in Texas, Anne had started as a GS4—pretty much the lowest level for any government employee—and worked her way up to a GS7, only to have to take a sizeable demotion to move out to California to be with Jeff. But when she got a shot at working in microbiology there, she took it, and let her work ethic, skills, and attention to detail shine. She also wasn't stingy with her charm around the doctors, and within a few short years, she had defied the conventional wisdom that a degree is necessary to run a laboratory, and she'd become the supervisor of the microbiology and serology sections at Fort Ord army base.

When Anne was hired at Walter Reed, it wasn't to keep running her own lab, but to work as a lab tech in immunology, performing tests for rheumatology and other special diseases. She had hoped to stay in microbiology, but the lab at Walter Reed was packed full of people who'd been there for years and weren't going anywhere. But again, Anne put her shoulder to the wheel and soon re-earned a reputation as the best and brightest. She got to know all the doctors, pathologists, and heads of sections personally; and slowly, she worked her way back up.

Anne's section was inspected every other year by the official certifying organization for labs. When the inspectors would arrive, Anne would have everything ready and laid out. The inspectors would stay for a week at a time, eagerly looking for any little mistakes, but each time, Anne came through with "zero recommendations" and "zero deficiencies," meaning everything was absolutely perfect. It was rare to achieve that once in a career. Anne achieved it every single inspection.

Then one day, the head of her section sat down with her in the break room over a hot chocolate and a Snickers bar and asked if she might be interested in flow cytometry. Anne claimed she was—even though she didn't yet know what it meant.

That night, she had Jeff take her to a bookstore. They bought manuals on the subject, and she studied and read them well into the night. It was a highly technical, cutting-edge field, different from anything she'd ever done, and she worried that she wasn't up for it, maybe not even bright enough for it. As he always did, Jeff held her hand under the covers as they fell asleep together that night, but this time he whispered to her: "You've always been able to achieve whatever you set your mind to, so why not this?"

"Not always," she said.

"Every time I've seen you try, you have."

"That's nice of you to say." She was still staring at the ceiling, lost in insecurity.

"I'm not saying it's always a good thing."

"What do you mean?" she asked defensively.

"You get what you want."

"Are you saying I'm a battle-axe?"

"Well, I'm not saying you're not, that's for sure," he said, completely serious.

She let go of his hand and whacked him hard across the chest.

The next day, Anne asked to be mentored by the current supervisor of flow cytometry. The work involved a laser that helps count and sort cells, detecting biomarkers by suspending those cells in fluid and passing them through a machine that can read their characteristics at a thousand parts per second. Initially focused on blood cancers, Anne quickly grasped and then fell in love with this new, innovative work. And when that supervisor left the job many months later, Anne took her place.

Not every hospital has a flow section, and the military had only a few. Suddenly, Anne was the supervisor of the Department of Defense's high-tech, cutting-edge flow cytometry lab, and she soared all the way up to a GS12, far higher than she had ever dared dream.

She didn't show her pride often, but when it came to this new position, it was hard for her to hide it. The woman who had been told she would never go to college or get a real job was now running one of the most esteemed labs in one of the U.S. military's most prized hospitals.

I clearly remember her first big concern in this new job, likely because it frightened me too. She began working with blood from AIDS patients, doing their T cell counts on her machines, figuring out how rapidly these supposedly straight HIV-positive young men were losing their immune cells, trying with the doctors to find any treatment that might help slow their decline, and failing each and every time. She never mentioned what she must have known: that many of these boys were closeted gay men in a military that didn't allow gay people to serve openly. But she never outright judged them in front of me. She was wholly focused on keeping these boys alive for their mothers and their families for as long as she could. That gave me some hope.

Then one crisp afternoon in 1995, when I was back for a spring break visit, she came home with a serious expression on her face and a Band-Aid on her finger. She had put her hand into her lab coat pocket, forgetting she had a specimen in there, and jabbed her finger with an HIV-positive patient's syringe. Over dinner, she told us she felt certain she would be okay, that this wasn't uncommon, and that such a small amount of exposure was nothing to get too terribly concerned about. But I was now a frequent visitor to the gay ghettos in L.A. and occasionally in San Francisco, and on the streets of West Hollywood and in the Castro I'd seen the gaunt faces of those suffering with AIDS. I thought about my mentors in the theater world who had simply vanished, and of one popular young friend in our pack in L.A. who had never been diagnosed, but suddenly died of pneumonia in the parking lot of Cedars-Sinai Hospital. He had undiagnosed HIV that had progressed to AIDS and, untreated, took him without warning.

It would be nearly a year before I felt I could trust the tests saying my mom was still HIV-negative. She didn't know how turned the tables were over those months—the still half-closeted gay son of a straitlaced Southern military woman worrying that his precious mom might die of AIDS in the early '90s.

But like always, the greater the challenges, the greater my mom's sense of purpose. Jeff would walk into her lab at the end of the workday, and she'd be sitting at her machine showing doctors results, pointing out cells so they could determine exactly what kind of cancer their patient had. Sometimes crowds of doctors hovered over her, listening to her every word, and Jeff would just sit back and smile. "It was like she was conducting a symphony orchestra," he told me. "She had everyone's ears. All these doctors with all of their years of school and degrees, all listening to her."

Anne's flow section eventually garnered international interest. An entire NATO delegation flew in from Africa to learn about her work. The lead health officer for one country sat in Anne's lab listening with rapt attention as she talked. He was taken with her passion, impressed with her easy grasp of this new technology, and dazzled by her human touch. Later in the day, that same lead health officer quietly offered Anne a job. A big job. To come live in his country and help build and run its own flow cytometry lab. It would have meant a big raise, perhaps even a taste of wealth, and certainly some medical acclaim.

Anne was beyond flattered, but she couldn't imagine living that far from her family, and what really gave her a sense of pride wasn't a paycheck or even having studies printed in magazines. What the health officer had failed to witness was what occurred each morning and late afternoon when Anne walked in and out of this army medical hospital's front doors. What happened then is what made this home impossible to leave.

I I

Anne surely qualified to park in one of the handicapped spots up front at her work, but she never applied for a placard. She didn't consider herself disabled. So even in the winter, Jeff parked in the closest regular space, grabbed her crutches from the back of the truck, and walked them around to her door just as

I used to before he arrived. Anne took the crutches and carefully swung her feet forward in case any ice was hidden under the snow, slowly making her way toward the hospital's doors. Jeff worried, but she summarily dismissed any offers to help, and he knew better than to press. It took her an extra minute or two to make it to the entrance, but make it she did—with a little grin and a tip of the chin that said, "I told you so."

The hospital's automatic doors swished open, sending a blast of warm air to greet them as they stepped inside. Jeff gave my mom a kiss. "I'll see you in the break room for lunch."

"See you there!" she replied.

And off he went to the transfusion services area where he worked.

Anne now had a lobby and a long linoleum hallway to navigate to get to her laboratory, but first she sized up the other early risers filling the lobby's chairs. Walter Reed was a center for rehabilitation, known for its orthopedic work with the toughest cases: double, triple, and quadruple amputees. So the lobby, which was set up more like a coffee shop than an entryway, was already filled with impossibly young soldiers, many in wheelchairs, most missing limbs or with severe burns on their faces, arms, and bodies. These were the brave young men and women who had been injured in battle or training in the course of protecting our country.

As was often the case, one of the young men quickly wheeled past my mother, working his chair with the one arm he had left, headed for the front doors she'd just come through. Anne threw him a familiar, if not judgmental, look, and he grimaced.

"You know you shouldn't be doing that," Anne said.

"It's the last one, ma'am." He was headed outside to smoke.

"You promise this time?"

"Cross my heart, ma'am," he shouted back, not meaning it.

"If you won't do it for your own mom, do it for me."

That actually got a laugh out of the young man.

Anne started swinging her way through the lobby. More than a few of the young men smiled or shouted a "Mornin', ma'am!" Again, as was often the case, a young man with no legs sitting in a wheelchair offered to help her with her bag, a little flirtation hidden in his cordiality.

"I've already got a husband, sir."

"Bet I outrank him, ma'am."

Anne stopped and flashed a cold smile. "I don't need your help with my bag, sir. But when you're ready to get up out of that chair, feel free to come to my lab, and I'll show you how to work a pair of crutches the way a woman likes to see them worked."

"Yes, ma'am," he said with a little more color in his cheeks than before.

As she disappeared down the hall on her own crutches, I'm convinced those brave soldiers felt a bit more hope that some sort of joy and accomplishment might live beyond the tragedies that had robbed their bodies of mobility or reshaped their skin. And as Anne made her way to her laboratory doors, I know that privately she was beaming.

Anne had written letters to young soldiers in Vietnam from her own hospital beds as a little girl. She had ventured out on crutches to vote in every election as a young woman. Were it not for her physical state, she likely would have signed up for military service herself to protect the nation she loved. Her job at Walter Reed was how she served her country now, and by showing up and being tough, proud, and visible with her own crutches and braces, she'd become the queen of the lobby. She knew it. She loved it.

As esteemed as Walter Reed Army Medical Center was to the outside world, those in the know were well aware that it wasn't in the best condition. The story would land in the news in the years to come and hit the army's reputation hard, a mark of shame for how the U.S. government was treating its heroes. For now, though, the disrepair simply meant that the ceiling in Anne's lab leaked, and that sometimes the water came raining down so hard that the staff had to cover her instruments in plastic to keep them dry and safe.

One morning, as Anne made her way into her lab, she had no way of knowing that the night before, so much water had leaked down that the overhead lights were no longer working. That became clear as soon as she tried the switch just inside the door. Fortunately, she knew the space well enough that she didn't need the overheads to get to her desk and its lamp. But what she also had no way of knowing was that the floor had turned into a lake overnight. A few steps in and her crutch tip hit the water. Her crutch slipped forward and across her body, sending her legs in two different directions. With no muscles to correct their fall, they split apart in gruesome, unnatural fashion, sending her body crashing down. Her face hit the cold, wet floor incredibly hard.

The pain was immediate, excruciating, and unbearable—and for my mom that really meant something. Hot ribbons of hell shot all the way up and down her left leg and spine. Her chin, which already bore the scars of so many such falls, was now throbbing. It took all her will not to cry out for help, but she didn't. Somehow, she managed to get herself up off of the floor under her own strength.

But here's the miraculous part. Anne worked the entire day, her face and leg slowly turning red, then blue, purple, and black. She even had to walk over to the auditorium to attend a lunchtime lecture. She sat fidgeting through the useless talk, her leg throbbing, never telling anyone, never complaining, and never calling Jeff for help.

When Jeff came down to her lab at the end of the day, he saw her sitting on a chair, perfectly still—too still. He asked her what was wrong.

"I hurt my leg," she told him in a whisper. "I'm in a lot of pain."

"Okay, we're going to go to the emergency room," he said.

"Not here. I don't want to go here."

He pushed her to, but she refused. She only wanted his help getting back to her feet. He knew he was bound to lose this fight, so he gave in and helped her up. The pain shot down her leg and spine all over again. She pushed it back as best she could to keep him from insisting on the emergency room again. "Let's go."

As she walked down the long hallway and into the lobby on her crutches and her own two legs, she put on her bravest cheerful face and waved goodbye to all her boys. "See you tomorrow, Annie!" one shouted.

"See you tomorrow, sir!" she shouted back as if nothing in the world were wrong.

"You take good care of her, sir," one shouted at Jeff.

Jeff wasn't as good at playing along. He was damn worried about her. But he knew he'd be in trouble if he gave up her truth, so he smiled and nodded back.

Anne made her way to the front doors, clenching her teeth to bear the pain. She knew she was those boys' hope, and she knew how valuable and necessary that hope was, so she wasn't about to be taken through the lobby in a cast or a wheelchair and jeopardize any of it. Instead, she put on the best act of her life and walked out brave and strong. The minute she got into Jeff's truck, she broke down in tears.

Over an hour later, at an emergency room in Virginia, Jeff had to pick Anne up and put her on the X-ray table as she cried out in pain. It turns out that in addition to all of the bruising, she had broken her femur, and it wasn't just any old break: she had broken it in half, the bone turned and twisted. The X-ray was horrifying. The femur is one of the hardest, most painful bones to break, and not only had she snapped it, she had walked on it all day.

Today, Jeff still believes that Anne could have filed a lawsuit against the hospital and won big. "It was a problem the hospital knew about, there were no signs for that wet floor, and this had been going on for months, if not years. But she wouldn't file that lawsuit."

Anne told Jeff she didn't want to sue because she didn't want to get the people at the hospital she was so proud of in trouble. She didn't want to bring shame to her U.S. Army. And beneath all of that, she didn't want to seem weak or get any special treatment. "Someone with two working feet wouldn't have slipped like I did, Jeff." And she left it at that.

That night in the emergency room, Anne refused to let the doctors put a cast on her leg. A cast would keep her away from work for too many months. What she (and we) knew was that a cast would have put her in a wheelchair, and she was determined never to be "down there" in one of those. She tried mightily to convince the doctors that the full leg brace she already wore each day would be enough to keep her leg set.

The doctors pressed Anne harder, suggesting that she might not understand how bad the break was. But those poor doctors didn't know who they were up against. Anne stared daggers through them, and let them know in no uncertain terms: "I know my body better than you ever could. I don't want your cast, I don't need your cast, and you can stop looking at me like I'm some kind of child or idiot right this very minute, thank you *very* much." Silence. "Is that understood?"

"Yes, ma'am," the doctors said.

She never got a cast.

Instead, my tough mom would cry through the night with pain for many weeks, and get back on her feet far sooner than she should have to walk through the doors at Walter Reed again, to do her job and deliver her own brand of hope and courage to those soldiers in the lobby who she knew needed it. That's how she'd earned the title of "Queen" from the bravest GIs—those seemingly expendable young soldiers our nation's freedom depended on. And she'd be damned if she'd ever lose her title.

These soldiers, her military, and her country are what gave my mother purpose. I admired her deeply for her dedication. But come Christmas 1995, I was all too aware that her military's stance regarding my slowly slipping secret would put her in an impossible new us-versus-them position.

CHAPTER 15

Xmas Down

Marcus, Todd, and I were as invested as our mom was in the success of each Christmas. No matter how much hard living had hollowed out Marcus's cheeks, how typically teenage-rebellious Todd was becoming, or how long my rather expressive bangs were growing, we all made our way home, made fruit salad, and unabashedly indulged in every possible sentiment: the music, TV specials, handmade presents, cookies, and joyful tears. Christmas Day was our family.

And when night fell and our special day came to a close, Marcus, Todd, and I would always gather around our mom in her bed, her thin legs safely tucked out of sight under her electric blanket, and without fail, we would say these words: "This was the best Christmas ever." And we meant it, because every year, by stacking MasterCards on top of Visas, my mom somehow ensured that it was always true.

I was midway through my senior year at UCLA as Christmas 1995 threatened. With so many miles between us, I could hear my mom's growing excitement. Soon we'd be face-to-face, and she could hear all the stories of my latest adventures while looking me in the eyes. But my tales were mostly rainbow striped these days. I would have to keep them under wraps for fear of ruining our most special day. So I decided to minimize the risks by going home for the shortest time possible. Between touchdown and takeoff, I would only be with my family from Christmas Eve to the morning after Christmas. My mom was heartsick about it. But given her skills of observation, even two days would likely prove a challenging game of hide-and-seek. My secret couldn't survive more.

For my mom, this abbreviated Christmas schedule confirmed what she already suspected: that something was wrong. Since I had come out to Ryan, my twice-daily phone calls home had dwindled to every other day, then twice a week.

So on the cross-country flight from Los Angeles to northern Virginia, I tried my best to figure out what stories I could tell her in order to satisfy her curiosity. Outright lies would never work. Southern moms can sniff those out like hounds on a hunt. So how could I bend the truth just enough that she wouldn't see the twists? How could I lie by omission? Or was the best strategy just to vanish, like I'd done with such mastery in school and church?

Jeff picked me up at the airport, and we talked about additions to our old model train set and his new job as a phlebotomist as he drove me to the house. Jeff got my bag out of the back of his truck, and as I started walking toward the front door, it opened.

There was my mom, beaming, leaning forward on her crutches so her arms could freely stretch out toward me. Her hands grabbed at the air between us, gesturing for me to get wrapped up in her arms as quickly as I could. She was crying before I got to her. I can still feel her embrace, how she held me so tight, tighter than ever. I was the last son home that Christmas and I'd be the first to go, and she wasn't going to waste a single moment. But in that embrace, I wondered one thing above all else: Would she hold me this tight if she knew?

An even bigger challenge was standing right next to her: my big brother, Marcus, all six foot one of him, his rocker hair now past his shoulders. We were oil and water these days, and when I gave him a quick hug at the door that Christmas, I could smell the cigarette smoke on his Sears Auto Center work jacket, the smoke my mom refused to acknowledge. And I wondered if he, or anyone in this family, would ever be able to love or accept me for me.

I quickly put my plan into action. I utilized a chorus of "I'm exhausted"s to race through frosting cookies later that afternoon. After dinner, I hugged my mom and said, "I don't feel very good, and I still need to wrap presents" to win her dispensation to retire to my room early. She kissed me good night, and I was soon upstairs, isolated from the family I held dear, alone with my tape, wrapping paper, the few gifts I could afford, and my very big secret.

I used the same sleepy excuse Christmas morning to explain my quiet demeanor, but when I look back at photos from that day, I can't help but notice that I'm wearing a hat pulled down low like a poker player's. It must have been so obvious to my mom that I was doing everything I could to hide from them all.

Thankfully, Marcus had decided to deep-fry the turkey in the back-yard that year, and having read about all the disasters such a method might summon, everyone gave their full attention to his bubbling peanut oil in hopes of a Christmas morning explosion.

His distraction left me alone to chop up the fruit for our traditional

Christmas fruit salad. Then I raced through Christmas dinner, sharing only one story about a film editing class I was dreading, claimed exhaustion from jet lag, and was off to my room again, pleased that I had dodged any questions. If avoiding discussing anything personal or intimate with my once close family was the goal, well, I suppose you can say I was succeeding. But it felt terrible.

Up in my room, as I filled my suitcase with the many gifts my mother most certainly couldn't afford, I couldn't help but feel that in my attempt to save Christmas, I was losing the one thing that had always mattered most to me: my family.

And then I heard it, the sound I'd heard a thousand times before, the sound that had brought me comfort some days and struck terror in my heart others: *click-clack, click-clack, click-clack.* Coming closer, up the hallway, louder and louder, moving toward my room.

Even before I left for college, my mom and I used to camp out in my bedroom and talk endlessly about her work, my studies, the future, her past, and what kind of box our universe lived in. After I left home, on visits like this, we often maximized our time together by skipping sleep. I had hoped my repeated claims of exhaustion had been convincing enough to keep her away this time, but the *click-clack* of her crutches outside my door made it clear she had other plans.

There was a knock. Then three knocks. I said nothing, but the light in my room was still on and she could surely see it sneaking out from under the door.

"Lancer?"

I remained silent.

Softer: "Lancer?"

Another moment passed.

Even softer: "Are you awake, my baby?"

I couldn't bear it any longer. "I'm just packing."

She took that as an invitation and opened the door. A warm smile on her face, she stepped in and sat down on a corner of my bed, leaning her crutches behind her. She seemed so happy that I hadn't yet fallen asleep. Such an entrance wasn't unusual. In fact, it was the most normal thing that had happened this Christmas. This was what had always preceded us piling back into Jeff's truck come morning and returning to the airport, exhausted but full of new stories.

This time, though, I had no idea what to talk about, so I continued packing. My mom happily took the lead and started up a conversation about the headlines of the day. As luck would have it, the implementation of a brand-new policy that threatened to affect her military and its brave men and women was all over the front pages. It was called "Don't Ask, Don't Tell," and President Clinton was ready to sign it into law.

My heart found its all-too-familiar home in my stomach. At first, I feared that my mother's choice of topic meant she was on to me, but from her building fury over this new policy, I knew she had no idea I had a personal connection to it. To be clear, my mom wasn't angry that "Don't Ask, Don't Tell" barred openly LGBTQ people from serving in her military. Her anger was aimed at the fact that this policy let LGBTQ people serve in her military at all—even if they did manage to keep their "ailing lifestyle" completely hidden.

"How dare this president allow those kinds of people to join? Even if they do keep it quiet, it's still wrong. There is still such a thing as right and wrong in this world, Lancer."

There wasn't anything left for me to pack into my suitcase, and worried that my folding and refolding to bide time was becoming noticeably bizarre, I sat down, my back against the wall. Her feet were dangling off the bed beside me, her passionate sermon filling the room as if one of her Sunday school audiences were hanging on her every word.

"We've worked too long and too hard and made too many sacrifices to desecrate the service of so many brave men and women in our armed forces. Who does this Clinton think he is to destroy the good name of our military by filling it with sickos?!"

And on she went, growing more fervent about the possible secret inclusion of these "degenerates" we'd learned our entire lives were mentally ill, criminals, sinners, all bound for some orgiastic, eternal bonfire. But she wasn't talking about some nameless, faceless damned anymore. Now I had names for these people—faces, hearts, and stories. These were my friends.

I had never been slow to debate my mom if I disagreed with her. She had always encouraged that. Now, feeling the very first sparks of indignation, I wanted more than anything to stand up for my new friends, for Ryan, and for myself. But this time, I didn't dare to. So she took my silence as accord, and emboldened by it, she grew more passionate, more sure that these "unnatural people" shouldn't be allowed in "the greatest military in the world. Secret or not, it is a disgrace to our country's great history. How can we ask our children to dream and aspire if we set the bar this low?"

She was speaking from the heart now. Being a part of any family is what mattered most to my mom; being a part of the U.S. military family was a huge point of pride for her. She took pride in meeting the high bar the organization set despite her limitations. An attack on the sanctity of her military family was an attack on everything she valued, and these gays were not good enough, not perfect enough for the family of her highest ideals.

Even when I had chosen to stay behind in California, to go into the arts instead of becoming a mechanic or a scientist, I'd still felt close to many of my mom's conservative ideals. The idea that somehow I was inherently no longer welcome in this wider, particularly Southern, military family of Americans was heart-wrenching, particularly coming from my own mother's lips. So I tried hard to focus on the wall behind her, on a large cartoon mural I'd painted the summer before. I tried not to take my mom's words personally, but I did. My mom and I share a gift of the kind of passion that's tough to ignore. After all, we'd both been trained by the best storytellers on earth: old Southerners with Jack Daniel's on their breath, preachers leading congregations in Mormon and Baptist churches, and prophets beamed in from Salt Lake City to every LDS church on the globe. So her anger cut deep. And for the first time, I knew for certain that this thing I couldn't change about myself put me squarely outside of my mother's love.

I didn't want to come out to her that night. I wasn't ready. So I prayed. Not to any Mormon, Baptist, or Catholic God, just to God, whoever that might be. I prayed for my sensitive ears to stop hearing, for my breath to return to normal, for the burning around my eyelids to cool, for my tears to stay inside, safely hidden until this terror was over.

Those prayers weren't answered.

The edges of my eyelids began to burn hotter. That set my stomach trembling. My hands followed. And then I felt it. The tear hit my cheek before I knew it had even formed in my eye. One single tear had betrayed me. And once I felt it, there was another. Soon, decades' worth of long-held tears came tumbling out.

Then I did something quite brave: I looked up into my mom's eyes so she could see them.

The room went silent. Not a sound.

A good Southern mom can read tears like tea leaves. Right then and there, my secret was out. Her precious middle boy with his wide-open, flying saucer, blue eyes, the boy who she'd always said was put on this earth to teach her so many new things . . . he was now one of "them." He was one of those broken people.

Somehow, despite all the clues over two decades, this news came as a shock to her. And only after a long, agonizing silence—not the kind she purposefully deployed to convey disappointment, but the kind that meant she couldn't find any words—she parted her lips, her voice trembling, her eyes searching the room. "Why, my baby?"

With complete sincerity, I asked, "Why what?"

"Why would you . . . choose this?"

I sat with that question for some time and thought hard on my answer, on the most honest truth I could find. And when I tilted my chin back up, I looked to her crutches leaned against the bed behind her, and for the second time in my life, I really saw them. I looked at the braces on her thin, withered legs. I saw them clearly too, and differently now. Then I looked into her eyes, mine still shedding tears, hers now threatening to, and I acknowledged the thing we'd silently agreed never to acknowledge: "Why did you choose those?"

It took the air right out of her. Her tears fell fast and hard as she gazed down at her shrunken legs, as if she too were seeing them for what they were for the first time in decades.

It was the only time we ever openly acknowledged that she was "disabled," that she needed those crutches to survive. It was the first and last time we ever acknowledged how different she looked. How different she was. In that moment, all the pretending had vanished. For both of us. It was indescribably painful. She had no answer. She knew full well that those crutches weren't a choice. Her only choice had been to survive them. And when she looked at me again, I didn't have to tell her this wasn't a choice for me either.

Without words, I knew what she was thinking now. She was blaming herself: *How could I have done this to my precious boy? What did I do wrong?* And, *How can I ever fix this terrible problem?*

I don't remember her leaving my room that night. I think maybe the sun came up and we were still sitting there in silence. Sometimes feelings can be so raw and painful that our brains mercifully stop recording—that sweet mercy called forgetting.

What I do know is that we didn't fix anything on that trip.

The next morning, I returned to the airport in Jeff's truck, my mom sitting silently behind us. And there was a different brand of goodbye tears. It wasn't just the sadness of separation. Our most precious relationship in the world was teetering on the brink. Our tears held our mutual fear that we were losing each other to our increasingly different and divided corners of America.

And as I walked into the terminal alone, I remember the dawning realization that for the first time ever, us boys hadn't gathered around our little mom on her bed on Christmas night. That Christmas, for the first time ever, no one had said the words: "This was the best Christmas ever."

A
Hungry Jackal
Production

Produced at UCLA's school of
Theater, Film, and Television
1996

CHAPTER 16

Hungry Jackals

I

I've often felt alone in my life. Sometimes it's been a real relief from my social anxiety and shyness. But the loneliness of 1996 was different. Since college began, I'd lived to hear my mom smiling over the phone when I had any news that bordered on "good." And despite the growing chasm between us, I worked hard to impress my big brother, Marcus, and even harder to inspire my little brother, Todd. Hearing Todd's new dream of heading to college after high school put real pride in my heart. But after that Christmas, my little family of survivors, so used to being pressed together into life rafts, suddenly felt a million miles away.

By my second morning back, Ryan could tell that my bleak postholiday mood wasn't just jet lag. "Who pissed in your Cheerios?"

"Sugar Smacks," I corrected. "I'm thinking." I wanted him to leave me be.

"About?"

"I have a lot more to think about nowadays."

"Oh. Fancy UCLA thoughts. I hope I didn't just murder some earth-shattering idea." He was openly mocking me now.

"Go fuck yourself."

"Unlike you, I prefer to have others do that for me." Silence. He knew I was still a gay virgin. Still waiting for love to open that door. So that stung. He didn't relent. "Well, would you please give me a heads-up if there's gonna be another pallet of grass in our living room tonight?"

Again, he was mocking me. Just before Christmas, I'd filled our living room with rolls of grass to film an experimental short featuring a white lily being battered to death by wind and rain, with a man's deep breathing in the background. Color me artsy. Or call it what it was: I was listening to and reading far too much Morrissey and Dorothy Parker and had convinced myself that this floral horror film was an act of revolution. A month ago it had felt that way. Now I was in no mood to defend it, so I gave Ryan a quiet "There won't be."

He abandoned our usual banter. "I don't like seeing you like this."

With that warmth, I considered confessing, but I thought better of it and offered only a lie of omission. "I just miss my family . . . back home."

Ryan said nothing. He understood that missing one's mom was enough to push a mama's boy like me into the blues. Then and there, he likely began plotting how to remedy the situation, with no clue that my mom was now busy blaming herself for a long list of things that had turned me gay, including letting me climb onto Ryan's motorcycle a half decade earlier.

In the meantime, little struggles that I'd never minded began taking on water. Like parking my three-cylinder Geo Metro at UCLA. Others may have called it orange thanks to its severely oxidized paint, but I will maintain it was red to protect its honor. Problem was, the car's starter rarely worked. But it was a stick shift, and in one of our increasingly rare conversations, Marcus had taught me that if I had a friend to help push, I could get the car up to a healthy clip, pop the clutch into first gear, and the engine would roar to life. The challenge at UCLA was that I had no one to help. Suddenly sensitive to such solitude, this took on undue emotional weight as I hunted for hilly spots in Bel Air near UCLA's film school, a neighborhood with slopes just steep enough to do the job. There I would park, give the car a loving pat on the roof, wipe off the orange oxidation it kissed back with, and pray not to get a ticket in the two-hour-only zone.

Walking into the film school's halls after Christmas break, I didn't want any of my artsy classmates to know that my mom hadn't leaped from judgment to acceptance overnight when she'd learned I was gay—that she hadn't hugged me tight and professed her unconditional motherly love for her queer son. I didn't want anyone here to know that I suddenly felt like the black sheep in a family that had always been my strength.

My new film school friends didn't have a clue. We called ourselves the 4-Ds: Dustin, David, Deena, and Danny. David was Latino, gay, and certain that Annette Funicello was a goddess. Deena was a tough gal who favored overalls, and Danny was a straight guy from California with nerd glasses and a serious interest in special effects. We were misfits among misfits. We signed up for all of our classes as a pack. And on that first day back from Christmas break, my dear Geo parked, my face red from the uphill walk to campus, I put on a fake enough smile that the 4-Ds didn't wonder if anything was the matter, and together we unwittingly walked into the crap-storm that would temporarily distract me from my familial woes and help define all of my future productions to date.

I I

A young professor had recently been hired to teach one of two undergrad film editing classes. It was already clear that digital editing was the way the wind was blowing, and the school owned a handful of machines that could do it. But the rumors proved true that this new professor preferred using old-fashioned razors and tape to splice together actual celluloid. We walked in knowing we were about to spend an entire quarter (and a good bit of money most of us didn't have) taking a class focused on a skill that had no value in the film world anymore. Like teaching actual typesetting to modern graphic designers, it was nostalgic and a bit hipster before that was a thing, but the reality was that we needed jobs out of school, and this wasn't going to help. So I must admit, the 4-Ds may not have gone into this class with the most positive attitudes.

Soon it became clear that this new professor wasn't terrifically concerned about our attitudes, or much of anything beyond her own struggling films. She didn't lecture or instruct; she simply shot a short film from a script of her making and gave us all the exact same footage to edit our own versions. She was rarely around to review what we cut on the old Steenbeck editing machines, so we sliced up film (and sometimes our own fingers) and physically taped our little stories together. It may not have been terrifically practical, but it was crafty and creative, and we didn't end up hating it half as much as we'd thought we would.

I didn't especially care what grades I got at UCLA, because I knew I wasn't heading to grad school, and I was rather certain that Hollywood studio execs wouldn't be checking our GPAs before green-lighting our films one day. However, others in our class—many of whom had never seen a B in their lives—cared deeply, and for good reason: most needed top grades to win scholarships to pay for their master's degree dreams. So weeks later, when our films were turned in and grades were posted, panic swept the film department. This brand-new professor, who had paid us so little attention, had handed down Bs, Cs, and if memory serves, even worse.

The 4-Ds and the other eleven students in this class convened to discuss what might be done to remedy this calamity. First, we needed an explanation; some understanding of what had gone wrong so that we might right it. As the "quiet, sweet one" who had never made waves, and who had far less riding on the professor's inexplicable Bs and Cs, I was elected to show up for her office hours and extract any information that might help us rectify the situation.

I arrived early for her office hours, expecting to take a seat on the 1950s linoleum floor outside her small office on the second floor of the theater building. Instead, she was already inside, and a bit bewildered to have a visitor. It seems I was the first student to have ever stopped by. Initially, her youthful appearance—her untamed blond hair and baggy, relaxed dress—eased my nerves. She seemed like the type of person who would prove flexible and understanding. I thought I could help her see these grades from our perspective, and find a path forward that wouldn't jeopardize anyone's future.

I sat down in the plastic chair beside the leather one that she'd pulled up close in front of her cluttered desk. She said she was working on a project of her own, a documentary. I was genuinely interested, but she wasn't in the mood to share details. Small talk dispensed with, and thinking I had little to fear, I dove in, explaining that without reviews of our work, we had been surprised by the grades she'd posted and were left wondering what it was we'd done to deserve such marks. Then, of course, I asked if there was anything that might help our edits earn better grades.

My words likely came out more stilted than that. I was just a kid, nowhere near becoming a speech-maker or debater. And before I could even complete my thought, I saw her transform. Her lovely, youthful face began to turn red. Lines appeared where none had been moments before as she furrowed her brow and pressed her lips together tight. I was in trouble.

She opened her mouth, and raged. According to her, the 4-Ds-plus-eleven were untalented, entitled, petulant children who should have considered themselves lucky to have gotten the grades she'd assigned. She didn't want a discussion—she wanted me out of her office immediately—but she made it clear that this wasn't over. "Your behavior in this meeting violates the rules of this university, so now you'll face the consequences." Nowhere in my usually adept worst-case-scenario imagination had I seen this coming. She was threatening a hearing that could end in my expulsion on the grounds of grade coercion, and she didn't want to hear another word about it. "You can leave now."

I left her there alone in her office, still red-faced and raging. She had never had a film succeed in the real world, and it seemed to me that her insecurity had bred contempt for her students, students who showed real promise and had their entire lives and careers ahead of them. It's a tough thing to say, but she was a terrible teacher— a mountain of anxiety and self-loathing she chose to aim our way, and now I was enemy number one.

On the long walk back to my car, I kept rewinding the tape of that conversation. Where had I gone wrong? What had I said to spark such a reaction? How could I fix this? I'd risked so much to get here, I'd worked so hard to stay here, and now I might be expelled for poorly chosen words in a meeting I had been sure would be healing, not inflammatory. Perhaps I could apologize, but I couldn't figure out what I might apologize for and mean it. What if my fake apology was unmasked and it only angered her more?

I was so lost in thought that I hadn't bothered to pay my car any attention. When I lifted the door handle, the door wouldn't open. I looked down to see that the entire side of my red/orange beauty had been bashed in so severely that my door would never open again. Someone had run into it at high speed, leaving streaks of white paint up and down her side. I checked under the wipers for a note explaining who had done this and how they intended to make it right. Nothing. I could barely afford the legal minimum of insurance. I knew that didn't cover hit-and-run situations. I walked around to open the passenger door and climbed over the hand brake to the driver's seat. Tears fell, and I gave swearing a try: "Fucking *fuck off*!" Who were these people who didn't give a damn how they affected others? I sat there raging, wrapping every offender into one: my half-rate professor threatening the only thing I had left of meaning, my education, and the big white monster truck that had plowed into the only thing I had of earthly value, my crappy Geo Metro.

My mother had once described this city as filled with more ambitions than care, more aspirations than morals, and more ego than love—charges I fiercely decried in my first years in Los Angeles. Now it seemed that despite so much talk about helping this or that charitable cause, my mom was mostly right, the overriding care in Hollywood was to get ahead of everyone else, with little mind to who got clobbered while getting there. The brand of compassion often peddled here suddenly felt like cheap talk, and despite their own faults, I hungered for the neighborly love of my old church and neighborhood—where if a family went broke, anonymous envelopes of cash appeared in the mailbox, and if a kid wrecked his bike, the neighbors all ran out to help patch him up. An America where you'd walk on broken legs to give others hope.

I stopped crying. I stopped trying to find the right words to apologize with, and I told myself I would meet that young professor at her damned hearing if she was bold enough to call one. With the school's esteemed dean acting as judge and executioner, I would hear her out, and then do my best to take her self-serving pseudo-justice down.

III

A hearing date was set, and a painful week crept by. The 4-Ds felt for me, as did the other eleven editing students, but I didn't want their pity or advice. Like my mom, when I get angry, I get quiet, so I kept to myself.

When the big day came, I made my way to the dean's office. He had taught my favorite class to date: the Stylistic Study of the Moving Image. He knew every film that had ever reached a darkened hall. In addition to being dean, he ran UCLA's film archive, its only rival being the Library of Congress. When he had generously invited all of his students to a Q&A with a "couple of his filmmaking pals" at the Academy of Motion Pictures Arts and Sciences in Beverly Hills, we were all bowled over that his pals were guys named Martin Scorsese, Steven Spielberg, and Bernardo Bertolucci. Our dean was our hero; now I was here to defend myself against being kicked out of his film school.

A handful of other teachers joined this meeting, which quickly took on the feel of a court proceeding. I had arrived first and sat with my back to the wall. The professor walked in last, looking smug, and laid out booklets, manuals, lists of rules, and stacks of supporting materials. She'd come armed with evidence but refused anyone eye contact. I got the sense this wasn't the first time she had created such a dramatic scene, and she knew well how to slay it. I won't lie: my palms were sweaty, and I had to remind myself to breathe. I had passed out a year before during a routine doctor's visit when I'd forgotten to breathe, and I didn't want that to happen here . . . or did I? Might that garner enough pity from these professors that they would keep me on? I had never faced anything like this. I was reeling.

With a wizardly old huff, the dean got right to it, letting the professor go first. She explained that she had entered her grades into the computer system and they had been printed up by a staff member and posted on the bulletin board outside the equipment room like every other professor's for every other class. She then described how I showed up without having scheduled a meeting and proceeded to object to how she ran her class and the grades she had handed out. Her death blow: that I had demanded explanations of her grades, grades that UCLA's policy plainly stated were hers and hers alone to choose, and that I had made it clear that I felt the grade I had earned ought to be changed. It was obvious that she had practiced this presentation. She was determined not to lose this fight.

The dean was as impressed as I was. He turned to me and said,

"Well, that doesn't sound so good, Dustin. Is there anything you'd like to add?"

This was it. If I screwed the next minute and a half sideways, everything I'd worked for over the past half decade or more would be out the window. So I took a deep breath and asked the professor the two questions I'd been practicing all week.

Question one: "What grade do you believe I wanted?"

It was clear she hated the sound of my voice. In a tone I can best describe as the devil's after smoking two packs a day, she said to me, "You think you deserved an A."

I steeled myself and met her eyes.

Question two: "And what grade did you give me?"

I'll never forget the next few moments. Her raging, confident glare turned inward. Her eyes were still looking my way, but they had lost all focus; she was too busy searching her mind for an answer. Silence. More silence. Then, a few awkward moments later, the dean cleared his voice to snap her back into the present.

The professor finally looked down, then started digging through the mountain of evidence she had painstakingly prepared to have me reprimanded if not expelled, but she struggled to find the answer to this simple second question. When she finally did, she went as white as that lily I'd destroyed in my experimental film.

She began gathering her things, then launched up out of her chair and declared to the room, "You are all a pack of hungry jackals!" With that, she stormed out.

She had given me an A.

I wisely held my tongue. I'd known all week what the dean was now realizing: that I could have gone back to her office a week earlier and fixed this problem in private, but I had chosen this very public path instead. Now I wondered if this little show would also earn me some form of censure. The first hint to the contrary was a bit of laughter that escaped from under the dean's beard. His final ruling quickly followed: he gripped me by the shoulders and said, "I like you . . . You're a real troublemaker."

I had never been called such a thing in my life! I had always been the easy kid, the well-behaved kid, the quiet kid, the kid who would far prefer to disappear than to cause trouble. Now, according to the most powerful man in this esteemed institution—a man who I would later learn had toiled in the antiwar movement, had put himself on the line to defend his peace-loving views—I was a bona fide "troublemaker"! Coming from him, and given these circumstances, I didn't mind the sound of that one bit. On the contrary—I loved it.

Not wanting to push my luck, I hightailed it out of there. As I walked to my car, I considered this new label. It wasn't Los Angeles or the film business that had turned me into a troublemaking twenty-year-old. No. It was my mom, who had often told me to "stand up straight and tall." Her conservative values, and even the lessons from her Mormon Church, had taught me that you don't hang an innocent man at high noon, and that good folks stick up for themselves. Now I wanted more than anything to call my mom and share this win, to let her know that I had finally fought back and in tough Texan fashion, but I didn't. I couldn't. I was too afraid I'd be met with the sound of disappointment and the silence of unasked questions.

Instead, I opened the passenger door of my Geo, crawled over the hand brake, and settled into the driver's seat. I sat there very still for some time. I began to imagine a line, drawn from a shy child quietly standing up for his mother in shopping malls to a young man learning to stand up for himself, and I then imagined that perhaps one day I might grow bolder, and answer a call to stand up for more than just myself and my mom. Because I now understood that good things could come from making the right kind of trouble. And from this moment on, I knew I had it in me to embody the noble title of "troublemaker."

Later that year, when all of the faculty—that young editing professor among them—were required to watch and review our senior thesis films, the 4-Ds decided we'd build a logo that looked a lot like a drooling jackal. And we wrapped up all of our closing credits with this image and a title card that read: "Hungry Jackal Productions." Thanks to that editing professor, we were now and forever a pack of hungry troublemakers.

CHAPTER 17

Spinning Yarn

Where I grew up, spinning yarn, or telling stories—with or without two shots of whiskey (but often better with)—held the power to entertain, illuminate, bring families together, to give us poor kids some pride in our own, and maybe even a much-needed dose of courage. My Sunday school teachers had spun stories of Mormon pioneers making their way to Salt Lake City in covered wagons, chased by murdering militias wielding skin-scalding tar and feathers. At family reunions, my uncle James told the tale of my young mom making her way up a mountainside on crutches and braces. Each time, the mountain got steeper, and my mom moved up it a bit faster. Those storytelling lessons were reinforced when I shadowed playwrights at the Western Stage in my teens, studied English and Russian literature at community college, and fought my way into one of the best schools for stories told on screen. Since discovering the theater in junior high in San Antonio, I had begun to hope that "spinning yarn" might one day even pay my bills.

But entering my senior year at UCLA, I still wasn't sure what kind of stories I might tell. I was drawn to the likes of Fellini, Bertolucci, Scorsese, and Truffaut, but I wasn't Italian or French, or from any sort of gangster background. The films I had directed so far could best be described as experimental, impressionistic, and a touch too retro. After all, the French New Wave hadn't been "new" for nearly half a century now. When I showed my short films to friends, family, and professors, the most common response was, "Well, that was . . . wow." They never said "good" or "moving" or "funny" or even "special"—just "wow."

And thanks to that young professor who'd tried to get me kicked out of film school and had now made her way onto the scholarship committee, I wasn't going to see a dime from the long list of finishing grants when my diploma came. I was dead broke. I was a film-splicing yarn spinner from Texas with a week to go in film school and no hope of turning my interests into a paycheck.

But as troubling as it was to be dead broke, there was one more pressing concern on my mind. It sounded like this: *click-clack, click-clack, click-clack.*

Even with an apartment full of rowdy twentysomethings, and

standing in the far corner of our second-story kitchen, I could hear that sound coming up from the street. My mom had bought a ticket, boarded a plane in Virginia, and flown to L.A. to attend my college graduation the next day. We had shared a few careful phone calls over the last six months, but this would be the first time I'd seen her since Christmas.

I wiped the crumbs and butter from our garlic bread assembly line off my hands and rushed to open the door before anyone beat me to it. There were now three of us living together: me, Ryan, and a dashing, openly gay Spanish theater major named Javier. His nickname was Javi. Javi and Ryan had organized a little dinner party—a tame one compared to the kind Ryan normally threw, because he had specifically designed this one for my mom. Since the morning of our sullen post-Christmas breakfast, Ryan had worried that something dire had gone down over the holiday, and since he adored my mother, he hoped this warm reception might help mend things. Javi had heard many a story about my mom and was excited to finally meet her. If it seems as if my friends saw nothing challenging about my mom's arrival, it's because they didn't. To deny them this dinner party would have given them reason to press for the whole truth, and I didn't want to tell them that my own mom didn't accept me for who I was, mostly because I didn't want that to be true. So I copped out. I never told them how my mom had reacted when she'd discovered my secret. Ryan had no clue that she was privately pointing a bit of blame his way. And there was one other complication: I also hadn't told my mom that most of Javi's, Ryan's, and my own close friends were gay or lesbian.

So the moment before I opened the door for her, I could almost hear my big brother, Marcus, say to me, "Hey, chickenshit. Say goodbye right this fuckin' second to the last bit of love you'll ever get from yer mom. 'Cause she's gonna disown your ass after this."

I opened the door, and all of my many gay and lesbian friends laid eyes on the woman who, unbeknownst to them, thought they lived somewhere along a sliding scale of sick, wrong, and evil. *Your lack of courage built this moment, and now you must live it,* I thought.

What we called a dinner party was actually just a mess of teen and twentysomething college kids, dropouts, and party gays sitting on the floor with paper plates mounded high with overboiled spaghetti, canned pasta sauce, white bread with butter and garlic salt, and a surprisingly delicious salad Ryan had pulled together. I gave my mom a hug, put her bag in my room, and cleared a spot for her on the futon. She was quick to compliment Ryan on the weight he'd lost, but she willfully ignored his new tattoos, and completely missed that I had obviously (to me at least) spent a great deal of time in the gym since December. It was forgivable, I suppose. Jason—who was also in our apartment that fateful night—hadn't noticed either.

Instead of sitting with my mom, I retreated to the kitchen to help cook. That way I could keep a safe distance as it dawned on my mom that her queer son now surrounded himself with countless other homosexuals, and not just straight-acting ones—vibrant, colorful, pink-triangle-wearing, rainbow-flag-waving queens with proud lisps, and a handful of lesbians in Doc Martens. I tried to look as believably busy as I could, checking the spaghetti that had passed al dente many minutes ago, and stirring a pot as if it would make any difference to the dented can of sauce I'd picked up off the clearance shelf.

Ryan brought a plate to my mom and they talked for a moment. Ryan was warm. She was polite. But I could tell she was uncomfortable. Ryan soon gave up and moved on to other conversations. It broke my heart to witness.

From the kitchen, I watched my mom sitting alone on my futon now. I could see her disappointment settling in. So much of how I'd lived my life had been designed to impress her, to let her know that her hard work raising us hadn't been in vain. But I could see her using my "new condition" and all of my new friendships as evidence to erase the list of maternal accomplishments she'd long held dear. I had been her pride and joy. She'd told me so. Now all of that seemed to be evaporating.

She didn't sit alone for long. My mom had always been a magnet. People loved to talk with her, tell her their stories, and share their fears and joys with her. Partly it was her laugh, her smile. Folks could tell she was listening, engaging. Partly it was her tears. She was quick to those. Folks could tell she cared. Partly it was her good old-fashioned Southern nod. She could nod, and nod, and nod, even when someone went on, and on, and on. She could nod you to death and you wouldn't even know it; you'd just think she loved your story like none other. It's a particularly Southern mother's skill, and she was a master at it.

My friends approached her one by one, sat beside her, and started asking her questions. A small circle began to form; then it grew. And when it did, my heart dropped like a lead fishing weight. As I washed the saucepot for the third time for no reason, I realized that because I'd said nothing to my friends about my mom's reaction to my being gay, they just assumed this dinner party meant she had no problem with our kind. They assumed my mom was forward-thinking, open-minded, and dare I say: a liberal. Thanks to my cowardice, they assumed my Jack Mormon, military, Texan mom loved and accepted her gay son.

Here's the thing: this was still well before *Brokeback Mountain* broke hearts, and way before *Will & Grace* and *Ellen* won them. For a mom—especially one with my mother's background—to accept her gay son in this way at this time would have been huge. So now my friends were looking at her like she was some kind of queer-loving Mother Teresa. *Holy fire and balls,* I thought.

When they were done listening to her harrowing tale of traveling to "this big, loud city" that morning, they took the opportunity to share their own stories. They told her where they were from—cities and towns across the country, including those in our treasured South, where some had been kicked out of their homes when they came out. How they had made their ways to Los Angeles to become refugees in a sunny city where they might not freeze to death at night if they couldn't find a job and a home. Some told stories of the Christmases they'd missed, of the families they hadn't spoken to in years, of birthdays with no phone calls and phone calls that went unanswered. These stories weren't uncommon back in the 1990s. Depending on what part of the country or faith one hailed from, they were the norm. My new friends and I had simply grown so used to hearing such tales that they hardly affected us anymore. It's who we were. Such rejections felt like a necessary trial in the initiation into our tribe.

I watched in horror as my mom did what she did best. She nodded. She acted like she was listening without judgment. I had seen her do it so many times before. When a "priesthood holder" at church would try to teach her something she understood far better than he ever would, she would simply nod. When a drunk army boy would spin a yarn of heroism at a lobster boil, she would nod as if believing every detail. When Marcus would tell her he was on the mend, no more smoking, drinking, or drugs, she would nod, and try her best to believe him. And there she was, nodding again, but my friends couldn't read her nods like I could. They thought she was actually listening, that she actually cared and felt for them, that she wasn't mentally damning them all to some lonely hell. So they just kept talking . . . and talking . . . and talking.

As the night grew long, the wine in the bottles got low, and with the courage of booze and the comfort of her bobbing head, my pals veered into more personal territory. They started asking my mom for dating advice, then sharing their own stories of romance and missed connections, and when she kept nodding, they pressed on, telling my good Southern mom about their breakups, their heartbreaks, their make-out sessions in bathroom stalls of gay nightclubs; a lesbian couple explained how scissoring worked, and an older gay friend described the unique challenges of gay hygienics. I wanted to vanish. Correction: vanishing could have meant reappearing. I wanted to die.

Knowing this would have been a bit much for any parent, Ryan and Javi did what I wished I could have and sought the safety of their respective rooms. Busying myself with cleaning, I watched my friends begin to leave one by one and two by two, many to get ready for our graduation the next day, others to hit the gay clubs, all saying goodbye to my mom with a kiss on her cheek, a saucy wink, and for more than a few, a heartfelt hug to thank her for listening to them with such compassion. Little did they know.

Soon it was just my mom and me in the apartment's small living room. With the echo of traffic outside bouncing off our bare wood floors, the paper plates and plastic cups still strewn here and there, the absolute lack of grown-up furniture, and my little mom perched on my futon, the space suddenly felt cavernous and cold. She let me pick up the last of the mess, then patted the spot next to her. She wanted me to sit down with her. It wasn't a request. It was a demand.

My mom was rarely at a loss for words. She had long flirted, reached out, intimidated, and even moved mountains with them when her body couldn't. But now, save for her clearing her throat a few times, she couldn't find a sound to fill this void, and we just sat silently beside each other.

Finally, she said: "I met your friends." I felt sure that she wanted me to read every bit of her disdain in that one sentence, and to apologize then and there.

"Yeah. I know," I said, hoping that was enough of an apology and we could get on with not talking about anything else that mattered.

"They seem nice."

"Yeah," I said. Again, I meant it as an apology. How long was she going to drag this out?

We sat there for another silent minute, my guts tying themselves in knots. I imagined she was somewhere between tears and fury too, ready to lash out and damn Ryan, Javi, and all our new friends to some everlasting hell or to beg me to enter into some arcane, scientifically disproven therapy to change this terrible "choice" she thought I'd made, to get me off this path she wrongly believed Ryan had led me down. I was on the verge of losing it, of screaming or leaving, but instead she said this: "I met the actor, or . . . writer, who you write scripts with."

Oh God. Right. Jason had been there that night, and I had hardly even noticed. The truth is, I was more enamored than ever, though he still couldn't be bothered to care.

"Right. Yeah. I know the one you mean," I told her. This was torture.

"Well . . . ," she said, then stopped.

"Well . . . ," I said, then stopped.

"Well . . . I told him that the next time he went out with my son, he might think about treating my baby boy with a little more . . . warmth. And he's older, isn't he? So I hope you don't mind, but I also told him that when he finally does wise up and take you out on a proper date, well . . . that he should pay."

I dared not trust my ears. I dared not look at her in case I had just imagined her words. So we sat in silence again, both of our eyes welling up. Hell, mine are welling up right now just writing this down two decades later.

Then my mom mustered the courage to turn and show me her eyes, so I turned and showed her mine. We looked at each other like that for as long as we could . . . about one second. Then she wrapped her arms around me and held me tighter than I think I'd ever been held. At least that's how it felt then to my heart and now in my memory. And she didn't let go.

I knew right then and there that for the first time in my life, my mother was holding me for me, all of me, and that she not only loved me with all of her heart but also loved me for all of mine.

In that embrace, in that moment, I suddenly felt stronger than I ever knew I could be: more courageous, liberated, seen, and loved. Her embrace that night lit a fire that would change the course of my life.

But how and why had her feelings so suddenly changed?

Because yarn had been spun.

What I thought had been less than worthless—our gay lives; our stories of tribulation, loneliness, and loss—had been spun into pure gold in that room that night. For the very first time in her life, my mom had heard actual personal stories from gay and lesbian people while she looked them in their eyes and gauged their truth. Those stories had little to do with statistics, activism, movements, politics, law, or the Constitution. My friends didn't think she needed to hear those stories. They thought she was already on our side. If they had known she was some enemy of equality, they likely would have dug their trenches deep and entered into heady debates armed with numbers and scientific and legal jargon. Instead, they talked to my mom like she was family, not a person from some "other America." They told their stories with open hearts—universal stories of family, love, and loss. And in one night, those stories set straight generations of myths and distortions. They erased every lie told by our church, our country, our own treasured families back home; by my mom's friends, her noble military, and our good neighbors. In one night, I witnessed generations of my mom's hand-me-down misconceptions be replaced with love, understanding, and acceptance. In one night. Thanks to storytelling.

I wish I could say that I had planned the night, but I hadn't. Ryan had. Its outcome was an accident. But thanks to this happy accident, I learned the value of speaking to the heart from the heart. I witnessed the absolute and undeniable power of the personal story.

The next morning, I donned my cap and gown, shook my troublemaking dean's hand before throwing him a wink, and graduated from UCLA's School of Theater, Film and Television. It was an impossible dream come true for me and for my mom. I was the first in our immediate family to get a college degree. Perhaps her childhood doctors had been right that she would never get one herself, but now her son had, and so she added this to her long list of maternal accomplishments, a list that had somehow survived the past six months and could now grow long and strong again.

I wouldn't get a job writing or directing films right away. They don't hand those out with film degrees. Instead, I would serve a lot of orange juice over the next few years, wearing an impossibly tight black T-shirt and short shorts at a rather gay West Hollywood breakfast and lunch spot. It was the same restaurant Jason worked at, where we knew all too well that if we let the men flirt, our tips would grow, and that was money we could put toward our films.

After a long day of work and one very long night of trying and failing to write something of merit together, Jason said I was free to stay the night. I lived far away, we'd had a glass or two of wine, and it was very late. So I climbed into his bed. It was big enough that we didn't have to touch. I lay there sleepless, perfectly still, minutes turning into an hour, not wanting to miss a moment of how close I was to my heart's desire. Then I felt his hand touch my body. Over that long hour, he had slowly, imperceptibly, been inching closer. I felt his breath on my cheek, and over the course of many more minutes, as if locked in slow motion, I turned my face toward his. Then, in the most loving way possible, Jason kissed me. I repeat: *he* kissed *me*. I'm not kidding.

That night a whole host of other things transpired, with varying degrees of success. I won't describe them here because my mother wouldn't want me to, but let me tell you this: it was all far better and more right than I'd ever hoped or dreamed. And Jason did take me out on a proper date soon after, and he did pay. Even better, a week or two later, he cooked me a homemade dinner: tortellini alla vodka. Years after I had fallen for him, Jason became my very first boyfriend. I still adore and admire him, and without giving too much of his privacy away, I'll say that more than a few aspiring young filmmakers in Hollywood these days likely call him "sir." Turns out I had good taste. This handsome old charmer now helps run a major TV studio.

Thanks to that night of pasta, salad, and stories, I began to find my voice. If personal stories had the power to change hearts like they had my own mom's, and if changing a heart had the power to change a mind, then how could I turn away from such lifesaving power? I couldn't. From that night on, I knew what I was called to do. I wasn't put here to re-create the French New Wave in the year 2000. No, sir. I was here to help tell the personal stories of diverse people who are treated differently under the law and by their neighbors because of their differences. Because that's what I knew. That's where I was from. It was in my bones. And by sharing such stories, maybe I could help move the needle for a group of people who truly needed that— a people I was fast coming to see as new family members, my LGBTQ family. I felt called to this new kind of mission the way the South and our church had taught me to defend our own, and to fight for my mother and brothers.

That's what Hungry Jackal Productions would become: not just a middle finger to a teacher watching our senior thesis films, but a production company with a philosophy; a troublemaking machine built to try its damnedest to move the needle toward understanding, compassion, and greater social justice for people of diversity. I had learned from great masters of yarn spinning, and now I was determined to use those skills to spin gold out of all of the lives and loves that had been made invisible for too long.

CHAPTER 18

Milk Calls

I

```
INT. SAN FRANCISCO APARTMENT - MORNING / 2008

A CELL PHONE rings on a COFFEE TABLE. In no big hurry, a
blond, youngish-looking WRITER, 30, finishes pulling on
JEANS, then a warm COAT. The call goes to VOICE MAIL. He
seems relieved. He looks at the phone. He's missed three
calls from this number this morning.
```

Somewhere in the eight years after I graduated from UCLA, I got up the guts to come out to Marcus and Todd in a bar in Wildwood, New Jersey. Two shots each of Crown Royal, and neither seemed too concerned. In that time I also came out to my once Special Forces military stepfather, and he just gave me a big supportive hug. It's a surprising truth to some, but genuinely straight guys rarely give a damn if someone is gay. Less competition for them, right? It's more often closet-cases who act on and/or vocalize the self-loathing homophobia that lives in their conflicted heads.

In that time, I also wrote countless scripts that went unread by anyone of influence. Then, after self-financing two documentaries with high-interest credit cards and parading them around film festivals, I landed a real job: directing and producing episodes of a reality TV show for TLC and the BBC called *Faking It*. Now I had checks coming in—not big ones, but big enough to attract an agent happy to take a percentage. That agent was now obligated to read my scripts. Thanks to him and the venerated, openly gay director Paris Barclay seeing value in one, I got my first paid union writing gig. It was exactly what I was looking for—a biopic for MTV and VH1 about the gay, HIV-positive activist Pedro Zamora. I flew to Miami, met Pedro's friends and family, and wrote a script that I hoped would inspire others to activism. It was happening. I was beginning to share LGBTQ stories with the world, at least on the small screen.

But what mattered most to film industry folks was that I was now

a member of the Writers Guild of America—a "working writer"—
and with that label came an even bigger opportunity. HBO had just
green-lit a new TV series about polygamist Mormons called *Big
Love*, and I was one of the only writers in Hollywood who had been
raised Mormon and was willing to share the details. Despite my short
résumé, my Mormon roots made me valuable enough to land a staff
writer position on what would become a hit HBO show. I spent the
next few years sharing what it was like to be LDS—yes, the dietary
requirements, the clothes, the homophobia, and the misogyny, but
on more than one occasion, I found myself in the unexpected position of having to defend my childhood faith. On long calls each night
with my mom to confirm old church memories, I was occasionally
reminded of the little things I missed about it.

Employing the LDS thrift I'd learned as a kid, I soon had the
required down payment and good credit to buy my first home. It was
a cozy nine-hundred-square-foot, two-bedroom bungalow in the
Hollywood Hills with a terraced backyard. Sitting up there at night,
I could hear the concerts at the Hollywood Bowl. It was a dream
come true. And although this milestone had taken nearly a decade
to achieve, I was branded an overnight success by LGBTQ magazines like *The Advocate*. I was grateful, but I wasn't satisfied. As suddenly successful as I may have seemed from the outside, I was far
from satisfied writing on a polygamist-themed drama series. I didn't
just want a paycheck; I wanted to make films that moved the needle,
and that was never *Big Love*'s aspiration. But with this steady HBO
job, I now had the stability and confidence to dedicate nights and
weekends away from Bill Paxton, Jeanne Tripplehorn, and our heady,
experienced *Big Love* writers' room to telling an LGBTQ story I felt
strongly had been lost for far too long. This was a story that I had
only learned of thanks to a big turn of luck fifteen years earlier—
a story that had saved my life when I first heard it in that Salinas
community theater called the Western Stage.

I I

Back in 1988, with no car to actually escape Salinas, I decided I would spend a second summer working at the Western Stage. I'd been asked if I'd like to shadow an artist in the company. I considered my options and chose a Latino director who had caught my eye with his confident swagger and style—long, colorful scarves wrapped over and around his denim overalls. But that wasn't the only reason I chose him. He was also expert in every department of our theater, and as I was increasingly interested in directing, I wanted to learn every aspect of the job. He already had a handful of other apprentices, but thankfully he agreed to take me on as well, and he quickly set out to teach us all the meaning of the word "possible."

In his strong feline manner, he circled us all, saying: "I look at some of you, and I can tell that a few already realize that anything you imagine can be made real. I look at others of you, and I can see that you don't know your own power, but that you're already exercising it, out of instinct. The rest of you, you don't know your own power at all. You're not using it. And we're going to fix that."

I immediately worried about which group he felt I was in—and I knew that this worry probably landed me in one of the latter two.

The following Monday, he padded into the theater lobby carrying a big silver boom box and a cassette tape. I don't remember anyone's having said anything homophobic, but perhaps one of us had used "gay" as a pejorative. Or maybe he could tell that at least two of us in his group might personally benefit from the words we were about to hear. Who knows? But he plugged that boom box in under the bench in the lobby, had us circle around, and before he played the tape, he offered this context:

"*This! This* is a speech by a man from New York City. But *this* was given in San Antonio. Texas! Ten years ago, when you were all just tadpoles."

That got my attention. I had once been a tadpole in San Antonio, a terribly confused tadpole swimming in Tim's aboveground pool. San Antonio had been my home when this very speech was made.

Our director hit Play. Through the static of his third-generation tape, we heard a voice:

> Somewhere in Des Moines or San Antonio, there is a young
> gay person who all of a sudden realizes that he or she is gay;
> knows that if their parents find out, they will be tossed out of
> the house; their classmates will taunt the child; and the Anita
> Bryants and John Briggs are doing their part on TV. And that
> child has several options: staying in the closet, and suicide.
> And then one day that child might open up the paper and it
> says "Homosexual elected in San Francisco" and there are two
> new options. One option is to go to California, or stay in San
> Antonio and fight. . . . You've got to elect gay people, so that
> thousands upon thousands like that child know there is hope
> for a better world; there is hope for a better tomorrow.

I swallowed my tears so they wouldn't be seen. In so many ways, I was *that* kid. This man was talking to me, about me, and from a stage in my own hometown, no less. I had already realized I was gay back when he'd delivered his speech, but with no way to hear his words, I had lived with the terror of losing my few friends and my treasured family. I had considered suicide and imagined being chased from my house. And until this moment a decade later, I had never heard someone be so confidently "out," or dared imagine there was such a thing as an "out" gay politician who had actually been elected to public office. I had always believed that being "out" was something AIDS did to gay men before they died. I thought being "out" was an unbearable situation brought on by accidental exposure or vicious attack. This man sounded downright proud about it.

Sitting there on that orange community theater carpet, the taste of salt burning down my throat, I trembled inside as my world cracked open.

I had just heard a man leading with love, not division or hate, with hope, not fear or terror, and for the very first time in my life, someone's brand of hope actually included me. The man's name was Harvey Bernard Milk. And on that day, ten years after his assassination, and thanks to this third-generation cassette tape, he had just given me hope.

Now, he didn't give me enough hope that morning to run go wrap myself up in a rainbow flag and start kissing boys, but it was enough to stop considering ending my life. And with that, I began to hide a bit less, to shrink a bit less, to start working toward my dreams again, and to quietly grow brave enough to believe that one day I might be seen as I truly am, and that when that day in the spotlight arrived, it might not be a tragedy. Harvey Milk's story was that powerful for me, and that it had taken so many turns of luck for me to finally hear it—that was a true tragedy.

III

A film project about Harvey Milk wasn't a new idea. By the time I was a writer on *Big Love,* I had watched from afar for years as a film about Milk based on the book *The Mayor of Castro Street* struggled to get made at Warner Brothers. In my film school's archive, I had also found a documentary from 1984 called *The Times of Harvey Milk,* but it was tough to locate in the real world. Few people outside of San Francisco, and almost no one my age, had ever heard of Harvey Milk. At that time, even when I'd ask LGBTQ activists and organizers, I would most often get blank stares.

It was frustrating to watch Milk's story slowly vanish. It seemed as if other minority communities knew their heroes and had seen at least some of their histories in libraries and on movie screens. They had a foundation for inspiration and hope. But save for a handful of books and films in scattered queer bookstores or niche film festivals, popularized versions of our own proud history seemed to have been stymied, buried by centuries of laws banning our lives, by the fear of repercussion for creating such work, and by concerns that shame and fear might keep gay stories from proving commercially viable.

Then something magical happened. In 2006, a composer friend

of mine told me he'd been searching for a man named Cleve Jones and had just found him in Palm Springs. I was thrilled to hear that Cleve was still alive—although he was only in his fifties, many, if not most, of the great activists of his generation were dead now thanks to AIDS. While watching his friends all disappear, and battling AIDS himself in the 1980s, Cleve had conceived the NAMES Project AIDS Memorial Quilt—a massive folk-art quilt made out of grave-size panels sewn for those whose lives had been taken by AIDS. It would eventually fill the entire National Mall in Washington, D.C. The quilt helped render this plague undeniable, and opened the hearts of Americans to their dying family members and neighbors. My friend wanted to do a rock opera about Cleve's powerful quilt. He would write the music; I would build the story.

But I had a secret secondary interest in meeting Cleve: I knew that he had been one of a handful of scrappy young Castro kids to intern for Harvey Milk in the 1970s. He had become Milk's political protégé. He knew the real Harvey Milk, and I wanted details and personal stories about this man I'd never met but whose story I felt could save and inspire more lives. A week later, we were in my friend's car headed to Palm Springs.

When I walked into Cleve's sparsely furnished home, I was struck by the smell of cigarettes and the pale gray skin of a man who looked far older than his age. His face had been ravaged by AIDS. His hands shook uncontrollably from his medications. But he wasn't weak. He was a tough, wizened survivor who spent our first hours together sizing me up. Was this blond kid up to the task of telling the story of his generation and the quilt?

Cleve pulled a chair into the living room, set an ashtray down on the floor beside it, lit up the first of dozens of cigarettes, and began answering my questions about the NAMES Project. Occasionally he would turn the tables and ask me something: where I was from, what my politics were, and what I understood about the movement. His questions weren't superficial or easy to answer, but his wasn't the first research interview of my career. I knew that the smart ones took caution with what they shared, with whom, and when.

An hour into this tennis match of an interview, the sun finally set, and my composer friend got up to pour himself a glass of wine from the three-dollar bottle we'd picked up on the way there. I seized the opportunity to ask Cleve what I really wanted to know. I asked him about Harvey Milk.

Cleve's tired eyes lit up like a boy's. "You know who Harvey Milk was?" I told him that I did. I told him how I had first heard Milk's story and the effect it had had on me. He laughed, but there were tears in his eyes. He sprung up then and there, marched into his garage, and returned with a box filled with objects and images that held his Milk memories. In the stories that followed, Cleve transformed back into the determined teenage boy who first met Harvey Milk on a street corner in the Castro in the 1970s. He began to answer all of my questions, freely and with personal detail. I was in heaven. My composer friend gave up on his quilt questions and finished one bottle of wine alone. Then the three of us went out for margaritas, and the stories kept flowing.

On our second research trip to Palm Springs, I passionately argued to both my composer friend and Cleve what was becoming patently obvious: that we ought to write a rock opera about Milk first. They both agreed.

In the research that followed, I learned a great deal about the real Harvey Milk—a very human man, not a legend: a man who failed more than he succeeded but never gave up on his dream that an openly gay man could be elected to public office. I also began to learn about what a real civil rights movement looked like: the value of diversity, of coalition building, of agitation and theatrics, and why asking for crumbs was a pathway to less than crumbs. But as I got more and more excited, my composer friend slowly stopped returning my calls. On the rare occasion I could get him on the line, he sounded faraway, strange. Eventually he would be found dead in a hotel room from a methamphetamine overdose—a brilliant, beautiful mind extinguished.

I couldn't keep moving on a rock opera without him. Despite years of Mormon-mandated piano lessons, I could hardly tap out a tune. I gazed at our half-finished outline and the two songs my friend had managed to compose, and I knew that this dream was done for.

Then a chance turn: come that winter, Bryan Singer, whose goatee was now shaved but who still donned far too much flannel, somehow landed the job of taking over Warner Brothers' Milk project. I swallowed my pride and invited Bryan to dinner at a Japanese steak house. It happened to be Valentine's Day. To be clear, Bryan was not my Valentine; I just desperately wanted to write a movie about Harvey Milk. I laid out my pitch. Bryan seemed to respond to it, and he sent me to Warner Brothers where I pitched my take again. They were interested, so they sent me to their project's longtime producers. I gave these two gay men the same spiel, but with even more details and heart. Still, despite the tears in their eyes, and my growing résumé, they told me I was too green. "The truth is, we're looking for a writer with an Academy Award, Dustin." I didn't bother offering them my more familiar name as they showed me the door. Nine months of meetings and maneuvering for nothing.

I got in my car, drove off the lot, and headed to nowhere in particular—an L.A. version of a thoughtful hike, but without the sweat. And somewhere on the 101 Freeway, with little clue as to where I was going or what it would take to go head-to-head with two of the biggest producers in Hollywood, one highly self-possessed director, and a powerful, celebrated movie studio, I told myself, "Forget those producers, screw Bryan Singer (not literally), and to hell with Warner Brothers." My rage and tears had turned into my mother's favorite brand of foolish courage. Thanks to Cleve and my research, I had now befriended many real people from Harvey's life. I still had the credit card I'd used to finance my first documentaries, and if I needed more money, I now had a home I could leverage. If I knew where an inspiring, hope-filled, lifesaving story was buried, didn't I have a responsibility to excavate it, no matter what the personal cost? Isn't that what my mother, with her broken leg and all her brave young soldiers, had taught me?

By the time I pulled into my garage, I had made a decision. I would go to war with Warner Brothers. I would quietly create a competing project—not because I felt slighted, but because thirty years after Milk's assassination, we were living in a time when the push for LGBTQ rights felt like it was stalling in the same corporate equality culture that so many other movements had gotten stuck in. This story didn't just feel hopeful and personally inspirational; it felt like a timely, necessary kick in the ass.

That Friday, production wrapped on *Big Love* and I drove to San Francisco with Cleve. We camped out in the rough and restless Beck's Motor Lodge on Market Street so we could interview more real-life folks who'd known Milk. It took a while to get most to open up: I was a new kid, and they had been let down time and time again by people from Hollywood promising to share Milk's story. I bought them dinners and wine and, hesitantly, some agreed to share their often painful memories of their friend, mentor, and father figure. I made this trip weekend after weekend, and each time, more wizened faces stepped forward with more memories. I was winning trust; now it was my job to make sure it was well placed.

Within the year, I had completed a first draft of a script. But I knew I had to be careful who saw it. I had to keep it hidden from those producers and Warner Brothers for as long as possible or risk them trying to shut me down. In that time Cleve insisted there was one person I had to show it to before anyone else: the director Gus Van Sant. Gus had directed one of my favorite movies, *My Own Private Idaho*, and a few years earlier, I'd been lucky enough to meet him at a large group dinner. Cleve had met him in the '80s when Gus was briefly hired to write a version of the Warner Brothers Milk project. Cleve found his number and called him up, and it turned out that Gus remembered me from that big dinner: "Oh. You were the blond angel who bummed smokes off Matt Damon all night." (I didn't even smoke. I just wanted to get as close to Matt Damon as often as possible that night.)

I did one last polish of the script, and drove it into the hills above Griffith Park to hand-deliver it to Gus's house. He was home. I didn't know Gus well yet, so I didn't understand that he's a man of few words. I just knew that his long silences doubled my nerves. Maybe he didn't like me. Maybe I made him uncomfortable. And as I sat at his kitchen counter, watching him flip pages in my script, saying nothing, I grew sure that this was a mistake. Then he closed the script, looked up, and said, "Yeah . . . it's good." He was in.

When the news broke in *Variety* that some young writer on *Big Love* had landed Gus Van Sant for his Milk project, I had to forward some scary emails from Warner Brothers' legal department to my tough-as-nails lawyer. But I also got a congratulatory call from the openly gay, Academy Award–winning producers of *American Beauty*, Dan Jinks and Bruce Cohen, whom I'd met at the Outfest LGBTQ film festival pool party they threw each year. When I told Dan that my only producing partner thus far was a Visa card, he and Bruce jumped on board.

Gus and I began making a wish list of actors who could play Harvey Milk, and in that search, we found several YouTube videos of none other than Sean Penn, the impossibly good-looking (and of course talented) actor from that Madonna music video that had once marked my darkest day in the closet in junior high. Sean was now giving passionate political speeches of his own, and after watching some online, we had our clear first choice.

Together with Bruce and Dan, we got the script to Sean, who it turned out called the Bay Area, Milk's old stomping ground, his home now. Sean already knew a bit about Milk, and after looking at the script, he was willing to meet. Still on our own dime, Gus and I drove up to Sean's home just north of San Francisco, where we watched a cut of the film Sean had just directed called *Into the Wild*. When the conversation turned to whether or not its star, Emile Hirsch, would make a good Cleve, Gus and I realized that this meeting wasn't about whether Sean would play the role but about what he needed to do the job right. He wanted all of my research. He wanted to meet the real people. He was 100 percent in from the start.

Last and certainly not least, we needed a brave studio to sign on. In 2007, networks and studios weren't terrifically interested in hearing pitches for LGBTQ-themed shows, films, or even characters. But Focus Features had just hit it big at the box office with a little gay film called *Brokeback Mountain*. We thought they might get what we were trying to do with our film, and equally important, they'd know how to get people to come watch it. So after attaching Emile Hirsch and James Franco to our cast, we sent our package Focus's way. They bit. After years of wanting to see Milk's story shared widely, after watching others try and fail, we were about to make it happen. And now it was happening incredibly fast.

EXT. SAN FRANCISCO / THE CASTRO - DAY / 2008

Set to silent, a CELL PHONE buzzes in the Writer's
pocket. With plenty of time before the DIRECTOR rolls
camera, the Writer checks his phone. The call is from the
same number as before, a 703 area code, but again, the
Writer doesn't take the call.

We shot *Milk* in San Francisco on the very streets where the real story
had unfolded. The city's residents showed up en masse to support our
efforts. Thousands poured into the streets when we called for extras.
Bruce Cohen, who had experienced a meteoric rise and unheard-of
success with *American Beauty*, put his arm around me on set one
night and said, "Enjoy it. It's not always like this." I'll forever be grateful to him for reminding me to soak in every moment of this experience. But Gus was more of a realist. "A happy set doesn't mean a good
movie," he told me. He and Sean wanted me to stay focused on our
work.

They were right. Even with a studio's backing, nobody was getting
rich on this. I was still in credit card debt up to my ears from research
trips, and with too many at Warner Brothers waiting for our film to
fall on its ass, I needed to avoid distractions to complete this improb-
able feat. Wearing my producer hat, I needed to focus on casting sessions, location scouts, visits to our production and costume design
studios—doing all I could to help Gus keep our film as authentic as
possible. And with a green light came more of Milk's contemporaries
ready to share their stories. I was eager to hear them, and thankful
that a writers' strike ended in time for me to incorporate some of
their memories into the film.

It was a remarkable time in my life. But here's the thing: in the
midst of it all, the moment that had the most lasting impact on me,
and eventually on many others, had little to do with rolling cameras.
This larger moment began with a phone call that would set the next
decade of my life in motion, and would ultimately bring the film's
value into sharper focus.

I V

```
INT. SAN FRANCISCO APARTMENT - MORNING / 2008

An impossibly sunny Bay Area Sunday. Considering his CELL
PHONE, the Writer is up on his feet, carving circles
around a COFFEE TABLE. Then, as if pulling a trigger, he
taps in that 703 AREA CODE PHONE NUMBER, returning the
call. After a few rings, a tough, tired voice answers.
```

MARCUS

```
        Hey, bro.
```

Hey, bro" was all Marcus said when, after a week of avoiding his calls, I finally rang him back. His voice was as tough as usual, maybe just a bit raspier from more than his usual share of Marlboro Reds, and he'd definitely had a few drinks the night before.

"Hey. What's up?"

"I, uh . . . I got a problem. I need to talk about it . . . with you."

Right. I had made the time: we had the day off from shooting, and I'd chosen not to hang out with the rest of the cast and crew in Dolores Park. Marcus had sounded vague but troubled in the latest messages he'd left; now he had my full attention. "What's wrong?"

He fell silent.

"You okay, Marco?"

"Yeah." But I could hear that he was on the verge of tears, and that wasn't normal.

"Whatever it is, we can fix it. I promise. Did you . . . get someone pregnant?"

"No, bro. No."

"Okay. I'm listening."

After a pause, his tone grew even more dire. "You know Larry, right?"

"Yeah, of course," I said. Larry had been one of Marcus's best friends over the past five years. They'd met in a Virginia bar shortly after Marcus hit rock bottom in California and my mom convinced him to move back into her home. Marcus and Larry were a natural pair. They both liked shooting animals, drinking beer, and watching cars go around in endless circles on weekends. Like Marcus, Larry was rough around the edges, rarely shaved, and wore the same pair of jeans for weeks on end. Unlike Marcus, Larry had a missing tooth. I had always imagined that he'd lost it in a fight and wore his gap like a badge of honor. I could easily hear him saying, "Yeah, well, you shoulda seen the other asshole."

So I asked Marcus, "What happened? Tell me. I won't tell Mom."

We had made this same promise a thousand times as kids: whenever he proposed we ditch school, the half dozen times we nearly burned down the house, and when we tried to kill our stepfather Merrill. I'd never spilled the beans to our mother. Not once. And so, when I said, "I won't tell Mom," he knew I actually meant I wouldn't ever tell a soul. Perhaps this reassurance is what helped him feel safe enough to finally let his own deeply buried secret surface.

"Larry, uh ... Larry ... broke up with me."

"What?" I said, as if suddenly unable to hear him.

I'd like to say that I handled this revelation like a gay pro, but Marcus was the most butch, redneck-and-proud, animal-murdering, NASCAR-loving Sears auto mechanic I had ever known. So it wasn't that I had gone deaf, it was that I couldn't process what I'd just heard.

He repeated himself. "Larry broke up with me."

This had to be a joke, a prank.

Reading the disbelief in my silence, he told me the story. "About a year ago, I went over to Larry's house, and we went down to his basement like we do to watch a race, and around the last few laps, Earnhardt was leading, which, you know, we were cool with ... and ... well, we had had some beers to celebrate, you know? And ... we were sitting next to each other, like we do. And ... well ... he leaned over, and he ... you know ... he kissed me."

I'm not sure if I said "Oh my God" out loud or to myself, but I said it.

"And . . . well, everything made sense finally. And I know he's skinny, and the tooth, and you know . . . but I love him, bro. I always loved him as, you know . . . more than a friend . . . and then . . . we made a deal not to tell anybody, and I'm breaking that now, but you know . . . we were together for a year . . ." He went quiet. I could hear him holding back tears.

Continuing to blow it, I said, "Wow," and sped up my circles around the coffee table in the top-floor San Francisco apartment the film had put me up in. I simply couldn't believe that my big brother, whose undeniable toughness had made me feel so lousy for so long about being so fey, was also into men!

But I didn't want to screw this up like I had when Tim told me he was Jewish, or when Ryan came out to me as gay, so I fought back every unhelpful phrase trying to leap from my lips—things like "Are you really sure?" or "Maybe this is just a phase" or "You just don't seem gay to me, bro!" Instead, I gathered all the "hope speech" language I could marshal and told him how brave he and Larry were, and how much better he was going to feel now that he'd given voice to this. I assured him that his life was about to improve, that I loved him unconditionally, and that he had strengthened our brotherly bond by trusting me with this. I even had him imagine me giving him the biggest, most accepting hug possible. *Done!* I thought. I felt sure that I had finally succeeded in not completely screwing up someone's big coming-out moment.

But there was still no hope in his voice. No matter how much love and acceptance I shared, no matter how many times I repeated my assurances, I couldn't hear in him what I had felt when I came out. I couldn't hear him light up the way I had when our mom had finally held and accepted me. Instead, he remained distraught, lost, and afraid.

Through quivering voice, Marcus went on. "Larry's scared. He told me we have to stop, and I don't know what to do to change his mind."

"Why does it have to stop?!" I wanted Marcus to put Larry on the phone so I could give him a healthy dose of hope speech too, but he wasn't with Larry.

"He's afraid of what will happen if people find out."

"Maybe people will accept him. How does he know? And if they don't accept him, what kinds of friends are they?"

"Yeah," he said. But I knew this wasn't him agreeing. This was what Marcus said whenever someone wasn't getting it and he was sick of explaining. He had a short fuse for such frustration and I'd already reached the end of it.

You would have thought my big brother had lucked out having an openly gay little brother armed with so much of our history, but his tone suggested otherwise. There was nothing I could say to give him hope, and if *I* couldn't, he didn't know who could. He made me reiterate my promise not to tell our mom, and I made him promise not to hurt himself and to call me back before he went to bed that night.

When he hung up, I sat down on the couch in disbelief, and I stayed there for a good long time as it slowly dawned on me what an arrogant jerk I had just been.

Of course I felt hope when I came out to Ryan: I came out in California, where at the very least we knew we couldn't be kicked out of our apartment if our landlord found out we were gay. Of course I lit up inside when our mother accepted me: I was working in the film business, where I knew I wouldn't be fired if my bosses found out. Marcus and Larry lived in the South, in Virginia, where even today they could *legally* be fired and kicked out of their homes if anyone found out they were gay. And they weren't looking to escape. They didn't want to move to New York, Los Angeles, or San Francisco. They loved the South; they loved their culture, their community, and the family they lived near. They didn't want to uproot themselves, becoming refugees of the America they held dear just because they fell in love.

The truth was, Larry had every reason to be afraid of the repercussions of discovery. They lived in an area where a lack of legal protections set the bar horribly low for how gay neighbors could and should be treated. Marcus and Larry had little reason to feel liberation, hope, or light.

For the first time, I saw it so very clearly. We didn't live in one America at all. Ours was and is still a checkerboard nation of wildly disparate tribes and laws—particularly the laws affecting my LGBTQ family. In some areas, we could come out to our landlords, neighbors, and coworkers, dispel myths and lies, and create new bridges of understanding. In other areas, we dared not come out for fear of losing our homes, our jobs, and our ability to survive and support our families. And so, where personal stories can't be told, the myths remain, and with them all the outdated prejudices and fears. And with those fears intact, too many places in our beautiful country remain truly dangerous for LGBTQ folks. Don't believe me? Do a quick news search for "gay bashing," or worse, look up the words "trans" and "murders" together.

I've always loved my country. I still do. So did Marcus. Hell, Marcus flew an American flag off the back of his truck, and stood tall and proud for the national anthem when he was lucky enough to attend a NASCAR race. But he knew all too well that the part of the country he loved most didn't care to respect or protect him in return.

On Monday night, I walked down to our film's set on Market Street, where we were shooting a re-creation of the enormously moving 1978 candlelight vigil for Mayor George Moscone and Harvey Milk, who had been murdered by the homophobe Dan White. Six thousand volunteer extras, many of whom had been at the actual march on this very street three decades earlier, showed up with their own candles, all dressed in '70s-style garb to help us replicate this moving moment. I stood holding a small monitor next to Gus and watched our actors march by, followed by so many LGBTQ San Franciscans and allies, who in reality, with their own bodies, blood, sweat, and tears, had fought so hard and for so long to get us to this point—where we at least had some safe areas, some free states, some places of refuge in our country.

Feeling the weight of what we were re-creating, much of the cast and crew began to shed tears. Even Gus did. But I didn't. My mind was busy straddling three decades of LGBTQ history: from 1978 to 2008. And as this endless march of silent heroes continued past us, I realized that this film wasn't enough. No movie would be. And my eyes began to burn in a new way. The South had taught me that families always come first and must be defended, no matter what. Now the South I loved was threatening one of my own family member's most basic pursuits of happiness. I knew I had to square this. I simply had no idea how to. Not yet.

V

While I was in the throes of postproduction on *Milk*, Larry made good on ending his relationship with my big brother, and Marcus decided he'd pack up his truck and give California a try. He was moving in with me. That same month, with Walter Reed Army Medical Center likely closing to merge with the local navy hospital in Bethesda, my mom's role as Queen of the Lobby saw its final curtain call, and she retired. With too much time on her hands now, she decided to join Marcus and his big black Labrador, Max, on their cross-country road trip to my house.

Marcus had come out to her and Todd within minutes of his phone call with me, and my mom's response seemed to have given him more comfort than all of my fervent hope talk. She'd simply said: "Well, what the heck do I know about anything anymore, Marco? I mean . . . good for you." When my mom shared the same sentiment with me on a phone call, I laughed and echoed, "What the heck do I know anymore either, Mom?"

Just as our family had mobilized before, mother and son set off across the country. This time, though, they were a touch less fearful about driving into Los Angeles because they knew I was waiting with open arms and a promise to take them to In-N-Out Burger. But somewhere in the Midwest, our tough mom's right breast began to ache. She'd felt the lump for some time, but like many in medicine, she feared a dire diagnosis and slipped comfortably into what some call denial, but when married to my mom's determination would be more aptly described as active refusal. By the time she and Marcus arrived in California, the tumor had grown so large and infected that it broke through the skin. She hid the blood. She hid the pain. None of us knew. This was her way.

Mom seemed tired when they arrived, but not too tired for a month's worth of saved-up hugs and kisses. I held Marcus tighter than I ever had, and I stopped only when he let out a "You okay, man?" That meant "Cut it out." Same old Marcus. Max ran around my little house and up the steps in the terraced backyard that looked out over the city. "This all the grass you got?" I could almost hear him protesting. Los Angeles isn't some claustrophobic metropolis, but it's not the wide-open space he was used to.

I set Marcus up in my spare room, put my mom on the foldout couch, and threw a barbecue that weekend to introduce Marcus to my many gay friends. Ryan showed up to welcome Marcus to "the family," and my mom held court in the living room, surrounded by eager ears. Back home, she openly called many of my gay friends her "adopted sons" now. So here, she was the queen of us queens and absolutely loving it. I listened to Marcus struggle to fit in, occasionally slipping a "girl" into the end of his sentences like Ryan did. But it didn't fit. He was a very different kind of gay guy.

I was busy packing my bags to head to London for the very first time to help record the score for *Milk*, but before I left, Marcus sat down in the backyard with me, lit a Marlboro Red, popped open a Budweiser, and asked, "Bro, are there any gays like me here?" I reassured him that there were, but I worried. He was a grease monkey with a pretty face and a twink body who liked heavy metal and killing animals. Los Angeles was home to plenty of self-proclaimed bears, twinks, jocks, cubs, daddies, otters, and leather queens, but to my knowledge, none knew how to gut a deer, and if you asked them what lube was best for, their first guess wouldn't be a squeaky suspension. It wasn't safe for Marcus to try to find love in the part of the country where he felt most at home, but after only a few days in Los Angeles, it was becoming clear that he was a fish out of water here.

One week later, I was in London, the then-unfamiliar city that I now call home, standing on a vibrant, bustling street in a doorway older than my hometown, when I got a call from the 703 area code. I picked up. I had been waiting all day for this call, waiting to hear my mom's voice, and thrilled to finally tell her all about this remarkable country and what a thrill it had been to watch Danny Elfman conduct an orchestra playing the score for our film in the Beatles' old studio. And as I did, I thought I could hear her smiling across the ocean.

Two years earlier, I had splurged at Christmas and, using *Big Love* residuals, bought her and Jeff a nine-day trip to Paris. I couldn't really afford it yet, but going to Paris had been a longtime dream of hers, and now the many pictures of her on a dinner cruise on the Seine, and standing beneath the Arc de Triomphe and the Eiffel Tower, were proof that it had been a dream come true. She had told me the story of my birth many times, how she'd looked into my eyes and said, "You're going to teach me so many things." I'd always known that this was my assignment, and now I was eager to play tour guide to the world for the Louisiana girl who once thought fruit from California seemed like a too-distant delight. Now I wanted her there with me to marvel at London. But surprisingly, she hadn't called to hear about my new adventures. "Honey, do you think you could stop by here on your way back home?"

Though there was no fear in her voice, it was a highly unusual request and came with no explanation, so I asked for one. She refused. That was startling. So the battle of bullheaded blonds began. I reminded her that I didn't need words to read her mind, that I knew something was wrong, and that now this was all I would worry about until I saw her. Finally, she relented.

"You can be a real pain in the rear, Lancer."

It's true. I admitted as much, and she continued.

"I went to the doctor. I have a lump in my right breast . . ."

I backed into the doorway, away from the bustling crowd, and leaned on a wall for support as I awaited the inevitable next words. And without worry or drama, she shared:

"It's cancer."

Full stop. Everything in my life. Full stop.

As my swirling mind struggled to process this news, we somehow got to the part where she revealed that it was stage 4 cancer that had already spread, so it was about as bad as it gets.

"We can fix this. You can beat this," I said by rote. But I meant it. After all, it had always proven true, so why not now?

She nearly laughed. "Lancer, you just think you can fix anything."

"With enough tape and glue," I said, knowing full well how absurd that sounded in that moment, but it managed to get a little laugh out of her.

Then, in classic Anne form, she took off her gloves and threatened that cancer with a helluva fight. "It's not going to beat me, Lancer."

Then as if talking directly to the tumor: "I'm sending it straight to hell. Thank you *very* much."

Making good on those words, she asked her doctors to hit her with all they had. She would undergo chemotherapy, then surgery, then more chemo, and top it all off with what proved to be painful, debilitating rounds of radiation. I flew home to Virginia immediately, and then every two weeks from then on as her body grew frailer but her spirit stayed just as strong.

One night, jet-lagged and nodding off in the very room where I had inadvertently come out to her a decade before, I heard a wailing sound from down the hall. I got up and walked to the master bedroom. Jeff was standing by the bathroom door, helpless. Something truly terrible was happening inside that bathroom, but she wouldn't let him in.

"What is it, Mom?" I asked.

Her crying quieted. "Lancer?"

"Yes?"

"Don't you dare let Jeff in here!" She sounded furious.

I looked at Jeff, who gave me a bewildered shrug. "Okay. I won't."

She shouted, "Jeff, go away!"

I nodded to Jeff as if to say "I got this," but God only knows what I had on my hands. Jeff left the room.

"He's gone, Mom."

"If you're lying to me, I'm going to be really mad at you, Lance!"

"I'm not lying. It's just me. . . . Can I come in?"

A quiet beat; then I could hear her pulling her body across the floor, then the sound of her unlocking the door, then more tears. I slowly opened the door, terrified of what I might find inside.

There she was, my tough mom who'd bravely slayed the world for her three boys, now looking so very small, in a lump on the floor with only a towel wrapped around her skeletal body and shaking. She looked up at me, tears streaming from her beautiful blue eyes, her favorite amethyst earrings still dangling from her ears—but no longer framed by anything. Almost all of her treasured blond hair, her "crown and glory," her secret weapon with doctors, nurses, and push-boys in all those children's hospitals, was now at the bottom of the tub. It had chosen to fall out en masse during her bath. Refusing to look away, she dared me to disagree when she decreed, "I'm a monster."

Like I've said before, I never learned how to lie to my good Southern mom. I knew even trying to was a path to pain, so I just said it like I saw it: "Mom, you look a lot like Gollum"—as in the pale, shriveled, mostly bald bog creature from *Lord of the Rings*.

"No . . . ," she blubbered out, desperate for this not to be true.

I had two choices: take it back or go full tilt. Knowing my mom, I really only had one way to go. "It's true, Mom. . . . And with those earrings in, you're Gollum in drag."

A burst of laughter, snot, and tears tumbled out of her.

I sat down on the floor, held her, and after asking permission, got Jeff's clippers out of the drawer and shaved what little hair she had left from her white, round little head. I'm not going to lie, it was incredibly difficult seeing my once indestructible mom like that, but I didn't want her to know that, so I didn't show an ounce of it. It was my turn to be shatterproof. And when the last of her hair was gone, I put a soft knit hat on her head and listened very closely as she beseeched: "I never, ever want Jeff to see me how you just did. Promise me, Lancer. Promise."

I held her, forcing back tears of my own, and made this sacred promise. For now, my job in this battle would be to help her hold on to whatever dignity she could, to help her stay beautiful for the man she loved. This was my family, this was my mother, and so of course I was up for this call to action: the many flights, tears, and hand-holding ahead. At that very moment, I had no real job, just a film premiere on my schedule. And so, I felt blessed to have unlimited time to share with my mom in this hour. But life is never generous with its time for long, and far too soon a second fight for our lives would erupt, this time out west begging my return to California.

CHAPTER 19

Cataclysm

I

Irony is a wicked little fellow who likes to pay me frequent visits. *Milk* was nearly finished and set to premiere in the late fall of 2008. Its story centered on an actual statewide California ballot initiative, Proposition 6, that sought to ban gay teachers and any who supported them. Now, on the eve of *Milk*'s premiere, a brand-new statewide proposition was on the ballot in California that sought to take away the rights of gay and lesbian couples to be legally wed. It was called Proposition 8. Months earlier, California had begun allowing such marriages, and with tears of joy and a helluva lot of rainbow bow ties, eighteen thousand couples took advantage of this opportunity, including Ryan and his now long-term boyfriend, Aaron. They too chose to strike while the iron was still hot and said "I do" with tears in their eyes in a West Hollywood park alongside hundreds of other devoted gay and lesbian couples. But now these unions, and all of that joy, were being threatened. And who was the main funder of this regressive ballot initiative? None other than my good old childhood pal the Mormon Church. Oh, life.

In *Milk*, and in real life in 1978, Harvey aggressively went after the proponents of Prop 6, built coalitions of other minorities and unions to fight against it, and boldly put gay and lesbian faces on the front lines of the debate to tell their personal stories, a demonstration of strength worthy of respect. Prop 6 was defeated. Milk's team won, and in a time that was arguably far more homophobic. But those fighting Prop 8 were almost exclusively putting straight faces forward, talking more about rights than lives, love, or families, and the LGBTQ organizers of the "No on 8" campaign had seemingly forgotten the power and necessity of building strong coalitions in a minority movement. Their campaign came off as cold, often confusing, and spineless.

I wanted more than anything for *Milk* to premiere before the November 4 election, so that perhaps the No on 8 campaign leaders, who refused to listen to criticisms, and the grassroots activists out working their tails off, might draw on Harvey's team's lessons and correct course. But moving up the release date proved impossible. As Election Day neared, I manned phone banks and roared at rallies. Yet witnessing the mistakes being repeated, I grew increasingly certain that come November 4, Proposition 8 would become the law of the land, and our right to marriage would be stripped away. Sadly, I was right.

The night after this devastating loss, I walked down into West Hollywood with Ryan and Aaron to join a rally to decry Prop 8's passage, but it turned out to be a stage filled with the very LGBTQ leaders whose tepid, mostly closeted tactics had lost this winnable fight. Frustrated with their rally's equally flaccid feel, Ryan and I asked each other, "What would Harvey do right now?" Once upon a time Ryan and I had felt sure that coming out would be the end of us. Now we were plotting an impromptu, aggressive, highly visible, unpermitted takeover of L.A.'s busiest streets.

With the help of at least one rowdy local elected official, we started a whisper campaign through the growing crowd to march north and away from the rally stage at 8:00 p.m. When that hour struck, one by one, and then all at once, young and old did just that. We turned away from that ghettoized stage and began stepping into Santa Monica Boulevard at San Vicente, immediately shutting down this major intersection. I'll never forget the supposed LGBTQ leader up on that stage shouting at us all, "Wait! Where are you going? I'm not done!" And how most refused to heed her demand to stand still. Not tonight. Not one minute longer. We marched.

My heart raced. Something very new for me and for my generation was happening now. Drawing on lessons I'd learned from Cleve. I quickly spoke with the police, told them our planned route (which I made up on the spot), and then helped lead our people and their anger up to Sunset Boulevard, out of the gay ghetto and into the "straight" area, then east toward Hollywood and Highland, a major city thoroughfare. We wanted to shut the city down. We wanted a peaceful but clear demonstration that our people were not going to hide in our ghettos, we were not going to lie down and accept this injustice. I remember looking back at the marchers behind me, our numbers growing exponentially, our hundreds turning to thousands. And with those numbers, we did shut down Los Angeles' streets that night, news helicopters hovering over our heads until the wee hours. It was fearless, shameless, and undeniably visible. So much of what the Prop 8 campaign hadn't been. And over the next several weeks, we all watched with gratitude and satisfaction as our anger and resistance grew and spread across the nation like fire—to New York, San Francisco, Boston, even Salt Lake City. And far beyond.

We could feel it in the air and in every conversation. Proposition 8's passage had sparked something in a new generation that had never felt the sting of discrimination before, while simultaneously calling an older generation back to the fight. Now, locked arm in arm—energy and experience—we were rising up together. But as aware as I was that this new fighting spirit was necessary, I also understood from history that it wasn't sufficient. Alone, our anger wouldn't create the change we needed.

So when I wasn't taking care of my mom in Virginia, I began researching what other civil rights movements had done when faced with similar circumstances. I started asking very different questions of those same folks I'd interviewed when making *Milk*: What had they done to win alongside Harvey, and what had they accomplished before the LGBTQ movement—in the civil rights movement, the women's movement, the peace movement? How and why were those battles won or lost?

There were two oft-repeated ideas from those in Milk's generation of activists. One: the only way to ensure equality for all Americans "in all matters governed by civil law in all fifty states" is to take the fight to the federal level. "Enough of this state-by-state chickenshit crumb begging," said eighty-year-old Frank Robinson, who had been Milk's speechwriter and right hand. "You beg for crumbs, you get less than crumbs." Two: it had to be done now. Cleve and I wrote an op-ed "manifesto" for the *San Francisco Chronicle* that said just that, plain and clear: "Now is the time for federal action."

By December, I felt called to fight for both of my families: my mother in Virginia, my big brother under my own roof, and also for my wider LGBTQ family, whose members were now hungry for ways to channel their new anger. A student of our history, I understood that if our energy was not directed soon, it would dissipate, and come to nothing, but who was I to help direct such fire and fury? No matter what I had in my head about how a movement worked, I still couldn't speak in front of five people without trembling, and nobody outside of Hollywood gave two cents what I had to say politically.

And then *Milk* premiered. And not only did it "not suck balls," as Marcus so eloquently put it on our premiere night in San Francisco's Castro Theater, the film received a helluva lot of love from critics.

Then, on January 23, I rose before the sun to call my mom and watch live on TV with her as *Milk* garnered a stunning eight Academy Award nominations, including for Best Picture and Best Original Screenplay. I'd hardly dared to dream that *Milk* would make it to the big screen. Now I was an Academy Award nominee. I didn't know it that morning—I was too busy screaming with my mom, calling Todd, jumping up and down on Marcus's bed, and popping champagne corks up at producer Dan Jinks's house—but with this unexpected success, I would have a shot at finding both the finances and the platform to help lead. The challenge now would be lassoing that opportunity and finding the courage to use its power.

I I

I drove into Beverly Hills and stepped onto Rodeo Drive, where, with the help of my fellow Academy Award nominee Danny Glicker, *Milk*'s talented costume designer, I picked out the most striking strands of pearls I'd ever seen. Not too big, because their recipient was quite small, but not too understated, because I wanted my mom, that girl from Lake Providence, to feel like the queen she was on the Academy Awards ceremony's red carpet. And we wouldn't be alone: thanks to the academy's generosity, I had enough tickets to bring Jeff and his mustache; Cleve, who with new medications and renewed purpose looked a decade younger than when we'd met; and Ryan, who had never wavered, and who now asked, "Girl, don't you think you owe me a house now?"

The day before the Academy Awards show in 2009, my mom and Jeff flew in from Virginia. When they arrived at my house, it was the very first time I'd ever seen my mom in a wheelchair. It was a punch in the gut. She had finished her first round of chemo, had a mastectomy, and was now undergoing radiation, which surprisingly to her doctors was taking the greatest toll on her strength. But she was still Anne: she wouldn't allow anyone to push the chair; she had to wheel it around herself, and she promised to be back on her feet the following night. She showed off the lovely blond wig she'd found, and an absolutely stunning black dress for our big night. She was tickled pink, so I forgot all about her new wheels and let myself go pink too.

But that night, I found myself sitting catatonic in the chair beside her hotel room bed. Usually she and Jeff would have stayed at my bungalow, but Marcus, Todd, Todd's delightful new girlfriend, Allison, and Max the dog were all filling those cozy nine hundred square feet. Here in the hotel room, our mom had her own bathroom and the privacy she needed to keep her pain and exhaustion a secret.

Studying me in that chair, my mom could tell that I was stressed out of my mind, and the caretaker roles flipped back to normal. My mom took my hand and gave me the same advice she had on my sixth Christmas Eve when I was sick with pneumonia on my aunt Martha's floor: stroking my eyebrows, she had encouraged me to breathe, and to dream of a better place. So now again, I closed my eyes, took a few breaths, and imagined the very best outcome for the following night. No, not golden trophies or champagne. If I'm being honest, I was more worried about winning than I was about losing. I was still very much the same shy kid who couldn't play percussion sticks in the Jingle Bell Band. A few weeks earlier, Sean Penn, who had already won an Oscar, described the moment of triumph as "like being hit by a freight train." I wasn't sure I'd survive that impact.

Following my mom's advice, I tried to stop thinking about the million potential disasters that might unfold and turned my attention to a fantasy: What would I have dreamed of hearing from the Oscars stage as a young boy in San Antonio, Texas, struggling in shame and isolation? I let words pass through that child's mind, and when a word or sentence felt right, when it felt hopeful, necessary, strong, and honest, I held on to it with my grown-up mind, saving it, just in case.

The next day, Focus Features sent a hair and makeup person to my house. Focus was treating me and my guests like absolute royalty, and my mom had no problem soaking it all in. It turned out that the makeup artist specialized in folks undergoing cancer treatment, and knew how to apply makeup to my mom's chemo-and-radiation-ravaged skin to keep her looking perfect for the many hours the show and subsequent Governors Ball would take. I put on the tuxedo Tom Ford had built for me, complete with a nice wide Milk-era lapel. Ryan showed up looking sharp as a tack, his head clean-shaven in solidarity with my mom, and a lot of hugs and laughs temporarily distracted me from the reality of the billion global eyes that would soon be on us.

The limo arrived, but first, I had a special gift for my mom: those Beverly Hills pearls. She protested that they were far too fancy for a Southern girl who used to make mud pies on a tenant farm, but she didn't hesitate a millisecond getting those bad boys around her neck.

Loaded into the limo, we headed down the hill to the Kodak Theatre, and as we rounded the corner on Highland, I laid eyes on a scene that helped measure the scale of *Milk*'s achievement. Not only had *Milk* proven a box office success in a difficult time for dramas, but now the Westboro Baptist Church had shown up with their iconic neon "God Hates Fags" signs to protest our film's many nominations and prominent status in this year's show. It was the same Southern church that had protested at the funerals of Matthew Shepard, Pedro Zamora, and so many other gay icons and heroes—the church that had become the symbol of homophobia and intolerance in the part of America my family hailed from.

I said out loud to no one in particular, "Looks like our people showed up," not expecting any response.

But my mom quickly shot back, "They aren't really our people."

I looked to her warm eyes. She wasn't divorcing herself from the South, she was divorcing them from it. I held her gaze in silence, so nervous, so grateful, and noticed that she had pinned a white ribbon, knotted in the center, to her dress. It was the new symbol for the fight for marriage equality—a quiet act of pride and support for my LGBTQ family from the same woman who had been so challenged years earlier when I had come out.

The limo's doors swung open without our even touching them, and there we were, at the edge of the most renowned red carpet in the world. *Pop! Pop! Pop!* A thousand cameras were flashing. The Latin boy with his pornstache, the soldier with the failed chute, the gay warrior named Jones rising yet again, and my itty-bitty mom from the poorest city in the nation were all heading into the Oscars together. When my mom got out of that car, despite the debilitating weakness brought on by the radiation, she did so under her own power, no wheelchair, just her and her trusty crutches. And together, we swung and walked that goddamn red carpet like the fierce and freaky outsiders we knew we were.

I was whisked away to do interviews, which gave me a chance to see Ryan, Jeff, Cleve, and my mom on the red carpet from afar. My mom's eyes darted about like a mouse's as she tried to soak it all in. It couldn't have seemed real to her; it sure didn't to me. As always, Jeff was more focused on her needs than on any spectacle before him. Ryan caught me looking and wagged his finger at me to pay attention to the news cameras. Ryan had a keen awareness that this moment shouldn't be the culmination of anything but the beginning of a larger fight. From what little I'd dared share of the words I might speak if I won, Ryan knew that there was a good chance I was about to declare war.

I was shown to my seat in the cavernous, majestic Kodak Theatre. The show's producers had put me in the front row of the second section—a row for nominees. Then a publicist from Focus Features came running up to inform me that the writing categories were coming early in the show this year. I tried to breathe. I reminded myself that, as luck would have it, the producers of this year's show were two openly gay men. I thought on that and decided that if I was invited up onto that glossy, intimidating stage, I wasn't going to pay any attention to the massive red clock at the back of the theater ticking down, shouting for each nominee to wrap it up. I would say what I needed to say and dare those producers to play me off.

What felt like mere moments later, the show was under way. Tina Fey and Steve Martin took the stage. They read the nominees for Best Original Screenplay, opened the envelope, and here's all I can really remember from the next few minutes:

Steve Martin opened his mouth and said, "And the Oscar goes to: Dus—"

Bang! I was out of my seat before he even got to "Lance." I wasn't wasting a moment. I can't say for sure what guided me in the next few minutes, but if I had to guess, I'd say it was a lifetime growing up with my tough, loving mom; all the dreaming she'd encouraged me to do, including the night before; and one big, healthy dose of whoever God is.

I don't remember taking the Oscar in my hand, but I do remember seeing that big red clock and its rapidly shrinking numbers, and getting myself to the microphone. Then, I somehow pushed down all the nerves that had crippled me way back when in the Jingle Bell Band and channeled the skills my mother and the South had tried to teach me along the way: I stood up as straight and tall as a writer can, and when I opened my mouth, I did my best to take the bull by the horns, to say the words I wished I had heard as a child, to stir up some good old-fashioned trouble, and lead.

FROM GLAAD'S 2009 OSCARS TRANSCRIPT:

Oh my God. This was, um. This was not an easy film to make. First off, I have to thank Cleve Jones and Anne Kronenberg and all the real-life people who shared their stories with me. And Gus Van Sant, Sean Penn, Emile Hirsch, Josh Brolin, James Franco, and our entire cast, my producers, Dan Jinks and Bruce Cohen, everyone at Groundswell and Focus, for taking on the challenge of telling this lifesaving story. When I was 13 years old, my beautiful mother and my father moved me from a conservative Mormon home in San Antonio, Texas to California, and I heard the story of Harvey Milk. And it gave me hope. It gave me the hope to live my life, it gave me the hope to one day live my life openly as who I am, and that maybe even I could fall in love and one day get married.

(He chokes up, audience begins to applaud.)

I want to thank my mom who has always loved me for who I am even when there was pressure not to. But most of all, if Harvey had not been taken from us 30 years ago, I think he'd want me to say to all of the gay and lesbian kids out there

tonight who have been told that they are "less than" by their
churches or by the government or by their families that you
are beautiful, wonderful creatures of value, and that no matter
what anyone tells you, God does love you, and that very soon,
I promise you, you will have equal rights, *federally*, across this
great nation of ours.

(Wild applause from the audience.)

Thank you, thank you, and thank you, God, for giving us
Harvey Milk.

My mind began recording memories again somewhere in the ele-
vator ride up to the press room when Jennifer Aniston kindly handed
me a much-needed bottle of water. Then I was ushered into a room
filled with previous winners, some of the most famous and accomplished film folks in the history of cinema, and the first sign that I
hadn't completely screwed up was when Whoopi Goldberg wrapped
me up tight in her arms and said, "You did it, baby."

In the massive press gathering that followed, I could feel the heat
of a thousand flashes, and I reiterated my call for the LGBTQ movement to take our fight for equality to the federal government, "in the
footsteps of every great civil rights movement." There was a new feeling in my bones, and it wasn't just the adrenaline or bubbly. Where
there had always been chalk, steel was beginning to form.

Nearly an hour later, I walked back into the Kodak Theatre during a commercial break and went right for my mom. She was still in
tears, positively shaking with pride. "You got out of that chair awful
quick, Lancer," she said. I gave her a tearful laugh in return, her shimmering eyes helping me begin to comprehend what had just happened. And then and there I made a decision. I put my Oscar in my
mom's lap and said, "Hold on to him tight, Mom. He's yours."

That night at the Governors Ball, my mom chitchatted with celebrities until she grew bored of their tuxedos, silk, and sequins, then
pulled Ryan in close. She wanted to finally speak openly about our
move to Los Angeles so many years ago—about her fears that he was
an unholy influence back then, and how now she understood more

and saw Ryan as a son. Perhaps painfully aware of her own mortality, she added, "Promise me you'll always look after him." She locked eyes with him. This was an order, not a request.

"I always have, and always will," he assured her.

The rest of that night was a dream. On a quick stop by my house to freshen up after the Governors Ball, I found that my neighbors' kids had painted me a "Congratulations" banner and hung it across my garage door. Marcus, Todd, and Allison, who had been watching from the Focus Features party, came home to scream, hug, and relive the moment from their perspectives before I was whisked off to the Vanity Fair party, then to Madonna's party, where P. Diddy was rapping my name as I walked in.

But the cherry on top was when legendary, openly gay CAA agent Bryan Lourd pressed me up against a wall at 3:00 a.m., a proud, paternal smile on his face, and said, "Do you realize what you've just done?"

He may have meant that my pay grade had just shot up, but what came to mind was that I'd just called on my wider American family to accept their LGBTQ children as a people loved by God. I had also called for what many considered too much: *federal action* from a movement that in my opinion had been begging for partial equality at the state and local level for far too long now. And I was no fool; I knew that what I'd said was bold, and I felt sure that a backlash was coming; I just didn't realize that it wouldn't come from those you might expect—the religious right, the South, or conservatives. Save for two online death threats, the America of my youth had little to say about my speech. Mostly I received letters from Southern moms and dads thanking me for opening their eyes to their sons' and daughters' plights. The real backlash came in whispers at first, then online, and eventually in emails and face-to-face confrontations— a chorus of criticism from many of my LGBTQ mentors and heroes who had begun privately and then publicly branding my call for *federal* action as too much too soon, naïve, ignorant, arrogant, and irresponsible.

I was disappointed but not entirely surprised. These were the same words my mom and I had heard our entire lives whenever we dared to dream too big. The same words Harvey Milk heard from gay leaders when he first ran for office. But I'm not going to lie: coming from the folks I respected and admired so much, these familiar words stung. Just not enough to stop me. I was hungrier for the sweeping nature of federal action than for anyone's approval, because I needed my big brother to feel the hope I'd felt. I wanted him to be able to return to the South, where he felt most at home, and be able to love who he pleased.

Since the pain of the passage of Prop 8, a fire had been lit. I had begun to dream that my brother and I might one day live in a less divided America—one willing to see its variety with a bit less fear and a touch more curiosity and compassion. Not "my" America, not "their" America, not some put-on notion of "one" America or the divisive ring of "two" Americas. I had no name for it yet, but I prayed for something more inclusive, accepting, and united than those labels suggested. And I wouldn't let anyone extinguish this dream. Not even heroes.

CHAPTER 20

SCOTUS Hiatus

The awards show had taken its toll on my mom. She was exhausted and faced more radiation back home, but she was eager to keep "kicking this cancer's tail" and get her retirement properly started. The good news was that the doctors felt the cancer was on the run. But polio had long since forced my mom to function with a severely compromised neuromuscular system, and the side effects of radiation were wreaking havoc on what muscle strength she had left. She already felt significant weakness and pain in her hands, and my mom's hands had long been her legs.

In the days that followed the Academy Awards, my agents at CAA were busy fielding incoming calls. I had left *Big Love* because the executive producers forced a decision between it and *Milk* when the productions' schedules overlapped following the Writers Guild strike. I missed my writer pals, the actors, and the delight-to-write characters of *Big Love,* but my work plate was still full. I was already hip-deep in a new project with Ron Howard and Brian Grazer's company, Imagine, exploring J. Edgar Hoover and the dire repercussions of staying in the closet—in many ways the mirror of *Milk.* This project would eventually team me with none other than my great teenage crush, Leonardo DiCaprio, and the former mayor who'd helped lure my family to California, Clint Eastwood. It would seem my wildest dreams were coming true, but the question now was whether I had the bandwidth for both Hollywood make-believe and the very real promises I'd just made.

Before leaving for LAX, my mom sat me down beside the big front window of my little bungalow in the Hollywood Hills to talk about my Oscar speech a few nights earlier. With her eyes glistening, her weakened hands held mine as she confirmed that, as I had said in my speech, she had never stopped loving me when I came out. She said that mostly she had worried for my future—in this life and beyond—but that those concerns had long since faded. Now she had a new concern. I leaned in, curious, as she reminded me of a lesson she'd tried to hammer home in my youth: "A promise is a big thing, Lancer. A promise is sacred."

Oh right. That. "I know, I know," I said, feeling the weight of my words from that big stage a bit differently now.

"We're only as good as our word."

"I know, Mom."

"Good. I'm glad. I'm so proud of you, Lancer." Her tears had dried by now, leaving behind salty streaks of sympathetic steel. She knew I was going to need all the metal my bones could bear.

Like millions of others around the world, my mom had heard the promise I'd made to young LGBTQ people, a promise for equality "very soon," and at the federal level. She wanted to make sure I understood the responsibility of saying big words on big stages.

With that in mind, the incoming CAA call that really got my attention wasn't the one from Warner Brothers looking for a fresh start to our relationship (they would eventually take over and green-light *J. Edgar*): it was from my feature film agent, Craig Gering, telling me that a man near my age from Arkansas who had worked in Clinton's White House when he was just a teen wanted to meet with me. Craig said, "Come to our office. Sit with him. I think you two might see eye to eye on a couple of things. Maybe you can make something of all of this."

When I arrived at CAA, I received a hero's welcome. I hadn't ventured out much since the big show, certainly not into any professional settings, and here I got the first taste of what such a win might mean for my film career.

Craig showed me to a conference room with a giant window for a back wall, a delightful arrangement of sparkling water, sodas, and coffee, and one striking fresh-looking face in a suit and tie. "Chad Griffin, Dustin Lance Black." Craig made the introduction and excused himself.

I remember being struck by how young and handsome Chad was. I had done my homework. I knew he ran a philanthropic and political consulting firm in Los Angeles that had worked with the likes of Rob and Michele Reiner and Brad Pitt and Angelina Jolie on issues such as stem cell research, big oil, and big tobacco. Impressive. And with all the calls coming in from LGBTQ organizations asking me to speak at award shows, sit on boards, or even start my own foundation, I thought that at the very least, this adorable Chad character might be able to help me make hay of those opportunities.

But when Chad opened his mouth, I was struck by two new pieces of information: Chad still had a bit of his Hope, Arkansas, twang. My aunt Josie and uncle James still lived in Texarkana, so Chad's accent sounded a lot like family to me. I immediately relaxed.

Then Chad made it clear that he knew exactly the position I was in at that moment: "I bet you've gotten an earful."

"Yes!" He didn't mean an earful of well wishes and congratulations. He knew I was fielding a good bit of criticism.

" 'Too much too soon'?" Chad said knowingly.

"In over my head, a 'neophyte,' mostly from gay folks in gay organizations."

"Nothing from lesbians?"

"Mostly just gay men. 'It'll bring on a backlash.' All that. Guess they think I'm dangerous." That last bit seemed so silly to me.

But I remember Chad pausing, perhaps sizing me up, debating whether it was safe to share what had been simmering.

I took that moment of silence to gaze past him out the window to the bright blue sky above Beverly Hills. A sky suddenly filled with so many new moviemaking opportunities. If Chad could explain in a way that made any sense to me why my ideas were dangerous, perhaps I could acknowledge what I privately feared: that I was indeed in over my head. Then, instead of trying for fifty-state marriage equality, I could get back to building the dream film career of my youth—my own company, with development departments for film, television, and theater—and our current LGBTQ leaders could all breathe a sigh of relief. Win-win.

Instead, Chad said, "I think you're right. I think we have to show a little self-respect and take this fight to the federal government."

He was the first person in a suit and tie to take me seriously. My gaze returned squarely to him.

We talked about several paths: creating a new organization at the grassroots level that would confront senators and members of

Congress in all 435 congressional districts, forcing our federal representatives to respond to our demands nationally. It was ambitious, would be very expensive, and would likely be seen as an attempt to unseat the Human Rights Campaign (HRC) in Washington, D.C., as the LGBTQ community's primary federal lobbying organization. Personally, I had donated to HRC, and I had enjoyed their black-tie dinners, but many on the ground felt that HRC had followed in the footsteps of other big corporate equality organizations: going soft, becoming safe, and getting too "patient." After all, if it's your full-time job, and you manage a massive D.C. office building filled with countless dedicated, hardworking employees, you might not be quite as eager to win equality and put a lot of those good people out of work. But building an organization to rival HRC was a goliath idea. And I wasn't sure this was the right time for such an internecine battle.

Chad had many other ideas, big and small, but now that he had a sense of who I was, he floated one more: "What about the United States Supreme Court?"

There were currently a half dozen different ideas swirling around about how Californians might fight back against Prop 8's passage, but most centered on when and how to get marriage equality back on the ballot. Only "crazy people" talked about taking such a fight to the highest court in the country. Given the mixed reaction among insiders to my simply uttering the word "federal," Chad was well aware that most in our movement would find any idea that included SCOTUS premature and dangerous.

Why would some find a U.S. Supreme Court case too bold? Because we could lose, and the message a broad constitutional loss might send about LGBTQ Americans' lack of fundamental rights and protections could have had devastating, unintended consequences nationwide. But the other side of the coin felt powerful. Just filing a case in federal court would demonstrate a mountain of pride and confidence, and as a Texan, I thought it might even win us some respect. When confronted by a bully in Texas, Arkansas, or Louisiana, you couldn't beg for half of your lunch money back. That would only earn laughter and a good beatdown. Where Chad and I grew up, we knew we had to stand up straight and tall, and have the guts to invite that bully out to a proper fight, usually on a dusty street corner just off school grounds, and ideally with everyone watching. The outcome of that fight mattered less than demonstrating confidence in front of your classmates. That's how you won respect where we were from: demand all that you're due and be willing to fight for it even if you think you might lose.

To my ears, the compromises set forth as progress by LGBTQ leaders of the time had been sending a clear and dangerous message: "We gays believe we're only half as worthy as you straight folks. That's why we're down on our knees in just a few cities and states asking for selective slices of equality. The whole pie? Well, that would be way too much for us." I could almost hear my uncle James saying, "Guess ya don't think yer half as good as us straight folks, 'cause all you seem to want are scraps." The U.S. Supreme Court wouldn't be scraps.

Chad could tell that my interest was piqued. I wanted more details: who, how, and when. Instead, in as casual a way as possible, and with a little chuckle thrown in to offset the enormity of the decision he was about to ask me to make, Chad said, "You know, I represent people in your business, and the thing is, I'm not sure you can do both activism and film well, not at the same time."

Sitting in CAA of all places, filled with agents eager to help build me a cinematic empire, Chad knew exactly what he was up to. He was asking me to choose between doing all I could to fulfill the promise I'd made on that stage and all of the glittering new opportunities in front of me: the new films waiting to be born, the financial stability I'd never known as a child. I could almost touch it all. But then there was that steel my mother had poured into my bones, and her words before getting on that plane back to the South. Not to mention all the scars I could still see and feel from my own childhood lived in fear and shame, and my determination that kids should no longer have to endure those injuries. So honestly, when it came down to it, this wasn't a tough choice to make at all. It was quite simple.

"We're only as good as our word," I said.

Chad agreed.

Hollywood was on hold.

I I

Afcer less than a year living in my house, it had become clear that Los Angeles would never feel like home for Marcus. My big brother missed his friends, his music, his food, his sports. His dog, Max, missed all the open space he'd had in Virginia. Although my friends were endlessly entertained at our frequent barbecues by Marcus's "y'alls" and his charming country ways, he never really connected with them. Instead, he started spending more time on the internet than out of the house. And when he met a gay man in Michigan online, a man who shared his interest in NASCAR, Marcus fueled up his big white truck and bid me and California farewell.

This wasn't a simple decision for Marcus. In Michigan, he would have to be careful again about who knew what about his personal life. Like every other LGBTQ person in Michigan at the time, my big brother would have few legal protections once he crossed over its border. He was taking a chance on love, and his roll of the dice would add even more personal stakes to my federally aimed equality work.

Chad and I shared a goal that we knew others didn't yet agree with. Certain that now was indeed the time for bold action, we also felt it was time to start laying our chips on the table. OutGiving, a biennial conference of major LGBTQ donors, invited me to speak in Las Vegas, and with Chad's encouragement, I got to work crafting a speech that wouldn't directly call for a federal case challenging the constitutionality of Prop 8 but would suggest donors refocus their efforts on strategies with an all-fifty-states aim. It sounded to me like a prudent baby step. Boy, was I wrong.

At this point in my life, giving speeches was not my forte. Without the adrenaline from the Oscars, I much preferred to be behind the camera—directing the spotlight, not in it. And so I endlessly reworked the speech, practiced it, and shared drafts with Chad, who joined me in Vegas for support. Awaiting the start of the show, I snuck outside to have a cigarette in the courtyard. You could say I was a selective smoker: either borrowing from cute actors or bowing to nerves. My nerves were begging for one right now.

As I sat on a bench in that courtyard, alone with my cigarette held in amateur style between thumb and index finger, a small man made his way over to me. He was then and still is a man I admire, a man who fought for marriage equality before most imagined it was a possibility or even saw the value in such a fight. I don't share the following story out of animosity. I share it so that young activists might understand that the first point of real resistance to any new idea likely won't come from your perceived opponents; it will more likely come from those on your side, perhaps even from your heroes.

This man sat to my right, neither particularly warm nor antagonistic. Knowing his long history in the marriage equality movement, I thought he was just the person to talk to about our idea of a federal course of action: I could test the waters; he could help me look for blind spots. But in this instance I indeed proved myself naïve.

The more I spoke, the more closed off he became, folding his arms across his body. He started looking out into the distance instead of making eye contact, masking his anger with condescension. He let me know that there was already an incremental plan in place for achieving nationwide marriage equality within the next three decades, and that this plan (his plan) was clearly laid out in his book if I would only read it, and show the "patience" he had during his long fight. My pushback was that his twenty-five-year strategy would likely leave him, me, most of our friends, and folks like my brother with little chance of experiencing the benefits of all of our work. "What about us?" I asked. "Are we not worthy of equality while we still have lives to live?"

He didn't appreciate that sentiment. Perhaps he found it impossible, or perhaps just selfish. Truth lived in both criticisms. I knew the path we were proposing held risk, but even today, I still believe that our goals and strategies for achieving equality and justice ought to address our lives now as well as our broader future, no matter how dreamy those goals may seem. After all, I am my mother's son, and she never did spend much time on realism lessons. Sadly, despite all the wisdom this man could have brought to our federal effort, he made it absolutely clear that he was refusing, and unceremoniously huffed off. I watched him grow even smaller as he stepped away and into the hard Las Vegas shadows.

I made a beeline for Chad's hotel room and told him the mistake I had just made. "Are you sure I should still give this speech here?"

Chad thought about it, and then said, "That's exactly the response I'd expect, and it tells us one thing above all else: this is the right thing to do, and these are the people who need to hear a different perspective."

In the ballroom, I was seated at a table next to a very wealthy man whom I also admired. He was and is one of the most generous donors to LGBTQ causes in America. To get an invite to this dinner, one has to pony up at least $25,000 a year. Needless to say, the linen-covered tables were mostly populated with wealthy, white, gay men. The man I was next to proved to be witty, kind, and warm. But just as I was beginning to feel at ease again, I saw the small man from the court-yard cross the room, making his rounds and shaking hands. He knew everyone here, and they all knew him. That cranked my nerves back up, and at just the wrong time.

Before I had a chance to down a glass of wine, I was introduced. My trembling hands clutched my notecards like crutches—tools I've long since learned to do without. I took the lectern and shared the words I had written and practiced, filled with concerns and criticisms I was quickly realizing were aimed directly at many of the leaders in this very ballroom.

OUTGIVING SPEECH NOTES — 2009

Harvey Milk's message was simple: be proud, come out, represent *yourself*, and reach out. If you look at Proposition 8 this past year, there were almost no gay people in the ads or literature, and little effort was made to reach out and educate. In fact, back in September, when I called up some of the folks involved in one of the major organizations fighting Prop 8 and questioned their strategy, I was told, "Gay people do not test well in focus groups." That isn't just bad strategy, that is homophobia, and until we find pride in ourselves again, pride enough to come out, and to reach out, and educate, so that we *do* start testing well amongst our fellow Americans, we will *never* win this fight. Because the simple truth is this: if people don't *personally* know who they're hurting, then they don't mind taking away our civil rights on Election Day.

And after that election, what did I hear from another leader in another of our largest LGBT organizations? "If we just quiet down, 'they' (whoever 'they' are) will let us do whatever we want." These are the words of one of our leaders: "Quiet down." I don't plan on doing that.

There is no question we are at a critical moment. As Dr. Martin Luther King said on the steps of the Lincoln Memorial in 1963, "This is no time to engage in the luxury of cooling off or to take the tranquilizing drug of gradualism." And another quote leaps to mind. It's from Harvey's first run for public office in 1973, when many of the gay movement's leaders told him it was too soon for an openly gay elected official, and not to push too hard, and Harvey said to them:

"Masturbation can be fun, but it does not take the place of the real thing. It is about time that the gay community stopped playing with itself and get down to the real thing. There are people who are satisfied with crumbs because that is all they think they can get, when in reality, if they demand the real thing, they will find that they indeed can get it."

At this point, most in the crowd laughed and cheered. In fact, throughout the speech, there were rousing rounds of applause, but in the back, the wealthy man who had just been so warm now looked none too pleased, and the small man sat stony-faced, his arms folded again. Chad was watching from the wings; his arms were also folded, but he offered a nod that said, "Keep going." The truth is, he couldn't have stopped me if he'd tried. Those stern expressions in the face of my generation's fire, desire, and demands to feel freedom in our life-times had hardened my resolve.

It has been thirty years since Milk gave his life in our struggle
for equality, and we will not wait thirty years more. It is time
for us to stop asking for crumbs and to demand the real thing.
It is time for the LGBT movement to follow in the footsteps of
every successful civil rights movement in this great country's
history, and finally, at last, name our dream:

*We, the gay, lesbian, and transgender people of America
demand that the promise of our constitution and declaration
of independence be honored. We demand that the federal
government act immediately, decisively, and unequivocally
to ensure equal protection under the law for LGBT people
throughout the United States of America.*

Full and equal rights federally. That is the dream.

We must dream bigger than Prop 8's which even in victory
would have denied us full federal marriage rights. We must
instead look back to the example set by *Loving vs. Virginia* and
the Civil Rights Act of 1964. They showed us loud and clear
that full and equal civil rights can only come from the federal
government.

We must name this dream in order to inspire the activist
generation of Harvey Milk to return to the fight, to inspire the
young people to join in, and lay their bodies on the line, to
inspire our straight allies: our mothers, our fathers, lawyers,
grocery store clerks, friends and those who do not yet know
we are their friends. I know this sounds lofty to some, but I
am a child of Harvey Milk, and he has inspired me to dream
and dream big, and big dreams are how change . . . really . . .
happens.

We must recommit ourselves so that when that gay kid out
there tonight in San Antonio, Texas, hears for the first time
that we are finally fighting for his or her *full* equality, federally,
he will know there is a brighter future ahead for him too, and
he will no longer think of taking his life. And that young girl in
Provo, Utah, tonight, she will know that very soon her love will

be just as valued and protected as her straight neighbor's love,
and not in some distant tomorrow. They will be equal citizens
in every state and county of this great nation of ours *within . . .
their . . . lifetimes.*

That is our dream. Equality. At the *federal level.* And together,
we *will* make it our reality.

At that point I received a standing ovation from most in the room.
But the small man refused to rise. My wealthy tablemate was equally
upset. My eyes stayed on them, and time would prove my focus well
aimed.

I I I

The next night, when I was no longer in Las Vegas, my once
warm tablemate got up onstage and gave his own address to
this very same crowd, attempting to dismantle my words as
misguided, impatient, and dishonest. Without question, his heart
was in the right place, and although he had long been a hero of mine,
for the next many years he and others in that room would wage active
campaigns against the plans and strategies that sprung from our
more aggressive philosophy, proving themselves to be devotees of
the "same old, same old" in a time I felt called for innovative action.

But to completely ignore their strategic concerns would have been
a mistake. They knew there weren't enough votes in Congress to pass
an LGBTQ civil rights act, and that a case in the Supreme Court
needed five votes out of nine to win. Most people felt secure that we
had four: Justices Ginsburg and Breyer, as well as Souter and Stevens
(who would soon be replaced by LGBTQ equality-minded Justices
Sotomayor and Kagan). But four is one shy of the five needed to win,
and most felt just as certain that Justices Scalia, Alito, Roberts, and
Thomas would vote against marriage equality. That left us with one
swing vote: Justice Anthony Kennedy.

Justice Kennedy was a conservative Reagan appointee who over the years had shifted slightly left on some issues, including with his opinion on *Romer v. Evans* in 1996, which struck down an anti-gay Colorado constitutional amendment because it failed to prove any rational basis for discriminating against gay people, so it didn't satisfy the Equal Protection Clause of the U.S. Constitution. Then again, in the landmark Supreme Court decision *Lawrence v. Texas,* Kennedy helped strike down Texas's sodomy law and made same-gender sexual activity legal across the United States. Kennedy had not only voted to legalize being gay, bi, or lesbian with his vote, he had also written the affirming opinion himself. His equality-minded words in these opinions gave me a good degree of confidence that he would vote our way on marriage equality as well. And the fact of the matter was, Kennedy and Ginsburg weren't getting any younger. I argued time and again that if a conservative president took the White House and replaced either of those justices with an anti-gay judge, even those small and wealthy men's great-great-grandnephews might never see federal marriage equality. If we were going to bring a case, I thought it wise and necessary to do so while we had any hope of getting five votes. Yes, we were short of certainty, but we did have a reasonable shot in that moment in time.

The small man and wealthy men seemed certain that the Supreme Court would only get more progressive with time. On this point, I felt sure they were being naïve—blind to our nation's history and its pendulum swings when it comes to presidential elections and civil rights. Yes, things move forward, but a pendulum also swings backward. They felt equally sure I was being a fool. At the time, who was I to say they were wrong? Neither side had a crystal ball. Looking back now, after Kennedy's retirement, their argument to wait has proven to be the shortsighted one, and most certainly would have killed marriage equality for generations. But at the time, their ability to persuade others that it was best to wait left us out on a limb. And partly thanks to my spilling the beans in that Las Vegas courtyard, they had a head start branding our strategy as foolish in the court of public opinion.

Back in Los Angeles, Chad and I were having lunch with famed civil rights leader and former head of the NAACP Julian Bond. Julian was nearly seventy then, a straight African American man who saw what many didn't yet: a clear connection between our movements. I was now in need of an authoritative, credible shot of courage to go head to head with my own people, so I shared our Vegas story with Julian Bond.

Julian leaned back and formed one of those smiles that stretches the skin tight over the face. Then, more to the clear blue sky than to me, he said, "Lance, good things do not come to those who wait, they come to those who agitate." His words were just what the doctor ordered. He saw the same value in troublemaking that my activist former dean had. Julian understood that this wasn't the time for "patience." He was encouraging us to use our troublemaking stripes to give history a big shove in the right direction while the iron was still hot.

IV

C had appreciated Julian's words, but he didn't need a shot in the arm like I did. It turned out Chad was a natural agitator with a big troublemaking ace up his sleeve.

A few days after our lunch with Julian, Chad sat down with me and some scrambled eggs in a West Hollywood courtyard café and in his classic casual style suggested something absolutely mad. Months earlier, Chad, along with actor and filmmaker Rob Reiner and his wife, Michele, had caught wind of a rumor that famed conservative Supreme Court lawyer Ted Olson—the man who won the White House for George W. Bush in *Bush v. Gore* in 2000—had a surprisingly pro-equality marriage stance. Chad had already met with Ted in D.C., and in theory, this hero of the right wanted to represent our very queer case.

"The man who gave us Bush?!" I let slip. Ted had argued in favor of almost every conservative case there was. He had been President George W. Bush's solicitor general. "That's insane!"

Unfazed, Chad added that Ted wanted co-counsel, and in that

search had suggested we reach out to David Boies, the famed progressive Supreme Court lawyer Ted had beaten in *Bush v. Gore*. That's when I caught the narrative by its tail. This combination had the power to cross the political divide, to reach from California and Massachusetts to Arkansas, Texas, Mississippi, and Georgia. It was a daring, tricky, but potentially brilliant design to create a new space that might grow acceptance where it was needed most: the places we'd once called home.

Better still, Ted and David were talking in "broad" legal terms about marriage equality—that it was a "fundamental right" guaranteed to all citizens by the U.S. Constitution. A favorable decision based on such arguments wouldn't just reverse Prop 8, it could bring marriage equality to all fifty states. That was important to me. Such a win would apply to my LGBTQ family in California but also to Marcus in Michigan, Virginia, or whatever corner of our country he called home.

Chad wasn't asking for my approval on any of this: he was showing his hand. Little did I know in that meeting at CAA weeks earlier how far along Chad's SCOTUS "notion" already was. Vegas wasn't just a test of our federal ambitions; it was an opportunity for Chad to test the courage of my convictions. Having passed that test, and now enthusiastic about this lawyerly design, I was invited to join the board of a new organization that would sue the state of California in federal court with the wildly unexpected combination of oft-foes Ted Olson and David Boise leading the charge together.

I began attending meetings with our case's other founding board members: Rob and Michele; *Milk* producer Bruce Cohen, who'd secretly been involved for some time; and Chad's esteemed business partner, Kristina Schake. Leaning into the red, white, and blue a bit more than the rainbow flag, we decided to name this new organization the American Foundation for Equal Rights (AFER).

But when the big day finally arrived to publicly announce our intentions, the ire from mainstream LGBTQ leaders and organizations multiplied tenfold. Bringing Ted Olson on board even made the stalwartly progressive ACLU oppose our case. According to many LGBTQ political insiders and opinion makers, we were dragging our people kicking and screaming toward a devastating courtroom loss that would invite a backlash that would set us back decades.

So, despite having been invited, most other LGBTQ civil rights groups and leaders refused to be in the room. They certainly weren't around the first time I come face-to-face with Ted Olson: tall, still very handsome at sixty-seven, with more floppy blond hair than a teen and a warm, resonant voice that must have proven quite helpful in his many wins in front of those nine justices on the nation's highest bench.

Our plaintiffs were in the room that day as well. After an exhaustive search for willing couples, we'd finally found Jeff Zarrillo and Paul Katami, who had been together for many years but hadn't dared marry before the Prop 8 vote for fear of having their marriage certificate ripped up, and Kris Perry and Sandy Stier. Sandy had two sons from a previous marriage that had reached a difficult end in her ex-husband's alcoholism. She'd found a happy new beginning when she'd met Kris. Kris had twin boys from a previous relationship as well. Together they made a family of six. But Kris and Sandy's marriage certificate had indeed been torn up when the California Supreme Court deemed then–San Francisco mayor Gavin Newsom's move to marry gay and lesbian couples in 2004 illegal. Now all Jeff, Paul, Kris, and Sandy wanted was to be able to marry just like their straight siblings could. Lucky for us, they were also brave enough to bear the weight and scrutiny such a case was sure to bring.

Ted took the floor and outlined the path we would have to take to victory. It started with a California federal district court, where the lawyers anticipated the usual filings but foresaw no trial or testimony. "That would be highly unusual," Ted said. Then win or lose, one side or the other would appeal to the federal Ninth Circuit Court of Appeals. We would win or lose again, an appeal would likely be filed, and we would have to wait and see if the U.S. Supreme Court would "grant certiorari," the terminology for taking up a case. There, our case would meet the scrutiny of Justice Kennedy and eight others. We knew the risks, but confident that truth and the law were on our side, we were ready to take them.

Then came a revelation: this was not a one- or even two-year task. We were all likely being asked to put our careers and lives on hold for what might prove to be half a decade or more. That was a lot more time than I (or my agents) had expected. With Hollywood's short-term memory, I would likely be long forgotten by the time this was over.

Then came reassurance: flying in the face of all my assumptions and expectations, Ted didn't launch into a preprepared, rousing, Hollywood-style courtroom speech about how we had a "real shot" at winning our way up to SCOTUS. Instead, he listened. Ted seemed well aware that he had walked into this room an outsider to our gay and lesbian experiences, and he instinctively knew he needed more than just a legal certitude that marriage was a fundamental right if he was going to win this. He needed to know why we felt so strongly about the word "marriage," and how those feelings of being left out of its embrace manifested in our day-to-day lives.

I was impressed but not surprised. As a straight, white conservative, Ted had long argued in favor of family values. He knew how to do that effectively. The big difference between him and so many others on the right was that he actually included *our* families in his definition. So I took a shot that his curiosity was genuine and spoke up: "Well, this is about our lives," I said. "So I think this case should be about our lives too, our personal lives and our personal stories. . . . I worry that if this becomes a story about two powerful lawyers, or just the legal arguments, we won't get very far with the people I know back home. Not in Texas, or Arkansas, or Virginia."

That seemed to grab Ted's attention. So I carried on. I told him some of my own story, and then turned to our plaintiffs' stories and asked that we focus a bit less on the constitutional arguments outside of the courtroom—on TV, in lectures, on stages, or in op-eds. "I think it's important that as much as possible, we put our focus on personal stories: our love, our families, our children. On the experiences my own family and old neighbors back home might relate to. Legal talk won't change my aunts' or uncles' minds. But a good old-fashioned personal story, well . . . we've at least got a shot."

There's no telling how much my plea affected Ted and David's approach, but for the duration of our case, whenever anyone would start to tell their own story, Ted would stop what he was doing and listen. And when he and David took to the airwaves over the next many months, they often led with our plaintiffs' stories. I'm certain I wasn't teaching Ted anything he didn't already know about the powers of persuasion, but what mattered a great deal to me, and ultimately to the way our case was received, was that Ted was genuinely listening to us gay folks. He understood that the most important story in the room wasn't his own.

Chad was in agreement with this personal focus. We both knew that, win or lose, we had a responsibility to use this platform to make measurable progress toward acceptance throughout our country. With such progress, we could rest assured that lives had been made easier, even without a big win. We both understood that personal stories, not political points, move hearts. And I'd long since learned that hearts are what change minds. And if all those hearts and minds pushed statistics and newspaper opinion polls toward equality, well, that was gravy—after all, Supreme Court justices don't live in bubbles; they read the papers too.

No moment better defined the value of the assumption-shattering decision to hire Ted than when he penned a cover story for *Newsweek* titled "The Conservative Case for Gay Marriage." Instead of preaching to the converted along the coasts, Ted was reaching across what had seemed an impossible divide—to the right, and deep into states like Texas, Arkansas, and Louisiana, where Chad and I had our roots, and Michigan, where my big brother was struggling to replant his. We weren't using the language of any one part of America to argue this case—that was the myopic, if not arrogant, trap I'd seen too many worthy causes fall into. We were trying our best to speak many languages, to a varied and diverse people, living in every corner of our beloved country.

On May 26, 2009, our legal team filed our case against Proposition 8 in the U.S. District Court for the Northern District of California. Surprising even our own lawyers, the judge assigned to our case, Chief Judge Vaughn Walker, called for an actual trial. This was highly unusual. Now both sides would be forced to enter a courtroom in San Francisco, each team's witnesses made to raise their right hands and swear to tell the truth, the whole truth, and nothing but the truth under penalty of perjury.

After I shook off the initial shock of having to raise the funds to wage an actual court fight, it began to dawn on me that in a court of law, there would be no refuge for all of the lies, myths, or junk science that had been used in campaign flyers, speeches, and ads against LGBTQ people for generations now. Any shock soon turned to eager anticipation. With both sides under oath, the truth of who I was, who we as a people had always been, and what our families are would be laid bare for the world to see. Without distortion. Finally. Marriage equality, and by extension, our very lives, were about to go on trial.

V

"8": THE PLAY

BUILT FROM THE TESTIMONY TRANSCRIPTS FROM THE PROP 8 TRIAL

KRIS PERRY
I swear to tell the truth, the whole truth, and nothing but the truth—

SANDY STIER
The first time somebody said to me, "Are you married?" and I said, "Yes," I would think, "That feels good and honest and true." I would feel less like I had to protect my kids or worry that they feel any shame or sense of not belonging.

PAUL KATAMI
I shouldn't have to feel ashamed. Being gay doesn't make me any less American. It doesn't change my patriotism. It doesn't change the fact that I pay my taxes and I own a home, and I want to start a family.

JEFFREY ZARRILLO
I would be able to stand alongside my parents and my brother and his wife, to

be able to stand there as one family who
have all had the opportunity of being
married; and the pride that one feels
when that happens.

                    KRIS PERRY
If Prop 8 were undone, and kids like
me growing up in Bakersfield right now
could never know what this felt like,
their entire lives would be on a higher
arc. They would live with a higher sense
of themselves that would improve the
quality of their entire life.

                    SANDY STIER
And that is what I hope can be the
outcome of this case. I hope for
something for Kris and I, but other
people, over time, would benefit in such
an even more profound, life-changing
way. . . . That's what I hope for.

I sat with Rob, Michele, Cleve, our plaintiffs, their kids, and Chad in that courtroom's gallery over several weeks, listening to moving testimony and compelling political and scientific arguments delivered under oath by experts. The trial was a master class in the power of storytelling. The arguments made by those opposed to marriage equality began to fall apart when defended by people under oath. Opposition witnesses who had waxed poetic about the "dangers of homosexuals" refused to testify, and even hid from our side's subpoenas. The opposition's one and only remaining "expert on marriage" folded under David Boies's cross-examination, for all intents and purposes flipping to our side on the stand, and later confirming this flip in *The New York Times*.

By the second week of the trial, what LGBTQ people had long known was finally becoming crystal clear to courtroom observers— the opponents of equality had freely said whatever they wished in campaign commercials, no matter how wildly untrue. But now, in a court of law, those same opponents had to tell the whole truth or be thrown in jail. So with their right hands raised, our fates suddenly became aligned, because their physical freedom meant our liberation.

And as the trial drew to a close, no matter where one stood on the wisdom of our strategy, no one could deny the enormous, historic nature of this case. Slowly, some of the detractors in the LGBTQ community began taking baby steps back our way.

On January 25, 2010, after ten days of testimony, both sides rested their case. Judge Walker chose to delay closing arguments as he considered all the points he'd just heard—his personal preference. When he finally reconvened us on June 16, he welcomed us all back by saying, "It may be appropriate that the case is coming to closing arguments now. June is, after all, the month for weddings." That prompted laughter, and broke the courtroom's tension, at least temporarily. Ted delivered his stirring closing argument, making a case for a fifty-state decision, but demanding that at the very least, Prop 8 had to go. David Boise later commented that it was the best closing argument he'd ever witnessed. Then the opposition's lawyer, Chuck Cooper, with his slicked-back silver hair, gave his closing statements, interrupted many times by the judge, who struggled with Cooper's reasoning—that somehow gays and lesbians marrying "deinstitutionalized" marriage, and thus would keep heterosexuals from procreating. Cooper claimed that "responsible procreation," not animus, was at the heart of this marriage ban.

Less than two months later, on August 3, our team was given notice that a decision was coming the following day. We were each assigned cities to be in. In case of a loss, Chad wanted us to do our best to keep folks from rioting. I was assigned to Los Angeles with Bruce Cohen. I was in his living room when the decision was released.

U.S. DISTRICT CHIEF JUDGE VAUGHN WALKER'S PROP 8 CASE CONCLUSION

AUGUST 2010

Proposition 8 fails to advance any rational basis in singling out gay men and lesbians for denial of a marriage license. Indeed, the evidence shows Proposition 8 does nothing more than enshrine in the California Constitution the notion that opposite-sex couples are superior to same-sex couples. Because California has no interest in discriminating against

gay men and lesbians, and because Proposition 8 prevents
California from fulfilling its constitutional obligation to
provide marriages on an equal basis, the court concludes that
Proposition 8 is unconstitutional.

"We won. We won big," Ted said moments after reading an advance
copy of Judge Walker's sweeping decision. This was the kind of decision that could bring marriage equality to all fifty states if it survived
its journey to the U.S. Supreme Court. That thought made my heart
soar. The nationwide celebrations in the streets that followed its wide
release were also thrilling. My mom called from Virginia. "You're on
TV! You're famous!" The kid in me ate up her enthusiasm. Her gay
son had just popped up on CNN making a pro–gay marriage speech,
and that was *good* news? Boy, we'd come a long way.

But I explained that we still had to make it through the Ninth Circuit Court of Appeals before even dreaming of our case being picked
up by SCOTUS. We had a long way still to go.

One big challenge to the effectiveness of our myth-busting trial was
that those opposed to marriage equality had successfully fought all
the way to the U.S. Supreme Court to ban cameras from the courtroom. It seemed they knew they had things to hide. Their win to
ban cameras meant that only those in the courtroom or those willing
to read reams of transcripts understood the historic, revelatory, and
decisive nature of what had transpired. The rest only got glimpses—
what news anchors and papers shared.

But our opposition couldn't stop me from putting my storytelling
skills to use to help solve this problem. I briefly considered writing
a movie based on the transcripts, but a movie takes many years to
make and would've missed the moment. However, with the right collaborators, a play can be written and staged within a year. So with the
help of Jenny Kanelos, Rory O'Malley, and Gavin Creel of Broadway
Impact, we constructed a plan to premiere a new play on Broadway
based on the trial's transcripts as a benefit fund-raiser for the case,
then to use that play as an outreach and education tool in the areas
that most needed to hear the stories and evidence that had produced

such a sweeping decision. Hollywood wouldn't hear much from me for a good long time still, but my skills weren't going unused.

Ultimately, *"8": The Play* premiered in New York and Los Angeles with casts that included John Lithgow, Brad Pitt, George Clooney, Christine Lahti, Martin Sheen, Jamie Lee Curtis, Jesse Tyler Ferguson, Kevin Bacon, Yeardley Smith, and Jane Lynch, bringing our plaintiffs' moving stories even more attention and raising millions of dollars to support our cause. The show then took to the road, where our plaintiffs' stories and the trial's actual words would reach all fifty states and eight countries.

In this way and so many more, we were sharing our stories and making our case in every corner of our diverse country. We knew it would take Ted and David, red and blue, conservatives and progressives working together to move the nation's heart toward equality. And as every turn in the road made our journey longer, not one of us doubted that our sacrifices were worth it. Our little team had been called to mine and share the very best of our lives, our families, and our very different American journeys. Like I told my mom, even with this one big win in California, the road ahead was still long, and any victory was far from certain, but our efforts along this road would prove to be our greatest honor.

CHAPTER 21

Virginia Roads

I

My mom's voice was shaking when she called. It was tough to tell these days if that was due to emotional duress or to the side effects of the cancer treatments she'd long since finished but which had further harmed her muscular strength. Her days and nights were now filled with fibromyalgia pain, belabored breathing, and the blurring effects of painkillers. But, it turned out this call wasn't about her own pain. "Hey, Lancer, can you call Marco?"

And so I played my part in our increasingly flipped parental roles. "It's past midnight in Michigan now, and in Virginia. Shouldn't you both be asleep?" I asked her.

"Don't worry about how late it is. He needs to hear your voice tonight." She was firmly the parent again. This wasn't a suggestion. And it wasn't something she had asked me to do before. Even during our less connected days, Marcus and I were closer than most siblings, likely because of all we'd survived together. He'd always reached out to me if he needed something, or just wanted to talk. Since he'd come out, our talks had become even more regular. So I worried what calamity was so severe that he had held it from me.

In conversations here and there, I'd already deduced that the man Marcus had met online and moved out to Michigan to be with hadn't ended up ticking all the boxes Marcus had hoped. The guy struggled to make ends meet, and couldn't resolve the simplest of conflicts with anyone. Marcus knew his boyfriend was no Prince Charming, but no one could deny that being in a relatively closet-free relationship was yielding benefits. Marcus still had beers and smokes now and then, but the hard drug use suddenly stopped. No rehab needed. He said he'd simply lost the desire. For the first time since our father's abandonment, his self-esteem was on the mend. With that boost, Marcus had also quit his knuckle-breaking job at Sears Auto Center and started attending college to study design and architecture.

I had always known that Marcus was the smartest and most creative of us three boys. He had paved the way for my own entry into drama club, and inspired me to draw and paint, and now his sky-high grades in college were measurable proof that he was the best of us, not the bad seed, as too many had assumed. So as I dialed the phone, I secretly hoped that his self-confidence had improved enough that he was ready to unload his half-rate beau.

When I finally got Marcus on the line, he sounded down. He had been expecting my call. But instead of walking me through a breakup tale, he revealed something far more dire.

Around the time of AFER's win in federal district court, Marcus had begun peeing blood. Embarrassed that it might be an STD, he ignored the symptoms. Now a student instead of an employee, Marcus had no medical insurance for the first time in his life, and in a country and state with no decent public health care, this meant that when he could no longer ignore the pain and blood, he was forced to accept a cruddy free clinic's false STD diagnosis and ineffective antibiotics. When the pills failed, he chose to bear the pain until it became impossible to urinate.

By the time my big brother had waited his turn for medical care in an endless line of folks with no insurance, the tumor doctors found filled 75 percent of his bladder. When it was finally removed over two painful procedures that scraped it loose with a wire and dragged it out through his urethra, the doctors claimed the growth was nothing to worry about.

Within months, the tumor was back: bigger, bloodier, and more painful. When he finally told our mom, she had immediately put down a credit card to get Marco in to see a proper doctor. Only thanks to our mom plunging herself into debt she could never repay on a retirement salary did Marcus learn the truth: he had a fast-growing, aggressive cancer in his bladder, twice misdiagnosed by a failing health care system—and now it had spread to his prostate. He had wanted an education, a brighter future. His dedication to that goal had left him uninsured, and barred from good care. Now what had likely been a treatable condition was life-or-death.

The only feasible option was to completely remove his bladder, rebuild a new one from a piece of his intestine, and take out his prostate. If it turned out the nerves in and around his prostate also had to go, this would likely spell the end of the sex life Marcus had just begun to explore. It was an aggressive, risky surgery that, if unsuccessful, would result in my brother's having no bladder at all—just a tube running from his gut out the side of his body and down into a plastic bag that would hang off of him for the rest of his life.

During that phone call, I heard my very tough big brother legitimately terrified for the first time. "Why now, bro? I'm finally figuring shit out." I had no good answer for that, because there was none. This seemed senseless and cruel to me too.

I immediately flew to Michigan, where I met my mom at the airport. We sat by Marcus's side before his surgery. Marcus was busy blaming himself for this whole mess, and now the trauma he was causing my mom, who was in such a frail state herself. Marcus's doctor believed that the chemicals Marcus had fed his body willingly, and those he'd been exposed to at the Sears Auto Center, could have contributed to this cancer. If he had just drunk less, smoked less, partied less, gotten a decent job . . . "Fucking Sears, man. I'm gonna have a piss bag hanging out of my gut and no boners the rest of my life because of fucking Sears Auto Center?!"

"Watch your language, Marco!" our mom snapped back instinctively.

"Sorry, Mom."

She took his weakened hand in hers and reconsidered. "No. You've got nothing to be sorry for, my baby. You just 'f-ing' get better for me." She couldn't say the swear word, but this was as close as I had ever heard her get, and her sentiment was clear. It was his turn to kick cancer's ass just like she had, and he was free to do that however he liked.

After we kissed and hugged him, the nurses took my big brother into surgery. He gave my mom two big thumbs up, and when she wasn't looking, he opened his mouth wide, stuck his tongue out like Ozzy Osbourne, and flipped me off with both middle fingers. It was his way of saying, "I fucking love you, bro!"

I sat with my mom in the waiting room. As luck would have it, New York State passed their Marriage Equality Act that same day. Now all New Yorkers could get married and enjoy their state's marriage benefits and protections—but federal benefits would still be out of reach for them. That would take something like a sweeping federal court decision in a case like ours. Still, the scenes coming in from

New York City on CNN were jubilant, a reminder of our own celebrations months earlier.

But as I sat in that waiting room watching CNN, a brand-new concern settled in: that perhaps our case was taking too long to get to the Supreme Court. I began to wonder how many of those who first rose up and fought for gay liberation at the Stonewall Inn in Manhattan forty-two years earlier hadn't lived to see this day of freedom and celebration in their own state . . . and by extension, how many more of us today wouldn't live to see full federal marriage equality in our lifetimes.

When Marcus emerged from surgery, there was blessedly no plastic "piss bag" hanging off his body. The doctor had managed to build a new bladder out of Marcus's intestine and felt confident he had gotten all of the cancer out without having to remove all of the nerves in Marcus's prostate.

As he struggled for lucidity, this concern was Marcus's prime post-surgery query: "Will I be able to get a boner again, doc?"

"Well . . . not right away," the doctor replied, a bit discomfited by this line of questioning in front of our mother. "But eventually."

"Love you, doc." Marcus seemed quite pleased and erectile-hopeful. So we were pleased and hopeful as well.

In the months that followed, other signs of hope emerged. Our marriage equality case suddenly wasn't alone. The wife of a woman named Edie Windsor passed away, and despite the fact that they were legally married in their home state of New York, Edie received a big federal tax bill for the inheritance—a bill a straight person would never have been issued just for keeping what she and her spouse had shared. Despite pressure to keep quiet from some of the same nervous folks who had demanded our case slow down, Edie chose to fight back too. She found herself a brilliant lawyer named Roberta Kaplan and sued the United States in federal court claiming that the Defense of Marriage Act was unconstitutional. DOMA was the legislation that had barred the federal recognition of same-sex marriages since 1996, when President Clinton broke his campaign assurances to protect LGBTQ people by signing it into law.

Now two marriage cases were racing toward SCOTUS, ours making an argument for same-sex marriage in all fifty states as a fundamental, constitutional right, and Edie's making an argument that would kill DOMA and bestow federal benefits on gay and lesbian marriages, but only in states with marriage equality already, like New York. Edie's case moved fast. And after a long-delayed win at the Ninth Circuit Court of Appeals, our case was at long last on its way to Supreme Court consideration as well.

Now the high-stakes waiting game began: Would SCOTUS grant either of our cases "cert"? Would marriage equality soon see the highest court in the land?

I prayed that the answer was yes. We could all feel that a tide was turning. Those allies who had initially pushed back were now pushing with us, including the men I'd met in Las Vegas, the ACLU, HRC, NCLR, and GLAAD, all working nationwide—online, in print, on the ground, and on TV news shows—to share stories of more couples and families seeking marriage equality. And braver than any court case or organization, individuals across the country were coming out and sharing their stories on the most consequential stage there is: the family dinner table. It felt like Milk-style politics on a national scale.

Soon, polls confirmed our feelings, demonstrating that no matter what part of the country someone called home, most could now say they personally knew at least one LGBTQ neighbor, coworker, family member, or friend. And as the SCOTUS cert decisions drew near, news networks began reporting that a majority of Americans now favored extending marriage equality to gay and lesbian people—their friends, family, and neighbors.

To my heart, it felt like the nation I'd always loved was finally getting to know and love their LGBTQ children. And then, after publicly opposing marriage equality in his 2008 presidential campaign, even Barack Obama, a sitting president, came out vocally in favor of our right to marry, and not after but *before* his election to a second term. We were truly and measurably winning hearts and changing minds.

Then, at the tail end of December 2012, Adam Umhoefer, the executive director of our case's foundation, rang me up, his voice filled with excitement and nerves. Surprising many a pundit, the U.S. Supreme Court had just granted both our and Edie's cases certiorari. Nearly four years into this grand venture, we were headed to the United States Supreme Court.

I I

It was a cold March morning. There were no leaves on the trees yet, but the sky was clear. I had flown out to Virginia the night before, and my mom quickly criticized that I'd "packed like a Californian." So Jeff had lent me his thick winter pea coat when I left the house early the next morning to catch a train into Washington, D.C. With that pea coat on, and a bright blue scarf wrapped twice around my neck, this Texas boy was warm enough to walk slowly from the Metro to the highest court in the land, and quite slowly, taking in the Library of Congress, where Clint Eastwood, Leonardo DiCaprio, Naomi Watts, and I had shot scenes for *J. Edgar* just a few years earlier. It was the last film I had been hired to write before turning my full attention to this equality fight, and despite the draw of working with my teenage crush, I wasn't able to be there to help produce the film like I had with *Milk*. I yearned to return to filmmaking. I missed the thrill and challenge of those bright lights, of working with the great actors of our time. That all felt a world away now.

I turned my gaze across the street, to the Capitol dome, pondering the future, thoughts of serving this nation I love one day, perhaps even as a representative. A boy can dream. Then I looked past the dome to the Washington Monument—the same spire Martin Luther King Jr. must have looked up to at least once as he shared his great dream of equality at the March on Washington for Jobs and Freedom in 1963. Also in my line of sight was the vast lawn before the Capitol that had once been covered by Cleve Jones's quilt bearing the names of those AIDS had ripped from us. I was walking in the steps of so many noble men and women engaged in the struggles of our past, present, and future. And then I worried. As confident as those of us who had brought this case needed to appear to our brothers and sisters in the movement, I was far from certain what legacy our efforts might soon find in this city's history—a history filled with great leaps forward but also terrible losses for people of diversity.

It was early morning still, but supporters and protestors were already gathering outside the Supreme Court. With Chad now at my side, I joined the line south of the court's grand steps, alongside Bruce Cohen, Cleve Jones, Rob and Michele Reiner, and countless others now championing these marriage cases that were gripping the nation. Every news station, paper, website, and blog had been headlining these two cases for months. Their outcomes promised protests, riots, or massive celebrations—and we knew we had a responsibility to be prepared for every outcome, nationwide. We had made very public promises that taking this fight to the federal government meant everyone would have a stake, so we knew most would react no matter what corner of the country they called home, and the results of those reactions were on our shoulders.

The line began to move outside the court. My chest began quivering, but not from the cold. We all followed the court's guard, easing past an army of news crews setting up cameras on the steps for the morning shows. Reaching the first landing, I looked back. The crowd of supporters had already grown to hundreds; a stage was being prepped for a rally. I spotted so many familiar faces from across the country, people who had traveled to be here on this historic day, and as they watched us make our way inside, they sent up a cheer of encouragement louder than their numbers. Then one by one, we walked between those famed columns and through the front doors of the United States Supreme Court. We had finally reached our destination.

Stepping inside the U.S. Supreme Court is a humbling, if not religious, experience. It's a temple. A temple to history, to the rule of law, to the U.S. Constitution: heavenly white marble with deep gray ribbons of earthly complications, red velvet curtains that could provoke a queen's envy, and dark wooden chairs and benches that refuse to let visitors forget how many have come before. It is the architectural definition of drama.

Our little crew took our seats near the front. Our nerves were visible. It had taken four long years to get here, and now all the arguments for and against marriage equality would have to be squeezed into little more than an hour. Ted Olson would be making the case for our side, and Chuck Cooper for the other. Slicked-back-silver-haired Cooper, who'd been leading the opposition against us this entire time, would soon argue to nine justices that marriage was a step too far for Americans like me, my big brother, Kris, Sandy, Jeff, and Paul.

The justices entered the grand inner courtroom in their robes with an immense amount of gravitas. The sight of Justice Ginsburg easing into her chair was inspiring—she may have been eighty and small, but she wasn't frail or elderly, and her line of questioning suggested that she was on our side. Justice Kagan took matters a step further as she directly confronted the same "procreation" argument Cooper had been making for years now as he tried to make it land here.

SCOTUS "PERRY" CASE TRANSCRIPTS

MR. COOPER: The concern is that redefining marriage as a genderless institution will sever its abiding connection to its historic traditional procreative purposes, and it will refocus, refocus the purpose of marriage and the definition of marriage away from the raising of children and to the emotional needs and desires of adults, of adult couples. Suppose, in turn—

JUSTICE KAGAN: Well, suppose a State said, Mr. Cooper, suppose a State said that, Because we think that the focus of marriage really should be on procreation, we are not going to give marriage licenses anymore to any couple where both people are over the age of 55. Would that be constitutional?

MR. COOPER: No, Your Honor, it would not be constitutional.

JUSTICE KAGAN: Because that's the same State interest, I would think, you know. If you are over the age of 55, you don't help us serve the Government's interest in regulating procreation through marriage. So why is that different?

MR. COOPER: Your Honor, even with respect to couples over the age of 55, it is very rare that both couples—both parties to the couple are infertile, and the traditional—

(Laughter.)

JUSTICE KAGAN: No, really, because if the couple—I can just assure you, if both the woman and the man are over the age of 55, there are not a lot of children coming out of that marriage.

(Laughter.)

It was a reassuring moment, but then from the four justices we had assumed might be against us came darker confirmations. I watched Scalia gleefully poke at Ted Olson. If cameras were allowed in this courtroom, the country could have seen how Scalia chuckled between several of the inflammatory questions he posited, seemingly loving their headline-worthy, caustic nature. Or how the perpetually silent Justice Thomas whispered jokes into Justice Breyer's ear, spinning around in his chair after his own punch lines as if this were a playground—as if citizens' lives weren't at stake. So although we clearly didn't agree on the issue of marriage equality, I appreciated that at least Roberts and Alito seemed to be taking their jobs seriously that morning.

It was a lot to absorb and decipher, so I listened very carefully, marking the time we had left. TV pundits would soon offer their own "pivotal moment" opinions, but for me, the historic newsflash came exactly twenty-four minutes in. That was when my crinkled-up, overly sensitive ears heard Justice Anthony Kennedy turn to Chuck Cooper and speak words I will never forget:

JUSTICE KENNEDY: There's substance to the point that sociological information is new (re: gay marriage). We have five years of information to weigh against 2,000 years of history or more.

On the other hand, there is an immediate legal injury, or legal, what could be a legal injury, *and that's the voice of these children.*

(I stopped breathing.)

There are some 40,000 children in California, according to the Red Brief, that live with same-sex parents, and they want their

parents to have full recognition and full status. The voice of
those children is important in this case, don't you think?

Full stop. To my ears, this debate was over. My entire life, I had
heard arguments from my church and our state that LGBTQ people
somehow harmed children. Harvey Milk had fought such claims in
his battle to protect gay teachers, Prop 8 ads had sounded the same
alarm bells, and Chuck Cooper had alluded to such arguments in
this very case back in district court.

Now, hearing in that question from Kennedy's own lips a defense
of gay parents' children, our children, I knew that our combined work
and sacrifices over so many years had proven effective. Somewhere
along this journey, or perhaps well before, Kennedy had heard us, he
had seen us, and he understood that the recipient of injury in this
case was LGBTQ people themselves, and that the malfeasant was the
unequal laws that had reinforced so many false narratives and deemed
our families less than equal for too long and for no good reason.

Cleve was sitting next to me. I took his hand and looked him in the
eyes. I can cry at greeting card commercials. He isn't that guy. He had
already survived too many fights with greater consequences than this
one. But in that moment, his eyes were also brimming. He had heard
and understood what I had. He knew what lived just beneath Kennedy's question. The critical fifth vote on this divided court was ours.

When we walked out of the Supreme Court together, our little
team of fighters and plaintiffs, the rallying LGBTQ supporters and
allies out front had grown to thousands. They let out a massive cheer
for our plaintiffs. Although cameras weren't allowed, the court had
released audio from the proceedings. Many in the crowd had also felt
Kennedy's question on a deeper level than how the more dour political pundits were now spinning it for the cameras. Personally, I didn't
need any experts' opinions. If we didn't win a broad decision in one
of these two cases immediately, the words these cases had pushed
Kennedy to utter would surely set off an avalanche of new cases that
would give him the legal opportunity to give us all fifty states. So
even if it meant sticking with this fight a little longer to set that avalanche in motion, I felt certain that we would soon see fifty.

Now there was only one thing I needed: to talk to my big brother, my great protector for so much of my life, and to tell him that we had stood up for *his* life today. That we were now one massive leap closer to my freedoms in California being his too. That thanks to the eye-opening call to action he'd tasked me with in his coming-out phone call that sunny Sunday half a decade earlier, my joy would soon be his joy, my liberation would soon be his liberation, and that the light I'd felt grow inside when our mother had held and accepted me for me would soon be his light too—no matter where in our great country he chose to call home or whom he fell in love with. It was now, at long last, time to finish that conversation we had started in San Francisco. Except that now, this call was impossible.

I I I

One winter earlier, as we awaited a long-delayed decision from the Ninth Circuit Court of Appeals, my phone rang in Los Angeles. It was Marcus. I picked up, eager to hear about his healthful recovery as our case bobbed about in legal doldrums. Instead, he could barely form words through his new pain. "I need your help. Can you come to Michigan? Right now?"

Months after the very hopeful prognosis following his surgery, Marcus began experiencing back pain. He had seen physical therapists and chiropractors to try to figure out where it was coming from and how to heal it, but it just kept getting worse. He described it to me as the worst toothache he'd ever had, but deep down in his back. I did as my mother had taught me: I attacked his pain with optimism, no matter how foolish. I tried to convince him that there was a solution and we would figure out what it was. But I could hear that he was growing weary of the same old assurances. Our best efforts only seemed to open doors to new problems. So I got off the phone and booked another ticket to Michigan.

In the time it took me to get there, an X-ray revealed a shaded area on his spine where Marcus had been describing his pain for months now to doctors and nurses who kept downplaying it. One look from a

specialist and it was crystal clear that my brother's cancer was back—
and it couldn't have found a more dangerous new home.

Walking into Marcus's small Michigan apartment, I felt sick to my
stomach. The place was a maze of filth: dirty clothes, unwashed
dishes, and containers of rotting fast food stacked to the ceiling. Marcus's boyfriend wasn't simply a disappointment; he was a monstrous
narcissist. He couldn't be bothered to take care of their home, much
less my ailing brother. When I found my way to the living room, an
unbearable sight stunned me still. Surrounded by empty prescrip-
tion pills bottles, my big, tough Marco was in a fetal position, long
unshaven and unbathed, and in terrible pain on their soiled sofa.

When Marcus looked up at me, his eyes deeply sunken and ringed
in gray, he thought I was a phantom. He closed his eyes again, grind-
ing his jaw, forcing back what looked to be excruciating pain. I gently
eased my way down onto the couch beside him and started stroking
his hair. "Where does it hurt, Marco?"

His eyes opened again, this time meeting mine, trying to comprehend the fact that his little brother was beside him here in Michigan.

"Where does it hurt, Marco?" I softly repeated.

Slowly recognizing that I was real, he began to sob. He was in too
much pain for words. He pointed to an area on his lower back, then
gripped my hand so tightly I could feel his pain. His body was thinner
than I'd ever seen it, but his hands were still big, rough, and strong.

"Can I touch it?"

He nodded. I began massaging the rock-hard, severely cramped
muscles by his spine. Thankfully, my touch did relieve a bit of his
pain, at least temporarily, and he slowly regained some awareness—
enough to let me know what he needed most: water, food, a cigarette,
more medicine, better medicine, a doctor who gave a damn, and to
get the hell out of the home of this horrible, stinking man in whom
he had misplaced his trust.

I've rarely become so angry that I'd use a word like "vengeful" to
describe my feelings, but I wanted to kill. My goals in Michigan suddenly changed from care to rescue. I dropped everything, and started
sorting through the soiled clothes, garbage, and discarded medical

supplies for my brother's belongings. I called any and all of Marcus's old friends, people who he would trust and who might prove willing and able to lend a hand.

Trying to get care for my uninsured brother in Michigan was like hitting a brick wall repeatedly with my head, with no helmet and the entire state government pushing from behind to make my skull crack harder. At one point, a doctor who was supposedly a specialist in bone cancer looked at me as if I were a dusty old chalkboard, not a human being, and within earshot of my big brother said, "What do you want me to do, cut him in half?" And he walked away. Welcome to American medical care for the uninsured working class.

In the evenings, in an effort to sort my brother's lifelong treasures from his lover's stinking trash, I stumbled upon one heartbreak after the next. The deepest stab was a letter from Marcus's dean congratulating him on his fine performance and stellar grades, and informing my once underachieving big brother that he was now on the dean's list of exceptional students. The letter had come just a week before Marcus had called me about his new back pain. Marcus's old question of "Why now?" was becoming increasingly impossible to answer without cursing God.

And then a small glimmer of hope arrived. Correction: a rather sizeable glimmer. Marcus's old friend Steve was suddenly out of a job in Salinas, California, and was up for "kicking any asses that need kickin', and getting our boy outta that fuckin' bitch hole." I booked Steve's ticket, and he was with us in a day. The first thing I said when I saw him again was "You, my friend, are huge." I had forgotten how big he was.

"Why, thank you very much." He loved his big-boy size, and I was grateful for it. This was definitely the guy you wanted by your side in an emergency move scenario, and on more than one occasion, his three hundred pounds easily backed my big brother's neglectful lover out of the apartment so I couldn't literally wring his neck.

Steve and I came up with a plan, which we shared with Marcus as he clenched his jaw against the pain. Instead of continuing to do battle in hostile territory, we would get Marcus home: to the South, to Virginia, and to my mom. During her own cancer treatments, she had exercised her charm with the doctors and nurses, quickly becoming a beloved star among her dedicated docs—doctors who might prove more willing and able to help heal their new star's son. I added, "And we'll pull off this trip by Christmas, Marco. I promise." That got a huge smile.

But Christmas was only a few days away now, and there were some major hurdles to get past. Marcus couldn't sit for more than a few minutes without unbearable pain, and as his intestine-constructed neo-bladder was still healing, he was temporarily dependent on a catheter to help drain his bladder through his urethra, and that needed changing often. So sitting in the cab of his truck or in an airplane seat wouldn't work. He needed to lie flat. I tried to rent an RV, but in this area at this time of year, we'd have to wait another three days before one became available. That would mean missing Christmas. And that would mean breaking my promise.

So in his rough country way, Steve suggested, "We put a bed cover on his truck 'n' slide him in back on topa his mattress that's on topa his boxes. Put the dog back there with him ta keep him warm, and git walkie-talkies so he can chew our ears off up front if he starts freezin' or dyin'. And we drive this bitch home ourselves. You 'n' me."

It was the dead of winter in one of the coldest states in America, the back of Marcus's truck wasn't heated, and I'm so severely claustrophobic that such a plan sounded like an absolute nightmare to me. But to Marcus and Steve it just sounded like another survival stunt that fit in just fine with the thousands of others they'd somehow pulled off before. They were ready to go.

It was the middle of the night and it had started to snow. Nevertheless, we followed Steve's plan, trying not to hurt Marcus too badly as we slid him into the back of the truck. Max jumped right up in there with him, their bodies pressed against the new hardtop. Then Steve did something that really worried me. He put a battery-operated electric heater in back with Marcus—in what would soon be a very cluttered, tight, and enclosed space—defying every warning on the heater's label. I protested, but Marcus and Steve overruled me. It was that damn cold.

We fed Marcus a heavy dose of pain pills, shut the back gate, and tested the walkie-talkies. Steve took a giant swig of something I pretended was water but knew full well was far stronger, and we hit the road in the middle of a snowstorm to try to make it home in time for at least one last "best Christmas ever."

But my calculations quickly proved overly optimistic. Marcus had to stop every fifteen to thirty minutes to drain his neo-bladder, not once an hour. And on one of the early stops, he seemed frighteningly loopy. "Read the damn sticker!" I said to him and Steve. "It clearly states that this heater is not to be used in small spaces. It could be putting out deadly gasses, or catch the whole damn truck and my fucking brother on fire!" They paused, laughed, and called me a drama queen. But they let me throw that heater in a dumpster. Now it was truly freezing in back, but Marcus refused to let us turn back or get a hotel room. He was determined to make it home.

Up front, Steve and I burned through packs of Marlboro Reds on the long and winding roads into Pennsylvania's hills, snow falling so fast and hard we couldn't see most of the turns until we were halfway through them. Marcus stopped talking over the radio. I genuinely worried that he might die in the back of the truck, so now I was the one insisting on frequent stops—to shake him awake and make sure his heart was still beating.

A day and a half into our journey, running on no sleep at all but insisting he keep the wheel, Steve began to drift off while driving. My job became shaking him awake when his eyes got heavy. When my shaking stopped working, it became an elbow to the ribs; by the time we crossed the Virginia state line, I was punching him in the shoulder as hard as I possibly could to get any response.

Then a bit past daybreak on Christmas Eve, Steve pulled the truck up to the wide, welcoming porch of our family home.

For the first time in hours, Marcus radioed me from the back. "Let me out."

I pressed the button. "Ten-four, bro."

"No. Hurry the fuck up. I need out."

He sounded angry and desperate, so I rushed to the back, opened the gate, and started gently pulling him out.

"Come on. Pull harder!"

I did. Max leaped out, then Marcus emerged, and I hustled to pull his wheelchair out from under the mattress so we could get him inside.

"Fuck off with that."

He didn't need to explain. He didn't want his chair. Like mother, like son.

Then softer, "How do I look?" he asked.

"Horrible," I said.

"Then fuckin' fix me, asshole."

And in the freezing cold, with absolutely no respectable gay tools at my disposal, I did my very best to fix his hair, to adjust his clothes, to scrape the crust from his mouth and eyes, and to make him look as handsome as humanly possible given the circumstances.

"You done? I gotta go shove a tube up my dick and fake-piss," he said.

"You look perfect," I lied.

Then I quickly ran around the truck to intercept Steve. I begged him to stay in the truck until Marcus had been through our front door for at least five minutes, maybe ten. Steve was then and will always be my superhero, but at that moment he was a superhero stinking of booze and smokes. He didn't need an explanation. I left him with "I love you, Steve. If you weren't a bear, and maybe twenty years younger . . ."

He shot back, "And if you had tits, baby."

I turned around. Marcus was already halfway up the driveway, walking under his own power for the first time since I'd flown out to Michigan. And just then, the front door opened. Our mom was in a wheelchair with oxygen tubes in her nose, but her arms immediately reached out with strength for her eldest boy to be wrapped up in. Todd had come home the night before. He and Jeff were just behind my mom. Marcus glanced back my way, and I'll never forget the look. He smiled a genuine "Thank you" through his pain. This walk to my mom's arms would be one of his finest moments, perhaps the greatest, most selfless performance of his life. With each step, he was giving our mom the greatest gift he could this Christmas: hope. Like she had done for us so many times in our poorest years, he didn't want to ruin her Christmas with the painful truth.

They held each other for what seemed like forever, and as I watched them, a deep, unfathomable fear sank into my gut. A fear that would soon be confirmed.

After I'd helped Marcus with his catheter and into and out of a bath, we all went to one of the hospitals my mother had gone to for care. They loved her there. Despite all the challenging side effects from her aggressive treatments, she was indeed in remission. A survivor yet again. And at this hospital, with the promise that we'd pay cash to do things right, they finally provided what seemed like humane care for our Marco. A special bed was sent to our home, appropriately strong drugs were prescribed, and a plan of action was drawn up for an aggressive round of targeted radiation. But when it came time for a prognosis, the news was no Christmas miracle. "There's always a chance," the kind doctor said, "and we are going to fight hard for that chance, but if I had to guess . . . I'd say six months to one year."

I hadn't eaten any real food in more than a day, so there was nothing to throw up, but after days of denying myself tears, my grief began trying to escape in other ways. I remember repeatedly dry heaving in a hospital bathroom stall as quietly as I could. This had all come on so suddenly: my mom and now my big brother. I was doing all I could to help fix them, but nothing seemed to be working. Now, the thing that had always mattered most to me, that had helped me stand tall, that had fueled my courage, that made me strong, was slipping through my fingers. My family was dying, and with it, I feared, my own hope and strength would too.

I V

We enjoyed a glorious Christmas together. We hardly noticed the tubes in my mom's nose, the wheelchairs all around, or the new bed in the living room that kept Marcus more comfortable. And when my mom gifted Marco her treasured 1967 Camaro, which had been gathering dust and rust in the garage for years now, he burst into tears. She must have known he'd likely never use it, but we all knew he loved that car. And she understood the value of optimism, and how those keys in the hands of an old Southern grease monkey provided more hope than any words could. And for that small reason, and for so many larger ones, Marcus meant it with every ounce of his being when he said, "This is the best Christmas ever, Mom." Because he likely knew this was the last time he would ever tell her that. It was the greatest gift he could give.

In the weeks that followed, it became clear that my brave big brother wasn't getting better and likely didn't have six to twelve months. I had flown back to Los Angeles just before New Year's Eve only to receive a call from our mom that I needed to get back to Virginia quick. In the short time I was gone, Marcus had dropped half his weight, and one leg was so thin that it didn't look alive anymore. He could no longer walk and was struggling to maintain consciousness. The cancer was moving very rapidly up his bones and into his skull. It was clear now that Marcus likely should have died far sooner, still in the squalor of his Michigan apartment, and that the promise to get him home had pushed him to hold on long enough to feel our mother's warmth once more. Now time was not our friend.

Perhaps sensing what I still refused to see, Todd had stayed in Virginia instead of flying back home to where he now lived in Texas. Marcus, Todd, and Jeff had shared long talks about old NASCAR races and fishing holes, and then a New Year's Eve in the hospital when Marcus's pain flared so badly he needed an IV to help relieve it. There, doctors ordered a complete MRI but never shared the results with Marcus. It turns out the cancer now ran the entire length of his spine and pelvis. It was devastating news. Soon Marcus was headed back home for good, the IV drip at his side feeding him a steady dose of morphine. The only aim now was to make our big brother as comfortable as possible.

When a nurse came by the house to check on Marcus, I asked her about his pain, about his level of awareness. Sensing my paternal nature, and hearing the question I was refusing to ask outright, she showed me a button I could press to give my big brother more painkiller "as needed." But I could read in her caring eyes what she legally or ethically couldn't say: "It will be over soon. Help make this as easy as possible for him."

I expected to be in Virginia for weeks. Instead, a few nights later, it became clear that Marcus was slipping fast. He no longer wanted to suck the water from the lollipop-shaped sponge we held to his lips. He could no longer form sentences and struggled to find simple words. Then one night, after sitting by his side all day, my mom kissed his hands and told him how much she loved him, and Jeff carried her up to bed to try to get some much-needed sleep. Todd and I stayed by Marcus's side, mostly in silence, just "being there" with him.

Sometime just before midnight, when all the shops in the area closed, Todd and I looked at each other. Something about the solemnity of this night didn't feel right. It didn't feel like Marcus. We knew what we needed to do. For too long, the world had bristled at Marcus's bad behavior: the drinking, the drugs, the heavy metal and punk rock music, and then others must have mocked him as a fag or pervert. If ever there was a moment to fully embrace my big brother, well, there weren't many left. And it seemed to us that rule number one in Marcus's instruction manual had always been to break as many rules as possible.

Todd ran to the store and quickly returned with a package. I leaned into Marcus's ear and said, "Hey, Marco, hey, hey." His eyes fluttered open just enough that we could tell he was listening. "Hey, Marco . . . What if we stop dipping this sponge into water . . ."

I stopped my sentence halfway through to choke back the tears I didn't want him to see or hear. I didn't want to scare him more. But he took my pause as the end of my sentence and nodded. He was done with water. The thing is, I wasn't done with my sentence: "And what if we start dipping it in Crown Royal?"

Marco's eyes shot wide open in a way they hadn't in a week. He was wide-awake now! He put on a devilish grin that stretched from ear to rules-be-damned ear. So I dipped that sponge into the Crown Royal Todd had just brought home and put it to Marcus's lips. He sucked it down fast. Then it was Todd's turn to give him a shot, and then mine again. Our unresponsive brother now seemed awake, alive, and thirstier than a cowboy in the desert.

Todd took the party up a notch, searching for the Dead Milkmen on his phone and hitting Play when he found "Bitchin' Camaro." Like a punk Lazarus rising, Marcus raised his bone-thin right arm into the air, his index and pinky fingers extending out like horns, and shook that devilish hand to the crazed beat. Rock on, Marcus, rock on. When the song was over, we fed him more shots, played him more music, and I laid heavy on the morphine button until the sun rose.

Marcus waited for my mom to wake up. He waited for her to come downstairs and kiss him a dozen times, not knowing that those kisses were her goodbye. She went to the little bathroom downstairs for just a moment or two, and with Todd loyally by Marcus's right side, and just as I was stepping to his left, my big, brave brother, who at thirteen years old had defended my life with an aluminum bat, and at sixteen had tried to take our stepdad's life to save mine—who had just come out of the closet and for the first time glimpsed hope but never got to touch it—took his last breath.

A treasured, fundamental piece of who I had always been took its last breath with Marcus that morning. It died with him.

I've faced some tough days, but I've never cried so hard, not before and not since. I lost my big brother to tragedy. There was no explaining the "why." Death came for him in brutal fashion just as he was figuring out how to live. He had motivated and protected me for a lifetime. Now I felt sure that I had failed him.

V

Many months later, as our team stepped out of the Supreme Court and down its many steps, greeted by the sights and sounds of countless news cameras and supporters, my big brother was all I had on my mind, my phone untouched in my right pocket, our conversation forever unfinished. Yes, I was sure we were going to win this fight now, but my big brother would never taste the joy, love, and freedom this win he'd helped set in motion would bring with it.

When the decisions did come down, every news station in the nation trumpeted Kennedy's historic words and his vote that gave LGBTQ people a "double win" that struck down Prop 8 in California and killed DOMA. I felt a sense of accomplishment, but with it came anger. I was angry with the circuit court judges who had taken years to hear and decide our case. I was furious with those who had preached incrementalism and patience from their wealthy, privileged perches. I was furious at myself for not knowing how to get this done sooner, and not knowing how to keep my big brother alive long enough to taste it.

These two decisions didn't get us to fifty-state marriage equality quite yet, but they killed Proposition 8, brought back marriage equality to California, and bestowed federal benefits on any marriage in states that did have marriage equality. And soon, just as I had predicted, Kennedy's equality-minded opinion brought new marriage cases raining down like a June thunderstorm.

At AFER, we quickly sued again, this time in the state of Virginia itself. My frustration with the state our family now called home, where my brother had just died an unequal citizen, wouldn't allow me the luxury of easing off the gas. And in every other state still without marriage equality, new plaintiffs stepped into the fight. Then, very quickly, and starting with none other than the LDS state of Utah, nearly every state's district and circuit federal courts saw Kennedy's writing on the wall and ruled on these new cases in accordance with his pro-equality stance. But when a court finally did disagree with Kennedy, a brave, bighearted man named Jim Obergefell, who like Edie Windsor had been denied federal marriage benefits when he lost his spouse, had his case taken up by the U.S. Supreme Court to sort out any such lower court contradictions. Now SCOTUS would have to determine once and for all, and for all fifty states, whether marriage was a fundamental federal right.

On June 26, 2015, the decisive day arrived. By chance, I was in San Francisco, of all places. Once the Supreme Court had granted Jim's case cert, I had slowly started to dip my toe back into filmmaking, and I was in my favorite neighborhood in my favorite city, the Castro, with a house full of writers doing research for a potential new project about the wider LGBTQ rights movement called *When We Rise*.

I woke up early that morning to a text message from Jeff, with a photo of him surrounded by hundreds of marriage equality advocates at the Supreme Court, holding a sign telling those nine justices to "Let my son get married!" He'd made the sign, called in late to work, and crossed the Potomac River to join the rally that morning. It was a helluva way to start what promised to be a dramatic day. I logged onto Wi-Fi and refreshed scotusblog.com endlessly in hopes of reading the Obergefell decision the second it was released. When it finally came through, I saw that Kennedy had written it, and I felt sure we had won. My belief was quickly confirmed. That promise made from a very big stage a little over six years earlier had finally found an ending, and for now a happy ending—at least as far as marriage equality was concerned.

I thought about that boy in San Antonio, that girl in Provo, and the hope they might feel on this morning. From this day forward—even on hot sunny sidewalks in that corner of America I grew up in and loved—when a young person realized he or she was gay, shame and fear weren't their only options. Now they could dream of wedding bells and happily-ever-afters. Butterflies of love no longer had to die, or turn to butterflies of fear. There were new options now, and with them had come measurable new understanding and acceptance.

But I wasn't feeling the joy I thought I would. I walked to a corner shop down on Castro Street and bought a pack of my brother's favorite smokes, and with sounds of celebration beginning to burst from windows all around me, I sat down on a step, lit that smoke, and quietly let my tears fall.

My brother would never hear these cheers. My brother would never know this victory. My brother would never see the promise he'd inspired me to help fulfill. He would never know the South as a place that accepted him for who he was and how he loved Larry. He would never rejoice knowing that the America he loved now valued him in return—and this was a man who had stood straight and tall for the national anthem, meant every word of the Pledge of Allegiance, and flew an American flag off the back of his truck. My big brother was a patriot—a gay patriot—and he died never seeing his country's promises include him.

So I sat there with tears running down my face, but not the tears of victory I had dreamed of and hoped for so many times over the past six years. These were tears of rage at those in comfortable places who had tossed about words like "patience" with self-satisfaction. Patience: "the capacity to accept or tolerate delay." To my ears, sitting on those steps that morning, listening to the cheers of the living, I understood "patience" in a new way—as a word that deserves no comfortable home in a nation that has yet to fulfill its promise of liberty and justice for all.

PART III

CHAPTER 22

Our Americas

I

"If you break something, take responsibility, and do your very best to put it back together again. Heck, even if you don't think you've broken something, leave it better than you found it, Lancer, not worse."

By the time I was six, my mom had learned to stock up on ample fix-it supplies: superglue, a hammer and nails, needles and thread, a screw gun and bolts, and every cleaner they had at Albertsons—all awaiting my attempted fix of whatever had sustained damage during my latest fit of inspiration. My fits came with chaos: scraps of fabric, construction paper, and thread in every corner; glue, paint, and glitter deep in carpets; bits of tape fused to floors and desks; cracked glass, scratched tables, stained walls. It became clear that chaos and destruction were creation's sisters. It was near impossible to build anything, least of all something brand-new, without them showing up. And I came to understand that building new things was a whole lot easier than putting back together what inevitably got broken.

In the weeks that followed each of our big marriage equality wins, my mom would comment that I must feel so proud to be a part of this struggle: "Imagine when gay people start getting married in Texas, Lancer." She was right. I would be thrilled. So she asked why I seemed to only get bluer with each win. I had been trying to convince myself that with this grand task's purposefulness filling my heart, of course victories left an empty space in their wake. But I knew that wasn't completely it. I'd never suffered from a lack of ideas or purpose before helping take on Prop 8. So was it the quiet concern that we might win marriage equality but, not getting any younger, I'd never enjoy the right myself? That may have been a small part of it. But the truth is, something deeper had long been breaking apart, and in the throes of creation, I just couldn't see the damage yet.

My first grown-up, decade-long creative fit helped manifest projects like *Pedro, Big Love, Milk,* and *J. Edgar.* That energy morphed into the struggle for marriage equality and wins in district, circuit, and at the U.S. Supreme Court. But a price had been paid. As when I'd raided the craft box in my younger days, unexpectedly precious things had broken in the creative process, things I wasn't even aware I'd begun missing. This list included my mother's family in the South, my own roots there, and even my relationship with the Mormon Church. In big ways and small, I hadn't left any of these relationships better than I'd found them. Now they were all quietly demanding repair.

And so, I started from the furthest away and worked inward.

A new friend named Troy Williams called from Salt Lake City. Troy had been a very good Mormon. He'd gone on a mission to help convince others to join our church. But he also knew that he was gay, and that to be honest with himself and the church he cared for meant his expulsion. Now he dedicated much of his time to securing LGBTQ equality in one of the toughest areas there was: the heart of Mormondom, Salt Lake City. On this phone call, he asked if I had any interest in meeting with some of the leaders of the LDS Church. It was a startling ask. I immediately booked a flight to Utah.

During the run-up to the Supreme Court case, I had helped a passionate journalist and filmmaker named Reed Cowan finish a documentary called *8: The Mormon Proposition,* which followed the money from an instruction by the LDS prophet to rank-and-file Mormons to help fund Proposition 8. Reed's documentary held our childhood church responsible for the divisive initiative, and the film brought plenty of negative attention to our old church's doorstep. That documentary, and my work on *Big Love,* likely had me on the church's list of adversaries. So this was a very surprising invitation.

Even more surprising, while I packed, I didn't feel the now-familiar pangs that signaled I was flying in for a fight. This trip felt more like a long-overdue reunion, albeit one littered with land mines.

As the small aircraft came in for a landing in Salt Lake City, I gazed out the window. It was a perfectly sunny day, and I could clearly see the Mormon Temple Brigham Young had broken ground on well over a century before—its five spires and golden trumpeting Angel Moroni reaching for the "Celestial Kingdom," an iconic vision for any good Mormon. I thought back to how I'd once dreamed I might get married in that temple, start a family, work my way up in the church, and perhaps become an apostle one day. I thought back on how that dream was cut short when I learned I was too different to be a part of the only thing I thought I belonged to as a six-year-old boy. I remembered the heartbreak of exclusion.

The plane's wheels touched down, and my nerves finally set in. I hadn't stopped to consider what these church leaders might want to confront me about. Should I have brought a lawyer? I must have seemed a sort of worst nightmare to them—most of my work to date had spilled the beans on our church's fundamentalist, polygamist roots, or pointed a bright light at one of its great political miscalculations, all of which branded the church too extreme to potential newcomers—and this was a church that still needed newcomers and their monthly tithing to thrive.

Troy met me at the airport, and together we headed to the Joseph Smith Memorial Building, the world headquarters of this powerful American religious institution. When we stepped inside, a very different kind of small man appeared—a soft-spoken, white-haired man in a simple navy suit. He was not so much physically small as tenaciously unassuming, a model Mormon. And although a man of substantial power and influence, whom most outsiders would have perceived to be my mortal enemy, he was deferential.

Over time, faced with LDS president Spencer W. Kimball's rejection thanks to my "homosexuality," I had rejected everything about my old faith in turn. I had thrown out any good with all of the truly bad, willfully forgetting the feel of this family's embrace. But when this soft-spoken man shook my hand and said, "Brother Black . . . it's so good to see you," I chose to believe him, and I felt a warmth I hadn't in many decades.

"Yes . . . Brother . . . I'm glad to see you, and to be here too." I was rusty with the old "Brother" and "Sister" this and that. He noticed but didn't mind.

He led me and Troy up a set of perfectly clean, pastel-carpeted stairs and into a boardroom where a half dozen more white-haired men greeted us with soft handshakes, kind voices, and more "Brother Black"s.

Now, as easy as it would have made things, I couldn't pretend there were no problems between us on this sunny day. There were. Big ones. It was still a sin to be gay in my old church, so LDS kids were at high risk of being kicked out of their homes—leading to high rates of teen homelessness, and one of the worst LGBTQ suicide rates in the nation. None of that was okay by me. And don't get me started on the church's treatment of women, not after how I'd seen my mother's pleas for help go unanswered in the name of honoring the "priesthood." I could still feel the sting of Merrill's punches, the shame of lying at school, and my own unanswered appeals.

And most certainly these men had big issues with me as well. Mormons don't like their history being trotted out for public inspection, a spotlight aimed at the most uncomfortable, tenuous "truths" of faith. What religion could withstand such scrutiny? And it's exactly the kind of public examination I'd been putting their baby-faced religious history through for years. Then, of course, there was the openly gay activist thing. That, and I really loved a good cup of hot coffee, which was also banned.

With Troy and me on one side and all that white hair on the other, I looked across a table that seemed far wider than its few feet—a canyon where bridges once stood, bridges that had sustained terrible blows in my youth and had been left to rot. Since then, both sides had stopped seeing each other, stopped speaking, stopped listening, and in fact lost all interest in bridges. That was the chaos and destruction left over from our respective attempts at creation. For them, a proposition called 8. For me, a right called marriage equality. But today wasn't for changing anyone in that room. I wasn't here to get them to wave a white flag, or better yet, a rainbow one. They weren't here to turn me straight or get me to switch to decaf. I had been invited to take a smaller step, to see if we might attempt what we so seldom do in our personal and political fights, to repair something we could agree had been broken in our opposing efforts, to build a bridge so that we might at least see each other again.

I was immediately heartened by a lunch menu that included a shocker: Pepsi Cola. It seemed caffeine was now allowed as long as it wasn't warm. Hallelujah! I was halfway home to a latte! Kidding aside, this signaled to my LDS brain that there might be some flexibility in this Mormon world after all, that these men might actually be willing to listen and be moved by an unfamiliar story. So I mustered my courage and shared some of my own personal stories from the years before and after I had been forced from their church. Troy did the same. They listened. Then the white-haired men took their turns, telling moving stories about their communities and LDS families: brave pioneer relatives, grandparents, parents, wives, and children. Troy and I could relate to much of their family histories, but we sat silent during the wife-and-children portion. We didn't have those stories, but I could feel the men's pride and joy, and I enjoyed feeling it. I had missed this most about my old church: the focus on community and family.

Then, hoping to break the ice even further, I took a big risk—I commented on the terribly dated drapes and paintings around the room, and suggested that perhaps the exclusion of gay men had hurt their church in more ways than they had even considered. "You could really use some new interior design in here, Brothers." There was a stunned silence. I let it linger, then reassured them, "That was a joke. You can laugh." And those white-haired men burst at the seams, any tension breaking into tearful laughter.

With the ice cracked, I described my own extended family: my LGBTQ family, the kinds of families some of us had already built, the families here in Utah too many had been kicked out of and missed, and the families of our own many of us still hoped to build "one day . . ." I was now listening to myself as closely as they were, feeling this thing I had missed out on, a thing this church had taught me to value: a family of my own that I felt sure I'd never have now. And right then I knew that for the first time in a very long while, these two opposing forces were gathered together talking about two not-so-different sides of the same coin, using a common language that I had spoken fluently in my youth, a language that men like these had taught me: the language of family and security. And at the very least, we were trying our best to see each other.

This next sentence may baffle some, but in that moment, I understood that in many ways, but not all, these men were also my people. That they felt similarly about me was made clear when they extended an invitation for my LGBTQ family to attend their Mormon Tabernacle Christmas Spectacular.

For those who don't know, the LDS Church's Christmas Spectacular is like the Mormon Oscars. It's hosted by a celebrity. It boasts big production values. It's televised. And it's a tough ticket to land. The church extended a handful of tickets for me, Troy, other LGBTQ representatives, our families, and guests. Soon, word began getting out that we planned to attend, and not unlike with our Prop 8 case, some in the LGBTQ community lashed out, calling us traitors. I understood their anger, but I'd felt my own community's wrath before, so instead of backing out, I invited someone along who wasn't afraid of a little heat: Chad Griffin.

By this time, Chad had accepted an offer to become president of the Human Rights Campaign, the big, national LGBTQ organization in D.C. I had once worried was too corporate, slow, and might need replacing. He had already begun focusing the organization on building new political power, launching the largest grassroots expansion in HRC's history, doubling its membership, and deploying grassroots organizers we had once only dreamed of to share our stories, mobilize voters, and fight anti-LGBTQ legislation in every state, including our home states of Texas and Arkansas. When I finally got Chad on the phone, I asked, "Hey, wanna meet some interesting people?" He immediately accepted.

I will never forget the feeling of walking into the Mormon Tabernacle with its famed pipe organ and its massive choir. Chad and I arrived flanked by several other groups of gays and lesbians with their families. And over the course of that truly spectacular show, I kept an eye on the "small," soft-spoken Mormon man I'd come to care for over the past many months. He was watching us closely in return, perhaps wondering if his trust was well placed, worrying that we might pull some grand theatrics to bring their show down like ACT UP had done so many times in the darkest days of AIDS to rock the nation out of apathy. He surely had seen the TV news images of ACT UP's protest inside St. Patrick's Cathedral in New York City twenty years before. But none of that happened on this night. What he saw instead was that even with our major differences, we still had much in common. We had tried our best to look nice (albeit in our own ways), we struggled just as hard to keep our children quiet, and we gladly sang along to the same familiar Christmas carols. Perhaps with even a bit more spirit in our glorias and *egg-shell-sees* (excelsis).

Call me easily moved, but I left that tabernacle buzzing with a Christmas spirit I hadn't felt since childhood. Chad had a thousand questions. I did my best to explain why our Christmas story was so surprisingly similar to the one at his church and what about the LDS Christian faith was different. It's not a conversation most might think two LGBTQ freedom fighters would enjoy, but we did. We were curious. And perhaps we'd both caught glimpses of some of what we'd lost when we stopped being welcome in our temples and chapels: the idea that family is primary to all else, the notion that we ought to honor our neighbors, and a daily kinship with the golden rule.

When I felt a hand take mine, I looked to my right. It was the "small," soft-spoken Mormon who had been watching us so very closely. "Brother Black," he said, as if he were considering asking a question he feared might offend.

"Yes, Brother?" I was getting better at that now.

"Do you . . . do you think you might ever want to have a family?"

"As in, what? Children?"

"That's right," he said, not yet able to look me in the eye.

I thought my answer must have been plain by now. What did he think we had been fighting for all this time? "Yes," I said. "You can kick the kid out of the church, but you can't take the church out of the kid. More than anything, I wish I had a dozen little ones. . . . Maybe you could say a prayer that I'll meet the husband of my dreams, Brother?"

Without the words to respond to that, he squeezed my hand. I waited. Then he said, "I think some thought perhaps you wanted marriage so you could . . . change it. Perhaps break its meaning."

"No," I said. "A lot of gay people, just like a lot of straight people, don't want to get married these days. Or have kids. But I'd love both. I'd love a big family. And we just want to be treated the same when we have those families and kids. So they're safe."

Now with tears in his eyes, he looked up at me and said, "I see . . ." Because he had seen. With his own two eyes. Because we had each been brave enough to try to fix one of the things that had been broken in our attempts at creation: a bridge, our relationship.

In this time, active Mormons began to organize a group called Mormons Building Bridges. Many of its members were mothers of

LGBTQ children, mothers who hoped for a better childhood for their kids than what I'd experienced. These moms called themselves Mama Dragons. The following summer, Troy asked me to grand marshal the Salt Lake City Pride parade. He drove the convertible I sat atop. Behind us, hundreds of these devout LDS members and moms in their Sunday best helped lead the parade past the iconic Salt Lake City temple holding aloft signs expressing sentiments such as "LDS Loves LGBT." Two very different kinds of Americans, marching as one. And today, when the latest LDS prophet has disparaged his LGBTQ members, those Mama Dragons have proven that they'll no longer stay silent. They've spoken out and helped correct his misconceptions.

Yes, it is true that much of the LDS Church and its leadership is still homophobic and exclusionary, but in 2015 Utah became one of the only red states to pass nondiscrimination protections in the workplace and housing through a Republican legislature, and it didn't experience the backlash of anti-trans bathroom bills that landed in so many other states. That was at least in part due to countless more meetings between LGBTQ people and the church that began with saying yes to a Christmas concert.

But on that special night in December, as I stepped toward the Mormon Tabernacle's exit, Christmas carols still ringing in my ears, I couldn't have known all that lay ahead. Then, it was just me and a soft-spoken Mormon leader walking together hand in hand. But in that moment, I understood that his faith, the faith that had once been mine, belonged to America. And thanks to Justice Kennedy, what had long been in my bones was also evident now: that I too belonged to America. We hadn't rebuilt a bridge across our divides quite yet—we were still feeling out the best place to lay the foundation for that bridge—but for the first time since our fighting began and all the chaos took over, we were holding hands. Literally. And we could see each other clearly across the rift. *This* was *our* America. Not one, not two, not only his, or mine. This. This moment was evidence that there was hope for the vision I'd long been reaching for: we, a nation of vast, seemingly irreconcilable differences— yet stepping forward together in a home we could embrace as *ours*.

I I

A step closer to home, my sweet aunt Josie in Texarkana had been battling blood cancer for a few years, and although her prognosis was fair enough, she had phoned my mom to say a sort of goodbye just in case. She was happy to keep fighting for her children's and grandchildren's sake, and she worried about how her husband, James, might get on without her. They had been together since their school days, and something told her that she didn't have as long left as the doctors thought.

When my mom called to tell me, I could hear a tightness in her voice like sticky gravel. She'd been holding back tears all morning. She'd lost her own mother just before I was born. In many ways, Josie had filled the maternal void. For me, Aunt Josie was the one person I'd trusted enough in my shyest days to come out from my hiding spot behind an armchair during a big family reunion. She took me into the darkened kitchen and we sat there alone together. She didn't mention my debilitating shyness; she just let me enjoy a bowl of strawberry ice cream in the safety of her silence. She was so strong and gentle at a time when the world around me was far too brutal. My entire life, she had been the matriarch of our good Southern family. But I hadn't seen Josie—or the rest of my mom's big family—in many years.

My mom was finding it near impossible to recover from the devastation of losing her oldest boy. She called me every day, wanting to know if she had been a terrible mother, apologizing for shortcomings I couldn't see, and breaking down when she'd land at the same conclusion: "I should have been able to keep him alive. Baby boys aren't supposed to go before their moms, Lancer." There was nothing I could say to convince her of the truth: that she had been a remarkable mother, and that perhaps we'd never understand the whys of Marcus's death, but it most certainly wasn't her fault.

With depression taking a terrible toll on what little health she had, the thought of losing her Josie was too much to bear. Now she admitted, "I can't get on a plane if it happens, Lancer. I'm on oxygen all night long now." Her spinning mind was keeping her from sleeping, and that lack of sleep left her too weak to breathe. It was a vicious, potentially fatal circle.

I could hear in her voice she was shaking from this rare admission of weakness. It was as if the cancer treatments had brought her polio back to life, robbing her muscles even further. But the truth was, her muscles had never been as strong as she had let on. Since childhood, she had performed and protested so others would allow her more freedom. And she'd come to believe those white lies about how tough her arms were because she was a crazy optimist who felt anything that could be imagined was possible. She had imagined being able to walk upright using her arms, hold a job, get married, have kids, and live until a ripe old age, holding grandbabies in those same eternally strong arms.

But after sixty years of optimism, she had taxed her battle-worn muscles to within an inch of their lives, then punished them all over again with chemo and radiation. What little strength her diaphragm had left was nearly gone. Coughing was excruciating work. Her new muscle pain demanded painkillers that further weakened her, and for the first time, she'd begun letting Jeff carry her around in full view of others; she'd stopped using her crutches and braces altogether and accepted her wheelchair as a necessity.

All of this worried me terribly, so I insisted she attend her checkups. She was happy to do so because they only proved her point. At each post-cancer checkup, the news was stellar. "If she sticks with the oxygen treatments, and we get her pain figured out, well, I'd say she's got ten years easy. That's a helluva strong heart in your mom." *Great, tell me something I don't know, doc.* But I feared she was performing for them too, and that no one was paying enough attention to the deleterious effects of her heartbreak.

The big call came within days. My aunt Josie had taken her last breath at home, in her sleep. She had gone peacefully, just as she had always lived. My mom was a wreck when she called me. She had to take long breaks between sentences to suck in oxygen from the little tubes going into each nostril, then return with another sentence or two. She was still convinced she would die if she got on a plane now, so she took a long breath, then lowered her voice: "But you could."

This was no simple observation. There was a helluva lot of subtext beneath those words: "Go in my place. Represent our family at my big sister's funeral. Our matriarch's funeral." This gathering promised to include all of the living family members who had gathered around me as a six-year-old to pray me back to health on Christmas Eve.

I knew this request showed great trust. It was an honor. But I hadn't been back to Texarkana in decades. Aside from one family reunion spent playing tennis with Todd, I hadn't seen my extended Southern family since well before I'd come out, and that was ages ago. Now, thanks to *Milk,* the Oscar speech, the court cases, and all the national news shows, I was miles from any closet as far as they were concerned.

I had long since convinced myself that I'd lost contact with my mom's family because of physical distance. "We moved to California, my mom moved to Virginia, so . . ." But that was bull. Todd had moved to Austin, Texas, a decade earlier to finish college at the University of Texas, and after a brief stint in California, he'd moved back to Texas with his girlfriend, Allie, so they could enjoy real Texas barbeque again. I'd made more than a few trips to see them. I could just as easily have made a pit stop in Texarkana. But deep down, I felt that when I'd come out, when I'd waged the public battles I had, I'd stepped into another country, and maybe even betrayed my roots. I worried that I'd be rejected by the people I'd once called home, and it's one thing to be rejected by strangers but quite another to be rejected by family. Thanks to my father's disappearing act, I'd had enough familial rejection for a lifetime. So I had chickened out. And in my lack of courage, I'd let something vital break.

I got off the phone with my mom and called Todd and asked if he'd come with me. He was in. I called my mom back: "I'll go. We'll both go. So yes, Mom, you will be there for Aunt Josie in spirit. Through us."

My tough mom wept with relief and pride. Yes, pride. Of all the things she might have felt with the death of her beloved sister, pride wouldn't have been my first guess, but if rule one is "family comes first" and close behind is "we show up for one another," then Todd and I were doing her proud.

So the odd blond kid who'd rarely said a word at reunions, and who was now an "unabashed homosexual" from "liberal Hollywood," was returning home to the South. But I didn't want those labels hanging off of me. Not for this trip. I wasn't headed to Texarkana to create any new understanding. All I wanted was to represent my mother well, maybe enjoy a bit of familial kinship, some pecan pie, fried chicken, and hell, if things went really well or tits up, a few swigs of our reliable cousin: Jack Daniel's.

I landed in Texarkana first, Todd drove in a little while later, and we made it to Josie's service just in time. Familiar enough faces filled the chapel, just recognizable through gravity-kissed skin, darkened eyes, and gray hair where blond or brown had been.

Josie's daughters, Debbie and Sandy, were so busy organizing that they kept their emotions at bay, but Todd and I received tight hugs and we shared ours and our mother's in return. Their brother, Lynn, kept his distance. I hadn't seen him in I don't know how long. I remembered him as an incredibly handsome, strong young man. He was a bit rounder now, but still tough and good-looking. His reception wasn't warm, but I thought, *Why would it be?* He'd just lost his mom, and he hardly knew me anymore.

Inside was a viewing. We'd held a viewing for Marcus months before, but I hadn't approached his casket. I already knew he was wearing his best jeans, his work boots, and his prized leather NASCAR jacket. I'd picked them out. But by his funeral, I only wanted to remember him as the strong, handsome man he'd been. With Josie, whom I hadn't seen in ages, curiosity got the best of me. I approached her casket. Inside was her body, much smaller than I had expected or remembered. I could only recall her through my youngster's eyes, when she had towered over me, easily able to keep me safe. So I looked away from this unfamiliar body and again chose memory over truth.

The rest was sound. Todd and I sat near the middle of the church during the service. I'm sure that words were said and songs were sung, but all I remember was the sound of our uncle James's pain, like a child gasping for air three or four times before forcing himself silent again. I felt like an interloper into something private and precious, an invader stealing the end of his love story. I had abandoned this family too long ago to be here now. I had denied myself this part of our American life, this American family of mine. I felt I'd given up the right to be there.

That feeling made what came next quite meaningful. Tough little Debbie, who had once taught my mom how to drive her yellow Chevy Malibu with hand controls, came up to me and Todd with two pairs of white gloves: "Now ya gotta help carry her, boys." This wasn't a request. This was a demand. We'd shown up; now there was work to do. We would be pallbearers for Aunt Josie. She had carried me as a child, and now I would carry her. So alongside our uncle Don and cousin Lynn, Todd and I helped lay our family's matriarch to rest. I had never felt so unworthy of such a great honor. And no matter how practical my inclusion was, I felt very grateful to have been asked.

Todd and I followed the rest of the mourners to the wake at Josie and James's house. When I walked in a side door, I was struck. Piecing together old memories, I slowly recognized this as the same house where I had once hidden behind the armchair, with the same kitchen table where Josie had sat me down with ice cream when I was still too afraid to been seen. It was like stepping onto a familiar stage, every object a prop from dreamlike memories, all right where I'd left them as a child, all right where they should have been.

There was no catering. Friends, family, and neighbors had cooked up their specialties and brought them by. I served myself up a tall plate and leaned against a wall with my aunt Martha, who was dazed with grief. My cousin Sandy soon approached, leaned on the wall next to me, and whispered for me to go look at what was pinned up right next to the toilet.

Doing as I was told, I walked down the hallway to the bathroom and stepped inside. There, next to the toilet, was that year's calendar. Written in by hand were every one of Josie's siblings', children's, grandchildren's, neices', and nephews' birthdays. I felt sure that I had long since lost my place in this family. And so I turned the calendar pages to June. But there I was, right there on the tenth was my name—and not Dustin, or Dustin Lance Black, but my familiar name: Lance. As far away as I may have traveled, Josie had never let me go. And I began to understand that all I had ever needed to do was to face my fears with courage and step back in, and I would have been home again.

Now I needed to visit our trusty cousin Jack.

The big Texarkana sky grew dark. Those of us left—my aunt Nan, Debbie and Sandy, Todd, and my big tough cousin Lynn—drank and spun yarn about Josie, her stories already growing into tall tales. Well soaked, Lynn laughed when he told me to go look under a toilet seat nailed to the side of James's old work shed. I did. Under the lid was a picture of President Obama. Yup, I was back in the South. I wasn't going to see eye to eye with everyone here, certainly not politically. So just as he'd unabashedly shown me who he was, I didn't hesitate to say I'd recently met someone who lived a long way away. An Olympian. A diver. A Brit. And yes, "A dude . . . named Tom."

The "dude" bit didn't come as much of a shock to anyone there, but the Olympic diver thing piqued the ladies' interest. I shared a few pictures and watched their eyes go wide. Tom didn't wear much to work, and he was very easy on the eyes. I wasn't too worried about Sandy or Nan's reactions; my eye was on Lynn, who remained unreadable. Still, when questions were cautiously asked, I dared answer. Yes, I was quite taken with this Brit; yes, it was a helluva long distance; yes, he was younger than me; and yes, he had me doing some crazy things: flying across the Atlantic, taking time off from work. "I've never taken a vacation in my life, and I'm on number three this year. Plus I'm living in the damn gym trying to find my abs again. He's gonna kill me. Literally. Or put me in the poorhouse. Or both!"

A loud laugh burst out of Lynn. "The good ones do!" he said. Then he pulled up pictures of the woman he'd been dating, and their last trip overseas. "She's gonna break my damn bank!" I knew it had taken a bit of courage for him to compare his love to mine. Without saying so, just by sharing those pictures of his girl, he was blessing my love as legit, perhaps even akin to his. Lynn wasn't about to lead any gay rights parades, but I started to think he might actually acknowledge me as family in public. The ice had cracked.

Late that night, after a few liquor runs, our tall tales growing taller and Josie nearing sainthood, I shared the story of how their mom had helped me peek out of my shell for just a moment back at a time when her care felt like life's blood, and how knowing someone like her existed in our family had given me hope. "People think tall, loud, and tough is strong, but she showed me another way, with her patience and silence and a bowl of ice cream: that kindness is what takes real strength. I try to pay that forward, some days better than others. I owe your mom for that." Lynn looked me over for a good long time, then he said, "Come 'ere, boy," and led me back out to his dad's work shed, where Obama was hiding under the toilet seat.

Inside that shed was a living, breathing shop. Long retired, James was now making picture frames out of old wood as a hobby. "Look. Dad's marbles," Lynn said, and he pulled a giant jar filled with marbles down off a shelf. I examined them through the glass. These weren't just any marbles; these were treasures, the prizes from every victorious competition dating back to my mom's childhood at least. And just as I was getting lost in the memory of my mom's old marble stories, there was a *crash!* Glass hit the floor hard, followed by the thunder of a thousand bouncing marbles looking for cracks and crevices to call home.

"What the hell?!" I demanded to know, suddenly feeling six years old again, terrified that we were in a mountain of trouble with Uncle James.

"Couldn't git 'er lid open, so I did it the old-fashioned way." Lynn had smashed the jar on purpose! Now he was picking up all the best marbles and handing them to me one by one. "Put 'em in yer pocket."

"I can't take your dad's marbles."

"Hell you can't. Some are probably yer mom's he stole. Take 'em!"

"Honestly, do you have another jar?" I wanted to conceal his crime.

"Just shut the fuck up and take 'em, asshole."

That was Texarkana code for "I like you, so don't say no." So I pocketed the marbles. I'd missed out on most of these sorts of country-boy shenanigans, the kind Marcus had lived for, the kind I might have taken part in if my crushes on boys hadn't chased me inward, or if my family hadn't run for our lives to California. Lynn was making up for my lost time—and fast.

"Come 'ere," Lynn said again, and he led me back outside, deep into his mom's backyard. It was very dark back there, but soon I saw the tin roof of a temporary-looking structure that had stood for a generation. When we got closer, I could see it stood on four chalk-white wooden stilts; beneath it was the rotting corpse of a 1965 GMC pickup truck. Lynn looked at it as if it were still brand-new. It reminded me of how Marcus had looked lovingly at any 1967 Camaro, no matter what sort of a rust bucket it was.

"My mom drove her. My sister too. And me. They took her away from me when I got busted with this and that. Used to drive her across the border to pick up, well, this and that, and git it back here. Now look; here she is dyin', meltin' into the earth."

"What color is she? White?"

"Yellow. Errr, yellow-orange. That's the primer you see."

But she was all primer now, all chalky white like she'd been whitewashed for spring along with the legs of her shed and a handful of the town's poorest homes. There was no orange or yellow left to be seen. No proof of glory days left. But Lynn could still see them in his mind. I gave him this: "She must have looked great back in the day."

"Fast too. To git away from the cops."

We sat there in silence for some time admiring her memory, Lynn reflecting on his war stories with her, his close calls with the cops, the car's secret compartment to hide "this and that" as he'd cross the border.

Then, committing Southern sacrilege, I broke this sacred moment with: "Well, I need to pee." And I really did.

"Well, hold it a fuckin' minute."

"What? Okay." I tried to pretend I wasn't bursting.

"Listen. If you promise to take good care of her, she's yours."

"What?" I had heard him, I just couldn't make sense of it.

So he made himself crystal clear: "I'm gonna put her on a truck, and yer gonna take her home, as long as you promise to take care of her."

I'd like to say I fought Lynn on his offer, told him he was too drunk to make such a mammoth decision, but holy mother of God, this was better than I could have ever imagined. This wasn't some first act of fixing a broken thing, this was no meager bridge over a ravine, this was a billion gallons of concrete to fill the whole damn divide in for good. He was giving me the Mosley family truck. It was the greatest reconnection a country boy could have ever dreamed of.

"I promise," I said. "And a promise is a sacred thing."

It's not like I had a choice in the matter. Where I'm from, if a man offers you his truck, you don't pansy around. You treasure it; you treat it like your child. You might even consider towing it to the best restoration shop you can find so they can get it running like a champ, paint it candy-apple red, chrome plate its rims, and give it a lacquered wood bed. And you should probably name it "Mosley" after the family you're so thankful to know again, that you were afraid lived in too different an America but that—politics and news shows aside—was right there with you the whole damn time. And with a pocket full of marbles, that's exactly what I did.

The thing about today's boxes, the ones created for the world's tribes to fit in by twenty-four-hour news channels hoping to sell us shaving cream or sleeping pills—well, those boxes must be built of rather angry blades, because instead of keeping us safe, they cut our families, our homes, and our world to pieces. And what's silliest about such boxes is that they aren't even real. My red-state, Southern cousin reminded me of that when he walked us back to his father's shed, and stepped us out of all the relentless political drumming we've come to call "trusted," "fair," or "balanced" news. And guess what quickly filled the void? Curiosity. The wonder we once had as children hunting for tadpoles or bugs together, praying for first kisses from cute boys or girls, staring up at stars, wondering what eternity and God look like, or stepping into woodsheds to raid Papa's marble jar—it's the curiosity that came naturally before too many of us were taught to fear and loathe folks living in boxes of different kinds or colors. With curiosity's return, it was plain to see that a far higher plane than politics lives right under our feet, or just across a road, down a river, or beyond a border. And curiosity has little interest in traveling down one-way roads—red to blue, or north to south—and even less interest in any boxed-in dead ends, because true curiosity would soon grow wearied with any one kind of America, or even two or three. Curiosity hungers for the kind of varied Americas that used to call us all to adventure.

It took years to blast away all the rust, to find the replacement parts Mosley needed, and treat her the way Marcus would have insisted upon and Lynn would approve of. It was late afternoon when I got a call from the auto shop that her last section of custom carpet had finally come in. Mosley would be finished that weekend, and I couldn't wait to show her the road again. But the call came just days before my fortieth birthday, and I'd already booked a flight home to see my mom, who had started calling herself a dinosaur. I had a flight to London after that to see Tom, the Olympian, who'd been happy to start naming our future children on date number two (that soft-spoken Mormon must have said a helluva prayer for me). So I wouldn't be picking up Mosley that fateful June weekend. She would have to wait a bit longer for her maiden journey.

Little did I know the world-shattering nature of the very first trip she would accompany me on, and how much sooner than expected it would occur.

CHAPTER 23

Mama's Boy

I

I arrived in Virginia just before my fortieth birthday, and to my surprise, my mom seemed in good spirits and relatively healthy. She didn't want to get out of bed, but that was nothing new: she had long since created a perch of pillows and surrounded herself with remote controls—for the TV, the ceiling fan, and now the electric blinds I'd bought her the Christmas before so she could let light in as she saw fit.

To many a gay man, turning forty feels like the end of something. A day to wear black, not celebrate. But since losing Marcus, I had grown more grateful for every candle on my cake. I was now one year under the highest number my big brother ever touched.

Jeff ordered us takeout from a restaurant around the corner. He and my mom got steak; I got my favorite chicken Parmesan. Caloric suicide. My mom sat up in bed and ate her dinner, Jeff sat in a big loveseat with his, and I was on the floor just below my mom, opening the gifts she had ordered online. Her big gift was a tube filled with memorabilia from the year 1974, the year I was born: a mood ring, '70s candies, and photos from the hit shows of the day. It was a time capsule that took us all the way back to that hospital she nearly died in trying to have me. For dessert, we had two cakes because my mom had forgotten which was my favorite: Black Forest or red velvet. I honestly don't have a favorite: I just love cake, so this was ideal. Then we topped it all off with some strawberry-cream-filled Oreos. It was the perfect way to spend my big birthday, in absolute gratitude for the woman who had risked her life to bring me into this world, and who despite every challenge had helped turn our lives into a dazzling ride thus far. Jeff told me she was a different woman when I was home. She was joyful. So was I.

But for the next two nights, she had to go to the bathroom constantly, and she couldn't sleep. Instead of fighting it, she and I took advantage. Jeff had work, so he went down to the couch in the living room and caught some z's. I stayed with my mom, watching TV, finishing the Oreos, helping her to the bathroom, and talking until the sun came up. In the middle of the day we would each manage an hour or two of sleep, but that was it. This trip was a window into her new life, ruled by a spinning mind that refused to let her body rest.

Now she had some sort of bladder infection that needed a doctor's attention, but she was hesitant to see doctors lately. That was new. She had felt something pop loose in her back a few weeks earlier, something the doctors couldn't explain, and I think she was afraid one might finally figure it out and let her know what she feared most: that the technology that had long held her together was outdated, and what was left of the metal in her bones had begun to give way. Modern doctors weren't studying polio anymore. Why would they? Who in America still got it? And most victims besides my tough mom had met their maker long ago. There were no good specialists anymore, no new surgeries or ideas to put a polio survivor back together. "I'm a dinosaur now, Lancer." That's how she put it. She wouldn't say it directly, but we both knew what had happened to the dinosaurs. I pushed that thought out of my mind.

But after three sleepless nights, and countless stories and Oreos, I convinced her to let me call Jeff back from work early to take her to a doctor as soon as I left the house. "You won't miss a moment with me. When I go to London to see Tom, you'll go to the doctor." She agreed to that arrangement. She was pleased that I was going to see Tom. Months earlier, I'd called her from a Heathrow Airport people mover on my way back to Los Angeles, tearful that I had to leave him behind. I'd never felt so strongly about anyone, and now I had no idea what to do about this unrelenting, long-distance heartache. It felt like madness. She sounded positively giddy about it. "Oh baby, I'm so, so happy for you."

"About what?!" I'd asked through a snotty nose. "I have so much work to do right now, Mom."

"Enjoy this, Lancer."

"You told me to always finish my work first so that I can enjoy everything else more." And then she laughed! Up to this point, I'd built a lifetime of workaholism around this ideal she'd instilled in me. I'd never once taken a vacation. How dare she laugh it off so casually now?

"I was probably just trying to get you to clean your room, Lancer."
Thirty-six years later, I was shaken by this revelation, but she had
deeper places to go: "I've been afraid to say it, but I was beginning to
wonder if you'd ever find *this*. It makes me so happy to hear that you
have. You're in love, Lancer, and boy, do you deserve it."

She'd met Tom at Christmas, when he'd made a special trip to D.C.
to frost Christmas cookies with us. Any young man who would cross
an ocean to take part in her treasured Christmas traditions was marriage material as far as she was concerned. And soon after, I caught
her Google Image searching pictures of Tom in swim trunks. Like
mother, like son.

So as I packed my bags back up for London, I called Jeff and asked
him to come home early. He arrived about thirty minutes before I
needed to catch the cab to Dulles. He seemed relieved that I had convinced my mom to finally see a doctor. His relief was mine. My mom
started ordering me around like the general she was, pointing fingers
and telling me to get her slacks, her socks, her blouse, her brush. She
may have been ill, but she was still a woman, and she insisted on
making herself beautiful.

I presented her with black socks, and she approved. I left them
draped across her legs like I always had, but this time, through her
weak voice, she said, "Help me with them."

It took a moment for me to really hear that request, but then I
carefully slid the socks onto her tiny feet as she watched, wiggling
her toes for show; that was the only movement she ever did regain.

Then, just as I was about to step away, she grabbed hold of my
forearm. Her grip was startlingly strong. When she looked straight
into my eyes with her striking blues, I could tell that she was still fully
present, still absolutely sharp. Then, with the intent and passion of a
lifetime of struggle, she gave me a singular order: "Fight for my life."

Chills ran through my body. It had been decades since she'd given
me such a command. I held her gaze and said, "I will."

"Promise me. Say it."

This felt so strange, so out of character, but I said it, I made the
promise. "I will. I will fight for your life, Mom. I promise."

She seemed to relax, to become herself again. I was deeply rattled. I told Jeff, and he said they were leaving for the hospital right

away. I told him I had hours before my flight and to call me with any updates: "I can always turn around."

I hugged and kissed my mom and told her how much I loved her. I could feel that something new and somber had begun to settle in, like she wasn't fully there with us. I hated it, so from the doorway I shouted an over-the-top, campy-as-all-hell "It's been a delight, Mother! We must do it all again real soon!"

Usually she would have caught my drift, laughed, and come back with an equally over-the-top, flying-in-the-face-of-tragedy send-off. Instead, she looked up and gazed at me for what felt like ages, then offered only a soft smile. And that was it. I had to go. The cab was waiting.

The call from Jeff came about eight minutes later, when I was well on my way to the airport. "It's bad, Lance, it's really bad. Come back now."

Whether with actual words or my heated gaze, I told my too-calm cabbie to "hit the damn gas" and catch up to the ambulance that was fast getting away from us, my mother inside.

It felt like an eternity until I was jumping out of the cab and tearing into the hospital's emergency room. Jeff had already told the nurses I was coming and to let me go directly in to see my mom. He was outside her room, likely in shock. He had put her in the passenger seat of the car and buckled her seat belt; then, as he made his way around to the driver's-side door, she had passed out, her head swinging forward and hitting the dashboard hard, her glasses breaking from the impact. Her heart had stopped. Jeff had pulled her small body from the car, laid it on the garage floor, called for an ambulance, and begun CPR. The ambulance arrived very quickly. The EMTs took over the CPR, pressing her chest with such force it broke ribs, but it got her resilient heart working again.

By the time I made it into her room, the doctors were intubating her. It was a horrible sight. I hoped and prayed she didn't know it was happening. But then her eyes shot open; she was fully conscious. Without her glasses, I must have looked like a blur—a familiar blur, but that wasn't enough, so I shouted, "It's okay, Mom! I'm here!" Now I felt sure that she recognized the blur as me and knew I had returned to fulfill the promise I'd made to her. The doctors asked my permission, and then gave her an injection to ease her pain and terror. She slowly relaxed and began drifting into unconsciousness, the horrible tubes down her throat now doing the breathing her body refused to. Her eyes were on mine, begging for her life, and putting that responsibility squarely in my hands.

Todd flew in that night. My mom's younger sister Mary arrived by car. All her life, my mom's body had stirred doctors' curiosity. That had sometimes led to special treatment—treatment we now gladly welcomed as the doctors put my mom in her own private room with big windows.

Over the next few days, when anyone "got practical" about the likelihood of anyone's coming off a breathing machine, much less my "fragile" mother, I refused to hear it. I was there to fight, not surrender. And I knew my mother better than anyone. She wouldn't have given me this assignment if she'd thought she couldn't survive. She was too kind, thoughtful, and loving to ever burden me with a failure of such magnitude. So I was going to fight, and she was going to live because it was the only thing that made her last words to me make any sense at all.

After the fifth day of sitting by her side, rubbing her arm and talking in her ear, as her vital signs ever so slightly slipped the wrong way, the doctor told me about a procedure he wanted to do to see how strong her heart truly was, to more accurately assess her likelihood of recovery, and come up with a path forward. Others didn't think it was necessary. They were giving up. I couldn't. A promise is a sacred thing. Besides, it was only a matter of money: this procedure wasn't going to cause her any pain, and perhaps it would shut the naysayers up.

So Jeff, Todd, and I went into a waiting room on the morning of June 16, and the doctor began running a probe down into my mother's irrepressible heart. Jeff and Todd waited through terrible nerves, knowing that the answers to come might very well break their hearts. I sat there stone cold, still trying and failing to make sense of this mission.

A nurse came rushing in, ending all our brooding. "You need to come with me right now." Her tone was soft but urgent. Her pace was swift. We got up and rushed behind her into my mom's room.

I knew it before her doctor could say a word. He had gone ghost white. I looked to the monitors, which showed my mom's blood pressure dropping, her heart rate slowing. Then I heard the doctor or the nurse or maybe heaven itself say aloud, "Talk to her; she can hear you."

Now? My strong little mom who had always conquered every single impossible challenge was dying? It made no sense at all, and I had no time to find any sense in it. So I took her right hand, leaned into her ear, and whispered what I knew she needed to hear. "I love you, Mom. You're the best mother there ever was. Ever. And because of that, we're going to be okay. I promise you that. We. Are. Going. To. Be. Okay. You raised us that strong. And now you can move again, Mommy. Now you can fly. Anywhere you want. I love you. And I'll be right here whenever you need to find me. So fly, Mom. You can fly now. Fly."

With those words, her impossibly strong heart stopped beating. And she flew away—away from the body that had been her greatest challenge and her immeasurable window into love and human compassion.

But I had just lied. I wasn't going to be okay. She had given me an order, a job, a holy assignment to fight for her life. I had made a promise, and I had failed to keep it. After all she had done and sacrificed for me, I had failed my precious mother in her greatest hour of need. It was a terrible ending to a spectacular love and it would take great pain, time, and an unexpected messenger to help that love find its home and purpose again.

11

The days ahead were a trial: I was privately wrestling with self-loathing while navigating a complex set of funeral challenges. My mom and Jeff had planned on moving back to California, where the mild weather would've made getting around easier for her. Jeff had long been looking for a job near Los Angeles, so we'd made what felt like a forward-looking decision to bury Marcus at Hollywood Forever cemetery—a lush, historic cemetery just behind Paramount Pictures where young people still flocked to watch movies projected onto its monumental mausoleum wall on summer nights. It had seemed perfectly suited to Marcus. So instead of a gravestone, we built Marcus a bench that revelers could drink and smoke and cause general havoc on when they came for movie night in among the graves. Most of all, my mom had liked the idea of being able to visit "his spot" after her big move back to the West Coast.

That terrible week of her death, Jeff said he still wanted to move to California, and the spot next to Marcus's was still vacant, so a unanimous family-of-three decision was made to fly Mom's body to Los Angeles like we had Marcus's, and bury her next to her firstborn. We were all a wreck, but seemingly the man of the house again in this moment, I was tasked with figuring out the arrangements: embalming, clothing, casket, a flight to Los Angeles with my mom's body in cargo, a service, a wake, and doing my best to get whatever remaining relatives she had out to Los Angeles to say farewell. I did all of this feeling like an absolute fraud, knowing I was the one who'd let the strongest woman in the world die. I kept running through every sign I'd missed, all the opportunities to save her that seemed so obvious now in hindsight.

In just a handful of years, I'd lost my dear composer friend, my great mentor Frank Robinson, most of my aunts and uncles, a step-grandfather, my big brother, and now my mom. I'd always kept my trusted circle quite small, and now it suddenly felt as if a plane had gone down with everyone I loved on it. I had always been able to find some light or wisdom on the flip side of such loss, but here there was only blur and darkness.

I don't remember many of the details. I believe we picked out a rosewood coffin. My mom liked the shade, and it only seemed right that our "Rose's" brave body rest in her namesake.

I remember insisting upon mint juleps at the wake. Like me, my mom wasn't a big drinker, but she had talked about having a mint julep together on my porch when she finally got back to California. I would have hers and mine that night.

And a little ray of hope returned when some of Aunt Josie's family flew in to prop me up. That reconnection with my good Southern family was now easy, joyful, and strong.

At the same time, in high-Hollywood fashion, Rob and Michele Reiner came to her service. My little mom never would have guessed that Meathead from *All in the Family* would help send her into the beyond. Chad also came.

And Ryan and his husband flew down from their home near Seattle. My mother's death hit Ryan surprisingly hard. I watched him weep openly, uncontrollably. Like folks had back in Lake Providence so long ago, many of my kind now told themselves, "If Lance's mom can make it with her differences, then I sure as hell can make it with mine." Now the light of her mighty example had gone out, and we all felt its absence deeply.

Instead of me flying to Tom in those weeks, he flew across an ocean and a continent to hold my hand and help give me strength. He had lost his own father to cancer a few years earlier. He knew what this was. He may or may not have been the answer to a soft-spoken, white-haired Mormon man's prayers, but he was absolutely a gift from God.

On the day of my mom's service, the chapel was jammed. My mother's life had moved and changed most anyone it had touched, so folks had made the extra effort to get to California in time for one last farewell. Those who couldn't make it in person sent flowers, and by the morning of the funeral, my home was jammed with hundreds of vases and thousands of roses.

On the outside it must have seemed as if I had it all under control. But even with the details coming together with the perfection of a well-planned play, I was more lost than I'd ever been—and for me that's really saying something.

What I do remember very clearly is struggling to figure out who would lead her service. My mom was still a woman of great faith, but she wouldn't have considered herself a Mormon anymore. She wasn't a Baptist or a Methodist either. She was still a Christian, but far more interested in Christ's compassion than in any one brand of Christianity. I needed to get that right, but I didn't know how to, so I made a call to someone who might know better how to thread this celestial needle.

I had met Bishop Gene Robinson during our long fight for marriage equality. He was a joyful man with little round glasses, most often cloaked in rich red or lavender Episcopalian shirts and robes. He was also the first priest in an openly gay relationship to ever be consecrated a bishop in a major Christian denomination. And while that mattered a great deal to many gay Christians and Episcopalians, I mostly remember the sense of peace he brought to the most trying days of our struggle. He spoke with a simplicity and clarity that cut through the clutter. I trusted him.

When I got in touch with Bishop Robinson, he was home on the East Coast. He wanted to know more about my mom before suggesting anyone, so I told him her story, this book's story: that of a tough Southern woman who'd refused to sit still, who'd led a life of optimism some called foolish, passed that optimism on to me, and more often than not proved her doubters wrong. She'd also loved and supported me and my brothers even when powerful forces had pressured her not to. She was a woman of great faith, but without a church that met her standards. And then I said, "Well, I'm not sure she was ready to go, Gene." He was the first person I'd shared this with, and I broke up inside putting words to my fear. "She wasn't done."

That was when Bishop Robinson told me, "I think I need to come do this myself." That wasn't why I had reached out to him. But he insisted.

The night before the service, Bishop Robinson arrived to a home filled with people from the South, the coasts, Texas, New England, the United Kingdom, and beyond. A house filled with food and roses. He found me in the backyard in a daze, my new normal. He gave me a good long hug, but I wasn't in a crying mood. Then he did something surprising: he pulled out a pack of cigarettes, popped one in his mouth, and offered me one. A smoking bishop? I'd never seen anything like this in the church I hailed from. But you know what, from him, a man of God, how could I say no? So I lit it up.

Then, like a skilled doctor, Bishop Robinson slowly coaxed my mom's final moments from me. He knew there was a shard of glass in there. It's likely why he got on a plane. But I had yet to tell anyone about my mom's final order, my promise, and my failure.

The words came slowly. "She grabbed my arm, looked me in the eyes, and told me to fight for her life. I promised I would, and . . . well here we are."

He took a long drag on his cigarette, looked up into the night sky, then blew a big white cloud up into it. When he looked back down, he had tears in his eyes, but he didn't seem upset by my tale. Instead, a joyful smile took over his face—as if he knew something I just couldn't see, something that was right there in front of me, that he could see with absolute clarity. With these words, he gently lifted the veil:

"She wouldn't have said what she did if she meant you had to physically keep her heart beating. She knew it was going to stop, and soon. She tried to tell you that, didn't she? In many ways, I'd imagine? And you just couldn't hear it?"

I thought back. She had been telling me she was a dinosaur for months, and I had refused to acknowledge or accept the only thing that could mean. She had begun refusing to see doctors because she knew that what they had to say was redundant. She didn't need a second opinion that she was dying. And when I had said, "We must do it all again soon!" she hadn't lied to me. She hadn't said her normal "See you soon, my Lancer!" She had told her most difficult truth with her silence. She knew she wouldn't be seeing me again.

Now tears started to fall in that backyard. I lowered my head to hide them from the guests, but the kind bishop tilted my chin back up and looked into my eyes. "Her life is what she told you to fight for. And you agreed. And she heard you agree. And she believed you . . . and so she knew she could finally let go."

I was starting to see the direction he was walking me, but I'd had no sleep for days, my heart had clouded my head, and I needed plain words.

"Your life and your mother's life were one. You told me that. You taught each other how to live when others said you couldn't or shouldn't. You taught each other what life can hold when you were promised so little. And even if you can't see it from here, she could. She knew it was a precious and powerful thing you created together. So maybe ask yourself, what did she give you, and what did you give her? What did you two discover together? What bridges did you build with her that no one believed could be built? And how did you build them? That is her life. That thing that was even more powerful than the sum of your two magnificent parts. And it's still right here, and now it's yours to hold and foster and pass along, if you're willing to keep fighting for it."

I thought back to the look in her eyes when she had told me to fight, the surprisingly sturdy grip on my arm—perhaps the very last of her strength—and she knew it. I heard her words again, and now they fit perfectly into the puzzle of her life. That gay bishop, that embodiment of the great contradictions of our time, could see so clearly what I had been far too close to see. Curiosity and compassion. Believing and fighting. Creating and fixing. Those combinations had defined her life and then ours even when it was difficult to find compassion, belief, and any bridges or fixes. And with dark clouds of division on the horizon, I knew the life I had to fight for, and the immeasurable building and fixing it would call for.

The next morning Todd, Jeff, and I went out to Mosley, who was sitting in my driveway, now candy-apple red. We fired her up. She was loud, bold, and determinedly Southern. Debbie and Nan had flown in for the day, and they whooped and hollered at Mosley's brazen *glug, glug, glug.* And together with Jeff and Todd, I drove Mosley, the great symbol of the reunion of my Americas, to Hollywood Forever Cemetery, and under a dazzling blue sky, we laid our brave mother's body to rest next to our big brother's. On her stone, covered in roses, are the words: "Roseanna Bisch—Sister, Mother, Wife—Her spirit made us grow."

I I I

Rose Anna Whitehead was born in 1948. She moved her legs for two years before polio robbed her of them. I was born in 1974. I had a normal enough childhood for six years, before I learned I was too different for our world. Now, having seen almost every continent and met countless, infinitely varied people, I know without a doubt that my mom and I are not the exception to any rule.

We *are* the rule. Every single person on this planet is different from everyone else in at least one remarkable way. Still, every day, children learn that for this reason or that, they're just too different, and then comes a list of what they'll never achieve because of it. Everyone reading this has probably experienced that terrible moment at some point in their lives, because sadly, this fear of difference is our current state of being—despite all the proof that it's our differences that make this world magical, delicious, entertaining, innovative, and downright livable. It doesn't help that we live in a world still led by too many men stoking the fear of difference for power and their own personal gain.

My mom had seen a storm coming. I'm not guessing at this; we'd talked about its clouds on the horizon. She had felt what I had, that forces were aligning to turn back the clock, to reclassify variety as inferiority, to reinforce divisions with fear: between North and South, West and East, coasts and valleys, left and right, red and blue, white and black, Christian and Muslim, disabled and able-bodied, cis and trans, gay and straight, and on and on until we live in little tribes in our own myopic versions of America and the world. Because if we are all divided into little tribes, a plurality of the selfish, who care little for the golden rule, might rise and rule from a place of fear again.

Those clouds were approaching when my mom gripped my arm. And in classic Anne fashion, she hadn't left me to wonder what it was I ought to do about them. She had been crystal clear. She didn't worry whether I could handle the heavy burden she was leaving me with. She knew we only rise as high as the challenges before us. And she knew, like I did, that all of those gathering clouds were filled with nonsense, that we didn't live in one America or two or even three but an America filled with infinite variety—variety worth fighting for. *Our* Americas. *Our* world.

"Stay in the fight" is what she'd told me with her last bit of strength, because she knew that the fight was fast approaching, and that it was worthy.

"Fight for my life," she said. And I promised I would. For a promise is a sacred thing.

Yes, I'm an optimist, just like my mom, but neither of us was a fool. From new laws and innovations to tough conversations, compromises, and paradigm-shifting storytelling, I know it's going to take great efforts to create what's needed to make this life more livable for folks like my mom, for me, and for all of us infinitely varied human creatures. And in that noble pursuit, so much will be broken and go terribly wrong, and it will require all of our attention to repair it. Because a life like my mom's isn't easy; it demands courage, vigilance, and damn hard work. But it is joyful, meaningful labor, and if you feel called to it, then as my uncle James would have told my mom, "Get yer tail in the fight, darlin'"—in any way you can. Big and small. Let's fight for our lives like that little Southern girl from the poorest city in America who couldn't take a single step but refused to believe she was too different to have it all. Hers was a life I was honored to witness and share, whose challenges I tried my best to rise to, and whose love I most certainly felt. But now, well . . . I can't keep her all to myself anymore. Because I made a promise when my mother asked that a life like hers be fought for, and thus shared. And a promise is a sacred thing. So now, it's my great honor to be a man of my word and to fight for that life, and to do so by your side—because now her life is yours.

A BEGINNING

Epilogue

On May 6, 2017, surrounded by family, Dustin Lance Black and Thomas Robert Daley legally wed at Bovey Castle in Devon, England.

On June 27, 2018, their first child, Robert Ray Black-Daley, was born in Southern California. He's so damn cute.

Lance's cousin Debbie flew in from Texarkana unannounced to attend Robbie Ray's birth. When asked why she didn't call ahead, she shot back, "'Cause you mighta said 'no,' and this is what families do."

One week later, the happy new parents asked Ryan Elizalde to extend his protective care to Robbie Ray as his godfather. Ryan cried, and then said yes.

ACKNOWLEDGMENTS

First, thank you, Mom, wherever you're flying tonight. Beyond what can be found on this book's pages, I'm deeply grateful for your keeping, stashing, hiding, and preserving anything you felt might hold some meaning from your life and ours—all of the sacred objects you rightly guessed might remind and inspire, particularly those that tell the stories of your most painful days, the occasions you never wanted to waste a moment of our living reliving, but that you must have known I would one day discover and put to use. I've tried my very best.

A big thank-you to my little brother, Todd Black, for reading early drafts, and sharing laughter and tears as you helped me fill in the blanks. To Ryan Elizalde, for digging out and poring through old photos, journals, and one rather dramatic manifesto to help clarify dusty memories. Your care and protection have again proven boundless. To Jeff Bisch, for making the time for long phone interviews at odd hours and answering every question, even when I tiptoed into some highly personal territory.

To my family treasures—Aunt Martha, Uncle Don, Aunt Nan, Aunt Mary, and my cousins Debbie, Sandy, and Lynn—thank you for facing the tears that inevitably rode sidecar with your favorite Anne and Lance humdingers, hardships, and humiliations. Debbie, Sandy, and Nan, thank you for letting me monopolize so many hours of your London visits/vacations with such probing. Lynn, thank you for reading this book, chewing me out, forgiving me, and letting me go to print without editing "one damn word" out of our family story. I love you all.

To my own personal heroes, Chad Griffin, Adam Umhoefer, Larry Gross, and Troy Williams, thank you for answering my political and LGBTQ movement questions, and for helping me refine this book's account of our shared LGBTQ equality work and history. More important, thank you for your tireless efforts in the struggle for LGBTQ equality. There is no doubt that you've all made lives more livable for LGBTQ people in Utah, the United States, and beyond.

To my agent, Joe Cohen, who felt it was about time I write this book. Thank you for introducing me to my superstar book agent at CAA, Cait Hoyt. Cait, you've proven to be a trusty navigator and sunshine on the cloudiest days (most every day here in London). You're also a damn good ball-breaker—particularly when I've proven too shy still to bust the balls that needed it. If my high school physics teacher was right and nothing moves without an outside force getting it going, well, you've been my prime mover. Thank you.

Tim, oh, Tim O'Connell. Perhaps it was the sugar high from all of the caramel corn I wolfed down just before our very first meeting, but you made me laugh from the get-go . . . sometimes with you, sometimes directly at you. I immediately fell for your spirit and felt sure you wouldn't let me lose the humor and heart in the shadows of my past. Thank you for your patience and willingness to talk through the same old ideas a thousand times on long international calls, and for doing so all over again a day, a week, or even months later. You're my favorite brand of nerd, and I am so grateful to have you as my editor.

Anna Kaufman, some may call you an editorial assistant, but we all know who holds the real power over there. Thank you for all of your keen insights, but also for the emails you wrote to Tim (emails he most certainly wasn't supposed to share with me). Know that your kind words, written behind my back, kept me typing on the days I was ready to throw in the towel.

Ellen Feldman, you brilliant production editor, you make me feel so very foolish when you highlight all of my countless mistakes. I suppose it would be wise to secretly accept your corrections and pretend that I'm as flawless as you make me appear, but, alas, I've just admitted your rescue work in writing. So, to hell with it: Ellen, you and your proofreaders Chuck Thompson and Bert Yaeger are my not-so-secret weapons. Thank you for seeing through what I wrote down to what I meant to write and leading me to the well.

I'd also like to express my appreciation for this book's team at John Murray. To my publisher Georgina Laycock, publicist Alice

Herbert, and editor Kate Craigie. To Diana Talyanina who has managed the production nuts and bolts, to marketing and social media guru Jess Kim, and sales director Megan Schaffer. To Ellie Wood in International Sales and Katrina Collett in the Australian office. To Will Speed for your inspired work on our UK cover. Your passion has been palpable. And of course, to Lucy Hale, deputy CEO at John Murray for believing in this book. Thank you all for listening to my pitches, reading my drafts, and going through a hundred photos, childhood drawings, and enduring a thousand more stories as you've all helped bring my family's story to my new home in the United Kingdom (and beyond).

And, of course, to the woman who has to put up with me each and every day, and in person: Tumi Belo, thank you for running our little office so well that I ran out of excuses to avoid my writing responsibilities.

To anyone I didn't explicitly name in this book but who may think it's you I was talking about, know that I made a decision early on not to criticize anyone by name who works and fights for a more creative and/or just and equal world . . . no matter how much I may disagree with the path chosen to achieve such goals. I believe it takes opposing forces with similar dreams, working together, but often at odds, to see our equality reached and our curiosities realized. I admire and sincerely thank you all . . . even as you are likely cursing my name all over again.

Finally, as my mom taught me to do, I've saved the best for last. I feel so unbelievably lucky to be able to thank my family: my husband, Tom, and our son, Robbie Ray. Tom, at our wedding you said in your vows that you would try to find the value in my sensitivity. This project has most certainly revealed new sensitivities and tested that vow. My tears, ruminations, insecurities, and insomnia must have seemed less than "valuable" on at least one occasion, but you always listened, coached, encouraged, and/or ordered us frozen yogurt. You are my best friend, my loving husband, and the greatest partner-in-crime a man could ever ask for. And to our precious Robbie Ray, thank you for the opportunity to pay my family's lessons and traditions forward . . . and for taking all of those long midmorning naps. Without those, I would never have completed my final pass. I can't wait for you to read this book one day and meet your strong, beautiful Grandma Anne. She would have loved you to bits and pieces, and somewhere out there, I promise you, she's doing just that. And a promise is a sacred thing, Robbie.

PHOTO CAPTIONS AND CREDITS

Captions to be read clockwise from top left

PART I

1. STILL WATER

- Cokie holding Don, with Victor, Josie, Faye, Buddy, and Billy Ray in Lake Providence, Louisiana, 1942
- Rose Anna with chickens on her parents' Lake Providence tenant farm, 1948
- Rose Anna with Cokie at a Vicksburg, Mississippi, Baptist church, 1951
- Rose Anna walking on a Lake Providence road, 1950

2. SAFETY'S SOUND

- Cokie and Anna outside a Warm Springs, Georgia, hotel room on Christmas morning, 1955
- Neighbors visiting Anna at home in Lake Providence, 1956

3. OUR SUFFERING

- Anne's March of Dimes portrait, 1958
- Anne with neighbors back home in Lake Providence, 1959
- Nan, Anne, and Mary in Lake Providence, 1962
- Anne, Martha, and Cokie, 1961

4. A BODY IN MOTION

- Anne in her marching band uniform, 1965
- Anne in her prom dress, 1966
- Anne with Raul at home in Lake Providence after their wedding, 1969

5. BEDROCK

- Marcus, Lance, and Anne, 1975
- Lance and Marcus with Anne's yellow Chevy Malibu Classic in Texas, 1979

- Anne's sisters Josie, Mary, Martha, and Nan, sister-in-law Faye, and sister Faye, with Anne, 1980
- Marcus, Raul, Anne, Lance, and Todd in El Paso, Texas, 1979

6. GRAND THEFT AUTO

- Marcus, Todd, and Lance in San Antonio, Texas, 1980
- A green-eyed neighbor with a cocker spaniel, 1980

7. CAN'T WALK, CAN'T TALK

- The Jingle Bell Band (Lance on far left), 1980

8. BULL BY THE HORNS

- Merrill, Marcus, Lance, Anne, and Todd in San Antonio's Olan Mills Portrait Studio, 1982
- Lance on a cow near Dallas, 1982
- Anne, Todd, Marcus, and Lance in San Antonio, 1983

9. HUNGRY DEVILS

- Lance in his Kitty Hawk Junior High football uniform, 1987
- Marcus with his punk band postcards, 1987

10. DELIVERANCE

- Jeff Bisch in his army uniform, San Antonio, 1987
- Jeff takes a photo of Anne in her laboratory, 1987
- Anne in Fort Sam Houston's Brooke Army Medical Center laboratory, 1987

PART II

11. WEST OF HOME AND EAST OF EDEN

- Jeff, Anne, Lance, Todd, and Marcus in Monterey, California, 1988
- Ryan and Lance visiting Big Sur, 1991
- Ryan photographing Lance in Big Sur, 1992

12. SECRET SOMETHINGS

- Ryan and Lance in their Los Angeles apartment, 1994
- Lance with his UCLA School of Theater, Film and Television acceptance letter, 1994

13. ALLEMANDE LEFT

- Marcus, Todd, Lance, and Anne at a Wildwood, New Jersey, hotel, 1994
- Ryan and Lance, 1996

14. QUEEN OF THE MA'AMS

- The hospital commander awarding Anne a commendation, 1993
- Anne with her laboratory team, 1993

15. XMAS DOWN

- Anne and Lance, Christmas morning in Manassas Park, 1995

16. HUNGRY JACKALS

- Lance and an Arriflex at UCLA's film school, 1996
- Cell for the first Hungry Jackal Productions credit, 1996

17. SPINNING YARN

- Lance and Anne in Los Angeles, 1996
- Jason and Lance shooting a short film, 1998

18. MILK CALLS

- Lance writing *Milk* at night in his Hollywood Hills bungalow, 2007
- Sean Penn, Gus Van Sant, and Lance at the *Milk* premiere in San Francisco, 2008 (ERIC CHARBONNEAU)

19. CATACLYSM

- Cleve, Jeff, Anne, Todd, Lance, Drew, Allison, and Ryan before the Oscars, 2009
- Lance on the Academy Awards stage, 2009 (PHOTO BY KEVIN WINTER/ GETTY IMAGES)
- Lance speaking at the Meet in the Middle protest against Prop 8 in Fresno, California, 2009 (GARY CLARK)

20. SCOTUS HIATUS

- Lance speaks at American Foundation for Equal Rights (AFER) rally, 2013 (COURTESY OF AMERICAN FOUNDATION FOR EQUAL RIGHTS (AFER))
- Lance, Ted Olson, David Boies, and Chad Griffin at AFER rally, 2013 (COURTESY OF AMERICAN FOUNDATION FOR EQUAL RIGHTS (AFER))

- The Los Angeles cast of *"8": The Play,* 2012 (PHOTO BY JASON MERRITT/
  GETTY IMAGES FOR AMERICAN FOUNDATION FOR EQUAL RIGHTS)
- Adam Umhoefer, Lance, and Cleve Jones at the Supreme Court, 2013

21. VIRGINIA ROADS

- Marcus at the Lincoln Memorial, Washington, D.C., 2010

PART III

22. OUR AMERICAS

- Lance as grand marshal of Salt Lake City Pride with Troy Williams (driving)
  and Mormons Building Bridges, 2012 (SCOTT SOMMERDORF/*THE SALT
  LAKE TRIBUNE*)
- Todd, Lance, Tricia Douret, Nan, and James at Aunt Josie's wake, Texarkana,
  Texas, 2012
- Mosley the truck makes it to a Venice, California, restoration garage, 2013

23. MAMA'S BOY

- Anne and Lance in Salinas, 1987
- Anne and Lance at the Getty Center, Los Angeles, 2006